60/41/59

THE

TOYOTA

LEADERS

VERTICAL.

The Toyota Leaders: An Executive Guide

Masaaki Sato

Translated by Justin Bonsey

VERTICAL.

Published by Vertical, Inc., New York.

ISBN 978-1-934287-23-1

Manufactured in the United States of America

First Edition

Vertical, Inc.
1185 Avenue of the Americas 32nd Floor
New York, NY 10036
www.vertical-inc.com

Table of Contents

Preface
Toyota and I—and David Halberstam

O N NOVEMBER 3, 2007 TOYOTA celebrated its seventieth anniversary. It was 1973 when I first began covering the automotive industry as a correspondent for the *Nihon Keizai Shimbun* (Nikkei), which means I've glimpsed roughly half of Toyota's history. During this time, of course, I have obviously not covered, as a front-line reporter, every last thing that Toyota has done. That said, even after leaving the auto beat, I've had the opportunity to rub shoulders with a long line of top Toyota executives. Before I knew it, developments at Toyota had become a part of my life.

The first Toyota executive with whom I became close was then-director Masaya Hanai. Hanai, said to be Toyota's moneyman, refrained from alcohol and cigarettes and, although he could claim golf as a hobby, he used only irons, which earned him the name "Iron Man" among his subordinates. Stricter than others when it came to mixing business with personal affairs, he was at the same time an ardent enough admirer of Eiji Toyoda to declare: "Eiji Toyoda is my hobby."

Holding that "if you have pride and affection for your company, you should own company stock," he purchased Toyota shares sedulously since joining the company and, as the years rolled by, he became the third largest individual shareholder next to Shoichiro Toyoda and Eiji Toyoda. Partly because he had no children, after resigning his position as a Toyota board member he contributed the entirety of his executive pension—upwards of several hundred million yen—to his alma mater.

It all began with Mazda's reorganization

Hanai and I first came to share common objectives through the issue of Mazda's reconstruction. Having failed in its response to the first oil crisis in the fall of 1973, Mazda lapsed into a financial crisis, prompting Sumitomo Bank (presently Sumitomo Mitsui Banking Corporation), Mazda's main bank, to launch reconstruction efforts. Ichiro Isoda, the managing director handling the case at Sumitomo Bank (later president), gave hope at an early stage for independent reorganization and was searching for a business partner with whom to ally the ailing company.

At the time I was pouring all my energy into covering Mazda. Every time Isoda came to Tokyo from Osaka, I used a variety of means to cross paths with him—twice a day, in the morning and in the evening and, if urgent, once in the afternoon as well. One time, a solemn-faced Isoda approached me with the following:

> The Japanese economy will take a massive hit if Mazda goes under. Toyota is the only domestic manufacturer capable of taking in Mazda. Even so, Sumitomo responded by raising funds instead of facilitating co-financing when Toyota was on the brink of bankruptcy in 1950. Since then we have lost all points of contact and all personal connections have been severed. But now is no time for such issues. I was wondering if you wouldn't mind putting out feelers to see if it Toyota, despite that past, would be willing to back Mazda.

Isoda thus attempted to use a journalist as an intermediary to resolve the situation. Sensing that this would turn into a headline story, I accepted Isoda's request. The most expeditious way to handle a story like this was to take it straight to Hanai.

Large Japanese companies, including Toyota, invariably require a public relations officer to be present and take notes on the proceedings of media newsgathering sessions. As soon as I brought up the Mazda issue, Hanai enjoined his PR officer, who had been present throughout, to leave the room. From that point on, it became customary for PR officers not to attend meetings or interviews I conducted with Toyota's senior management, whether with Hanai or anyone else.

Although senior managers tend to choose their words carefully in the presence of public relations officers, their tongues loosen up considerably when it is just the two of us. Perhaps because my practice of not taking notes during any kind of interview allows them to let down their guard, they often tip their hands on important issues.

As it turned out, Toyota did not make it to the negotiation table to consider a tie-up with Mazda. Consequently, Isoda switched over to revive talks with Ford, committed to reconciling previously stalled negotiations.

This occasion brought Hanai and I much closer together, and time permitting I was taught the fundamentals of leadership at Toyota, from the company's history to founder Kiichiro Toyoda's management philosophy, from third president Taizo Ishida's views on money to the secret of streamlining, Toyota fund operations, personnel development, and more.

While I met with Hanai almost every month during his tenure as executive vice-president and chairman, most hearteningly for me he suggested that I meet so-and-so for this, so-and-so for that and put in a word for them to meet with me, introducing me to a whole slew of important figures at Toyota. Even after leaving our respective posts, we continued to see each other until right before he passed away in 1995, and I was always able to sense changes at Toyota through Hanai's words and actions.

Behind the scenes of the Toyota-GM partnership

In the summer of 1980, Eiji Toyoda proposed to Ford a joint production venture in the United States as a decisive means for resolving U.S.-Japan auto-trade friction. However, negotiations made little headway and broke off one year later. Toyota lacked the confidence back then to set up a factory in the U.S. on its own, and plans for internationalization seemed headed for a dead-end.

Among the people to whom Hanai introduced me was Hideo Kamio, who handled overseas business for Toyota Motor Sales. As I routinely heard about Toyota's tribulations from Hanai, without much forethought I suggested to Kamio, "One of my friends was involved in negotiations for a business tie-up between Isuzu and GM and has continued to serve as an advisor to both companies. He's coming to Japan in November to see the Tokyo Motor Show. Would you like to meet him? His name is J.W. Chai, and his title is vice president of Itochu International, Inc."

It was November 1981 when the two of them and I met over a meal to exchange information. Kamio and Chai seemed to get along exceptionally well, speaking animatedly to one another as might friends of ten years. Kamio openly revealed Toyota's concerns, while Chai pointed out some of the problems with GM. Although they covered a wide array of topics during their conversation, the discussion suddenly took on a serious tone when the subject turned to the economic policy of the newly-elected Reagan administration.

"Reagan was elected on the slogan to 'make America great again,'" Chai held forth. "In order to vitalize private enterprise, he'll need to be flexible about applying America's antitrust laws, considered the toughest in the world. That's why a Toyota-GM pairing would..."

I had assumed, listening in from the sidelines, that a collaboration between the two countries' top automakers was a pipe dream given the antitrust laws, but hearing their conversation, I started wondering *what if.*

The partnership negotiations *de facto* began from there. While Kamio would try to persuade Eiji Toyoda, Chai would determine whether GM was willing to partner with Toyota. What with their own routine job responsibilities to tend to, along with a 14-hour time difference between Japan and the east coast of the United States, frequent communication between the two would be difficult. I therefore became their go-between, conveying to Chai Eiji's thinking as I heard it from Kamio and passing along to Kamio GM's policy as I heard it from Chai.

Once both parties' intentions had been confirmed, and based on the premise that antitrust laws would be applied flexibly, it did not take very long until the idea was floated to produce Toyota-developed compact cars in the U.S.

Although there would be twists and turns before the summit, Eiji and GM Chairman Roger Smith met privately in New York on the night of March 1, 1982. Their meeting, which took place at the Links Club in Manhattan, went on for four hours. Chai, who attended as GM's interpreter, escorted Eiji back to his hotel and promptly called me in Japan to give me the details of the summit's content.

On March 8, two days after Eiji had returned to Japan from a dealer convention in Canada, *Nihon Keizai Shimbun* ran in its morning edition the exclusive breaking story that the two companies had entered into partnership negotiations. Fortunately, the story earned that year's Japan Newspaper Publishers & Editors Association Award (Editorial Division).

The elusive president

I met up with Taizo Ishida, the third president of Toyota, at the Toyoda Building across from Nagoya Station on a number of occasions around the time of the first oil crisis. Already in his late seventies and retired to a consulting role, he was still as healthy as ever.

At our initial meeting, the first thing out of Ishida's mouth—he sat cross-legged on the sofa—was: "I'm already retired. If it's about today's Toyota, you should ask Eiji. He's far more knowledgeable about Toyota than I am." Perhaps because he'd asserted this right off the bat, I couldn't bring myself to ask about the current state of Toyota and instead listened to him go on at length about the inventor's life of Sakichi Toyoda, the founder of the Toyota Group, and the business vision of Kiichiro Toyoda, the man who brought Toyota Motor Corporation into being.

Eiji, meanwhile, was the most difficult interview during his term as president. It took forever for him to answer a question. Just when the reporter, assuming the president didn't want to answer a question, and also mindful of the limited time, moved on to the next question, Eiji would start to answer the first. From the outset both sides ended up feeling awkward, and this was the experience of most reporters. However, once you realized that Eiji's nature was to consider questions seriously, the next interview and on became a cinch. All you had to do was shut up and look out the window until he answered.

In 1983, while he was chairman of Toyota, *Nihon Keizai Shimbun* decided to run a story on Eiji Toyoda in its popular column "My Résumé"; I was to conduct the interview and do the write-up. I would ask Eiji about his life from the time of his upbringing to the present, put it together in writing, and finally Eiji would make any necessary corrections.

We proceeded to meet once a week over the course of six months. During this time I asked Eiji in detail about his life as a car guy: memories of his uncle Sakichi Toyoda (Eiji's father's older brother), the enthusiasm that his cousin Kiichiro invested in the automotive business, the turbulent postwar period, Kiichiro's resignation and reinstatement as well as his death soon after, his experience as an invitee at Ford and how it was reflected in Toyota's style of management, car-making geared towards the era of motorization, and so forth.

Eiji's "résumé" subsequently turned into a book and was even published in English. Even though people were familiar with Toyota vehicles, before then hardly anyone in the U.S. knew about Eiji, let alone Kiichiro, Toyota's founder. It is my proud belief that the English version of the book prompted Eiji's induction into the Automotive Hall of Fame as only the second Japanese honoree; Soichiro Honda, founder of Honda Motor, had been the first.

Going from president to chairman, honorary chairman to senior advisor, Eiji withdrew himself gradually from the center stage of Toyota management; yet, even today, I am blessed with opportunities to meet and talk with the man. Six years ago, when leg problems confined him to a wheelchair, he took the precaution and checked into the Toyota Memorial Hospital to spend his remaining years there, but every day, he not only eagerly peruses all the Toyota-related articles delivered to his room but makes unstinting use of a computer to follow Toyota's latest developments.

In addition, Eiji was the most devoted reader of a series of mine called "The House of Toyota" that was published beginning in 2002 in *Bungei Shunju*, a monthly periodical boasting the largest circulation in Japan. For the nearly three-year period during which my articles appeared, Eiji kindly and invariably pointed out any erroneous statements I made. Coming up to his ninety-fifth birthday in September 2008, he is still well and in good spirits.

The maverick president

Kamio first introduced me to Hiroshi Okuda, saying, "There's a maverick at Toyota Sales. Why don't you meet him?"

While behind-the-scenes moves to form a partnership with GM heated up, it had been decided for certain that the hitherto separate Toyota Motor Company and Toyota Motor Sales Company would be merged, and Hanai's selection of directors for the reborn Toyota was approaching a climactic stage. Hanai had reservations about appointing Okuda. Perhaps Kamio, apprehensive about this, thought to let a third-party observer describe the man Okuda to Hanai.

Okuda and I met over sake immediately after the partnership negotiations with GM came to light. My initial impression was in line with what I had heard from Kamio: a maverick. He freely badmouthed senior management to a journalist whom he was meeting for the first time. One could say he was only griping as any salaried employee might, but what set him apart was that he always suggested an alternative, stating what he himself would do. I was immediately convinced that if he ever became president, Toyota was definitely going to change.

Although he fared well, quickly climbing the corporate ladder at the new Toyota, no matter how high he climbed, it never went to his head. Moreover, he was curiosity on two feet. On the occasion of Prime Minister Keizo Obuchi's visit to the United States for a U.S.-Japan Summit meeting, Okuda, then chairman of Nikkeiren, was invited to attend a formal dinner hosted by President Clinton as a business figure. Sitting next to him was a middle-aged Japanese man who had also been invited to attend in his capacity as Hillary Clinton's fashion coordinator. The man said some interesting things. Okuda wanted to hear more, but the dinner ended and alas, they'd run out of time. Before parting, Okuda said that he would stop by the man's store in New York the next time he came to the U.S.

The U.S.-Japan Businessmen's Conference was held in San Francisco later that year. Okuda had a free day, so he flew six hours to New York in his personal jet, sought out the man's downtown store by foot, heard the continuation of the dinner talk at the White House, and immediately returned to San Francisco. What interested Okuda was the man's fashion sensibility.

We met less frequently after Okuda became president and then chairman, but we made up for it with a larger volume of phone calls. Although nowadays he calls me on my cell phone, before they were in common use he called me at work. He'd simply say, "It's Okuda"—and so, more than once, my assistant informed me after getting one of his calls that "a Mr. Okuda had called" and that "you were busy with a guest; I asked him to please call again." When he calls, we rarely talk about the automotive industry, developments at Toyota included. Most of the time, our conversation ranges from the state of the Japanese economy and trends in the U.S. economy to movies and books that we just read.

The following took place in August 1995. While covering a story in Dalian, China, I got a call from Okuda's private secretary asking whether we could postpone dinner plans in Nagoya scheduled for the day after I got back. Up until then, Okuda had never once cancelled an appointment with me. Instinct told me that he'd received informal notice that he'd be appointed president, so I asked Okuda's secretary to "give him my congratulations" and hung up the phone. Just as I had expected, the night before, Okuda had been given informal notice and strict orders from Shoichiro, Toyota's chairman, not to have contact with anyone outside the company until the board of managing directors made it formal.

An encounter with Halberstam

My encounter with David Halberstam, who unfortunately passed away last summer in a car accident, was the catalyst that prompted me to freelance after years working as a newspaper correspondent.

One year after the exclusive story on the partnership between GM and Toyota, Maryann Keller, who was known to be the most incisive auto-industry expert on Wall Street, asked me if I could talk to David Halberstam about the Japanese auto industry on the occasion of his visit to Japan since he was writing a book on the American and Japanese auto industries. Maryann Keller, by the way, is J.W. Chai's wife.

I gave Halberstam a day-long lecture on the past, present and future prospects of the Japanese automotive industry and introduced him to people I knew in the industry. After the lecture had wound down, I asked him what impelled him to take up Ford and Nissan Motor as opposed to other companies. His answer was lucid:

> My aim is to discuss the auto industry through the human relationships at representative U.S. and Japan firms. The reason I chose Ford on the U.S. side is that Chrysler is in too poor a standing and on the verge of bankruptcy. Conversely, GM is too enormous and financially well-off, and its backbone won't give out as long as there's no major sea-change. Since I chose the number two company in the U.S., I chose Nissan over Toyota on

the Japan side. Toyota would have been fine but, as far as I can tell, its management is faceless.

I was stunned by what he said because I had thought that no other company's management was as discernible as Toyota's. Afterwards, Halberstam offered some encouragement to me: "I heard from Ms. Keller that you got the exclusive on the Toyota-GM partnership. There must have been some sort of human drama that played out behind the scenes. How about writing something based on those personal relationships?"

The Reckoning, in which Halberstam contrasted Ford and Nissan to draw a lively picture of the ebb and flow of the U.S. and Japanese automotive industries, appeared in Japanese translation in May 1987. Back when we'd met, Halberstam had known hardly anything about the automotive industry, but upon reading his finished work, I was surprised anew by the New Journalist method, which brought past events back to life as though you were actually seeing them unfold.

Inspired, in the spring of 1993 I wrote *Kyojintachi no Akushu* (Handshake Between Giants), a nonfiction work replaying the events that occurred behind the scenes of the Toyota-GM joint venture. What I understood after sitting down to write it was that the automotive industry had become the bedrock of my life experience.

Twenty-three years have passed since Halberstam and I met. The vicissitudes of the automobile industry during that time have been intense. Unable to break free from a prolonged slump, the Ford that Halberstam wrote about has since been readily overtaken in size by Toyota, and in 2007 Toyota sales outpaced that of Ford in Ford's own home territory, the American market. A solid rival of Toyota for years, Nissan came under the wing of France's Renault at the end of the twentieth century. Finally, GM, which Halberstam described as "enormous and financially well-off," is seeing its backbone give out. After holding on to the World's No. 1 spot for 77 years, GM has been dethroned by Toyota.

There are no secrets to Toyota management

This book has been written especially for American readers. I've witnessed half of Toyota's history and this work is the culmination.

The point I try constantly to get across in this book is that there are no secrets to Toyota management. What there is, is simply effort.

For example, take the case of the Toyota Production System (TPS), which overseas automakers compete to adopt. Countless books on TPS have been published in both Japan and the U.S. Most of them, however, are technical instruction manuals. But TPS is not so sweet and easy that it can be mastered simply by reading such books. Rival automakers that take the trouble to visit Toyota's factories and follow the manual they receive from Toyota nevertheless encounter difficulties implementing the system because they have no idea how TPS was born in the first place.

I had the opportunity to get together with GM Chairman Roger Smith, who passed away in late autumn of 2007, when he visited Japan in the spring of 1984. "We thought that there was some kind of inconceivable secret to TPS, but there was nothing arcane about it," he insisted at the time. "Using computers, we'll be able to make high-quality cars that surpass Toyota's."

Prodded by Smith, GM built a separate high-tech computer-equipped plant in Tennessee and launched production of the Saturn line of compact passenger vehicles. It's been twenty years, but the project can hardly be touted as a success. Although for a time the banners of *kaizen* (modification) and *kairyo* (improvement) had been flying at GM factories, without knowing the origins, subsequent development and growth of TPS, it was all just empty theory.

The "secret" of Toyota's strength is that it has had a sound strategy since its inception and, more importantly, that successive generations of senior management have carried on the tradition. Kiichiro hoped "to use Japanese brains and skills to raise up an auto industry in Japan and make world-class compact passenger cars." Although this dream did not come to pass during the Kiichiro era, his cousin Eiji made it happen with the Corolla. Had they been satisfied with that, however, Toyota likely would have ended up a mere manufacturer of affordable cars. Eiji hoisted up the new goal of "Global Ten," or capturing a 10-percent share of global sales. It took a long time—two decades—to realize that objective.

After achieving that Global Ten, Toyota boldly declared that it would raise its market share to 15 percent by 2010. Fifteen percent is synonymous with being the largest automaker in the world. At the same time, so as not to be seen as hegemonic, it laid out the concept of "corporate virtue" or winning social esteem and responded promptly to the issue of global warming by developing hybrid-electric vehicles. Thanks also to its luxury brand Lexus, Toyota's image changed dramatically, spurring further growth.

Toyota's greatness is that quantity (scale) is accompanied by quality (revenue). Be that as it may, the company hasn't always been a high-revenue operation. It has been both driven to the brink of bankruptcy by a shortfall in financing and also condemned by the public for failing to meet the deadline for emissions regulations.

Automobiles are an international commodity, and management, too, is borderless. The business of management is conducted by people. This book may feel like difficult reading at first owing to the appearance of many names with which American readers aren't familiar. But if you want to know why Toyota has become the top automaker in the world, the quickest way is to familiarize yourself with its history and the leaders behind it.

Chapter 1

The Toyoda Precepts

Toyota Motor Company, established in 1937, was originally to be called "*Toyoda* Motor Company" after Toyoda Automatic Loom Works, its parent company, and the Toyoda family itself.[1] The cars it produced and sold during the Automatic Loom Works years bore the name "Toyoda." Following a prize competition for a logo upon the company's formation, an emblem consisting of a circle around "Toyoda" written in *katakana* (a phonetic script) had been adopted.

But Toyota's founder, Kiichiro Toyoda, objected to this, saying, "The original plan was 'Toyoda,' but that's written in ten strokes. Ten denotes perfection, consummation. But Toyoda's cars aren't consummate yet. We're going to progress, aiming for that level. Also, Toyota is easier for foreigners to pronounce than Toyoda."

To emphasize this aspiration for better car-making and to make clear to outsiders that the automotive enterprise wasn't a Toyoda family business, Kiichiro softened the final consonant and decided on "Toyota." (Incidentally, the city where Toyota is currently headquartered is written using the same characters as Toyoda but pronounced "Toyota," like the company.)

When Kiichiro entered into the auto industry, he proposed what sounded like a dream at the time: "We aren't just going to be dealing in cars. We're going to put Japanese brains and skills to work to develop world-class compacts." His insight was that cars are an international commodity and that if the business was to stand at all, the world had to become its stage.

---

1. Founded in 1926, Toyoda Automatic Loom Works is now known as Toyota Industries Corporation.

Corporate mission: contribute to society

Seventy years later, in 2007, Toyota produced and sold more vehicles than General Motors, matching in revenue terms the lord of the global auto industry of the last three-quarters of a century. Many speak of the "Toyota Production System" (TPS) as the source of Toyota's might. What forms the backbone of TPS is the "Just-In-Time" (JIT) production system devised by Kiichiro that takes economic efficiency to the limit by "supplying the right parts at the right time and in the right amount." According to Eiji Toyoda, whose role it was to provide on-site instruction in JIT since the construction of the first plant, "The JIT approach is the kind of production method everyone who's ever been involved in manufacturing comes up with. Refusing to let his thoughts end as theory, putting them into practice—there it was that Kiichiro excelled."

A textbook allocation of people, materials, money and time doesn't necessarily make a blue-chip company. A business is an organism that does not go by the book. Toyota was able to become the world's top automaker because, encountering various difficulties and surmounting them one by one, it continued to face reality and reform its business.

The origin of Toyota management—handed down continuously through its successive leaders since the founding until the present day—the Toyoda Precepts articulate the life and thinking of Sakichi Toyoda, master inventor and founder of the Toyota Group. Compiled by Kiichiro, the five-part precepts were announced on October 30, 1935, the sixth anniversary of Sakichi's death.

1. Be contributive to the development and welfare of the country by working together, regardless of position, in faithfully fulfilling your duties.
2. Be at the vanguard of the times through endless creativity, inquisitiveness and pursuit of improvement.
3. Be practical and avoid frivolity.
4. Be kind and generous; strive to create a warm, homelike atmosphere.
5. Be reverent, and show gratitude for things great and small in thought and deed.[2]

2. English translation of the Toyoda Precepts is as appears on Toyota's website: http://www.toyota.co.jp/en/vision/philosophy/

Many companies have a mission statement, but most of them are decked with fancy but dry words. Meanwhile, the Toyoda Precepts are the willed instructions of Sakichi, whom the Toyota man looks upon as an affectionate father. Sakichi's life had even appeared for a time in elementary school morality textbooks.

The first precept—"Be contributive…"—encapsulates Sakichi's life. Growing up in a poor family, the boy Sakichi felt motivated to aspire to the path of inventor: If inventions would benefit his country, he'd invent something no one else ever thought of.

Much of Lake Hamana's environs, Sakichi's birthplace, was dedicated to agriculture. In the off-season, farmers' wives customarily hand-wove cotton on the side. The looms they used were crude affairs powered by foot, and the entire weaving process was time-consuming.

"Clothing (cotton cloth) is a Japanese consumer good," Sakichi reasoned. "Increasing the production efficiency of cotton and offering it cheaply would benefit the country. The foot-powered looms used in Japan are too primitive. Upgrading them would allow for faster weaving." He decided this was an invention worth pursuing. It was 1885.

Sakichi accurately discerned the situation in Japan, which had cast off nearly three centuries of isolationism and was rushing to modernize. "Agriculture requires one hectare of land to support a single household. The same hectare, employed to set up an industry, could provide for an entire village. Japan, with so little land, has to engage in industry. So I focused my invention on the weaving machine and put it together with my own hands."

The undercurrent of Toyota management is this idea of "benefiting the country." Only twice has Toyota fallen into the red throughout its seventy-year history: its first year in business and during the labor disputes of 1950. A highly profitable and leading Japanese firm as early as the 1960s, Toyota subsequently continued to enjoy tremendous growth in both quantity (sales) and quality (profit).

When the first oil crisis broke out in the early 1970s, a backlash against the high economic growth era led to mounting criticism of businesses. Toyota was hoisted up as the symbol, and criticized for "making too much money."

A white-faced Eiji Toyoda, then president, countered, "The Toyota company is not just about making money. We're always

wondering what we might do to vitalize industry in our country. For
Toyota, contributing to society means properly profiting and paying
taxes for the country's sake."

Uniting quantity and quality, Toyota is by now a target of
emulation among Japanese companies, and big businesses around
the world hope to maintain blue-chip status over an extended period
"like Toyota." Lee Kun-Hee, chairman of Samsung Electronics,
Korea's largest company and a dominant player in the global market
in semiconductors, mobile phones, etc., once asked Hiroshi Okuda
(then Toyota chairman) point-blank what the formula is for long-
term prosperity.

Okuda's answer was clear: "A corporation's mission in society is
to contribute to it. If a company's goals can be made to match the
national interest, that company is guaranteed development."

"Invention" as an article of incorporation

The second Toyoda Precept—"Be at the vanguard…"—is a deeply
Toyota-esque principle of action. Though it's not widely known, all
Toyota-affiliated manufacturing firms including the Motor Company
include the word "invention" in their articles of incorporation.

There is a history behind this. When Toyoda Automatic Loom
Works was first established, it naturally listed "the manufacture
and sale of textile spinning machines and other machinery" as the
company's objective, but also, at Sakichi's insistence, "invention and
research pertaining to the above" as an important task. Valuing both
invention and profit is a mentality that has been inherited not only by
Toyota Motor but by each firm in the Toyota Group.

Fujio Cho—a protégé of Taichi Ohno, the white-collar father of
TPS, and Toyota chairman-cum-TPS evangelist—describes the late
Sakichi's invention:

> The loom that Sakichi invented was not simply an inspired
> invention but was actually productized with an emphasis on
> modification and improvement through field testing. He spent
> a substantial part of a quarter of a century developing the loom
> from scratch until it evolved into an automatic loom. My own
> interpretation is that an invention is about making possible

something that was previously thought impossible through modification and improvement. Sakichi accomplished this. It must have entailed a lot of painstaking work. It is precisely because Sakichi's genes have rubbed off on Toyota that we have been able to implement TPS through a long succession of hardworking efforts to modify and improve.

One of the things that has been productized in the spirit of Sakichi's inventions is the hybrid-electric vehicle, which combines electricity with a gasoline engine. From the late 1960s to the 1970s, photochemical smog became a significant problem in both Japan and the United States.

U.S. democratic congressman Edmund Muskie submitted legislation to Congress aimed exclusively at automobiles (Muskie Bill), which was then approved in December, 1970. In rapid response to the Muskie Bill, Japan drafted its own version of the legislation which included regulatory values consistent with those in the U.S. Honda was among the first to announce a bid to conform to regulations. But Toyota and Nissan, having developed a variety of different models, failed to meet the deadline. Finally, they successfully appealed to the government for a 2-year extension.

For Toyota this was nothing short of humiliating. The strength of present-day Toyota lies in how it used this humiliation as a catalyst to spend time pioneering the development of an eco-car to contend with global warming and the depletion of fossil fuels, which it released ahead of the field. Nowadays, eco-car has become a byword for Toyota and soon laid the groundwork for the "environmental Toyota" corporate brand. Like outflanking an opponent in a game of Othello, with a single stone's throw Toyota used its past mistakes as a springboard to dramatically rework the company's image altogether.

Genuine local flavor

The third precept—"Be practical and avoid frivolity"—is not unrelated to the features of Aichi Prefecture's Mikawa region, the home of Toyota's headquarters. Aichi Prefecture is positioned in the very middle of the long north-south orientation of the Japan archipelago. Toyota's headquarters and main plants are concentrated in Toyota

City, which itself is situated right in the center of the Mikawa area. Nagoya (Owari), the location of Aichi's prefectural government, and Mikawa are geographically back to back, which means that one can travel by highway from Toyota headquarters to the heart of Nagoya in about 40 minutes. Despite this, the two areas are entirely different in terms of climate, people and temperament.

As most of the Mikawa region is mountainous, life there is without pretension and the people are simple and hardworking, as well as enduringly honest. In *The House of the Conqueror*, a book portraying Ieyasu Tokugawa, Ryotaro Shiba, one of Japan's most prominent historical writers, describes the distinctive features of the people of Mikawa as "a strong sense of loyalty, remarkable integrity, an exclusive identification with their native place, a rustic manner, and simplicity."

Drawing on the natural and spiritual features of Mikawa, Toyota's corporate climate is genuine and sincere. Endowed with a down-to-earth and independent spirit, Toyota continues to embody the spirit of the Mikawa people, valuing content over form, substance over name.

After Kiichiro passed away, Eiji took the reins and built the foundation for Toyota's development. Although Toyota's head office— located at 1 Toyota-Cho, Toyota City—lies in the center of the city, on Toyota's own map the city centers around Eiji's home in the Tanimachi Yagen district.

From Eiji's garden one can just make out Toyota's headquarters and main plant to the east. In addition, lying in a radial pattern are the Motomachi Plant and Teiho Plant to the north, the Miyoshi Plant to the northwest, the Tsutsumi, Shimoyama and Myochi plants to the west, the Takaoka Plant to the southwest, and finally the Kamigo Plant to the southeast. In other words, Eiji's house is at the axis of a network of enormous factories stretched out in all directions. Moreover, if one were to draw a circle around this area on the map, Toyota's headquarters and 9 main plants in the Mikawa district would fit perfectly within a 5-kilometer radius of his house. It is from here that Eiji ironed out the details of negotiations to form the alliance with GM that shook the automotive industry around the world. Supporting Eiji from the sidelines since 1969 for the 15 years he served as president were two people, both Mikawans born and bred: Taichi Ohno, the father of TPS, and Masao Hanai, who could be dubbed head of the "Toyota Bank."

Honorary Chairman Shoichiro Toyoda has a house each in Nagoya and Tokyo, and Okuda has one in Okazaki, while both former president Fujio Cho and the current president, Katsuaki Watanabe, have one in Toyota City. Each thus resides in the Mikawa region, echoing many of Toyota's past and present leaders who lived in close contact with Mikawa's local features.

Employees are a company's treasure

"Be kind and generous…"—the fourth of the Toyoda Precepts— expresses an extended familism characteristic of Toyota. Throughout his life, Sakichi viewed his employees as family. Kiichiro witnessed this firsthand. When he sold the patent for the automatic loom invented by Sakichi to the British company Pratt Brothers, under the pretext of a special merit bonus he distributed ¥100,000 of the lump-sum proceeds of ¥250,000 to employees directly involved in developing the loom, and the remaining ¥150,000 to, not only Toyota Boshoku (Textile Manufacturing) and Toyoda Automatic Loom Works, but all 6,000 company employees that together formed the Toyoda *zaibatsu* conglomerate.

Toyoda Automatic Loom Works earned exactly ¥250,000 during the three years it was in business. This money was desperately important to Kiichiro, who had already determined to direct his efforts towards the auto business. However, he then announced to the public that he would provision the special merit bonus for a 100-day Buddhist memorial service to be performed in Sakichi's honor on February 5, 1931.

Distributing ¥150,000 equally amongst all employees yielded ¥25 per person. As the average monthly salary of female factory workers at the time was ¥28, this amounted to an interim bonus of almost one month's salary for employees.

The world was then in the midst of what seemed like an indefinite financial crisis. For this reason alone Kiichiro's tactic paid off. His provision of a special merit bonus was picked up extensively by newspapers and radically boosted employee morale. As a result, Toyoda Automatic Loom Works received a flood of orders when it released its high-draft fine spinning machine the following month.

With this, Kiichiro stabilized the automatic loom business and created an environment conducive to pursuing automaking.

Kiichiro freely and openly professed that "employees are a company's treasure." When employees repatriated to Japan in droves during the turbulent times following the war, he turned to making pots and pans—anything he could think of—because he could not provide for his employees with cars alone.

Eiji was charged with setting up a chinaware business, while Shoichi Saito, among the first group of university graduates to join the company, was assigned to farm-raise loaches. Just before graduating from university, Kiichiro's eldest son Shoichiro was sent to Wakkanai, Hokkaido, situated on the northernmost tip of Japan and referred to at the time as "the end of the Earth." His task was to mechanize a factory engaged in the production of fish sausages and fish paste.

Largely due to the severe fiscal austerity imposed by the Dodge Line in 1949, the Japanese economy was devastated almost past hope of recovery. Even in the automotive industry, rivals Nissan and Isuzu Motors were quick to move ahead with massive downsizing. Nonetheless, Toyota avoided employee layoffs out of deference to the Toyoda Precepts. They were able to do this because affiliated textile machine companies such as Toyoda Automatic Loom Works were doing well at the time and thus able to support Toyota financially.

But naturally there was a limit to this. Even while fully cognizant that Toyota's coffers had been cleaned out as of December 1949, Kiichiro exchanged memoranda with the labor union to the effect that he would remain firm in not laying off workers. In the end, however, the situation deteriorated into a sink-or-swim conundrum. Pushed to the very edge of bankruptcy by the end of 1950, Toyota was finally forced to fire employees the following spring. This of course developed into a labor dispute, eventually leading Kiichiro to resign as president to settle the situation.

Although nowadays the only person left at Toyota who knows about these grueling times firsthand is Eiji, over the years many of Toyota's leaders have been told of the strain of running a business during such a demanding age. Other than that once, at no time before or after has Toyota cut back its personnel. Refusing to layoff its staff no matter the circumstances remains Toyota's credo to this day. Knowing this provides Toyota's employees with the peace of mind to focus on TPS.

Turning Sakichi's world into a reality

The final precept is to "Be reverent…" For a large majority of Japanese companies, work comes to an end on December 28 and starts up again on the fourth of the new year. But at 8:30 in the morning on the first of January, Toyota's executive managers pass through a shrine gate surrounded by a grove of pine trees on the north side of Toyota's main factory and gather on the premises of Hoko Shrine, which is dedicated to the god of manufacturing. Nearly everyone lines up and raises a glass of juice in a toast. With the president leading the way, they perform a ceremonious rite before a small Shinto shrine in which all present put their hands together and offer a prayer for the future prosperity of the company.

Upon concluding the solemn ritual, they warm themselves over spirits and cold sake at a nearby gymnasium and wish one another a happy new year. On years when the northerlies are fierce and the chill cuts down to the bone, no one can possibly be in the mood for it. Toyota continued to perform this ancient ceremony up until when Shoichiro served as president, the third from the Toyoda family. Hoko Shrine was built by Kiichiro based on the Toyoda Precepts.

Ikichi, Sakichi's father, was an assiduous believer in the Hotoku Sect. Hotoku (moral requital) is a kind of "indigenous faith" based on the "reconciliation of economics and morality," a principle which Sontoku Ninomiya, a peasant who worked his way from rags to riches, called for throughout his life. Sontoku preached that "what one contributes to society, without regard for self-interest, will one day be returned." Sakichi heard much of Sontoku's ideas from Ikichi from a young age, instilling in him a deep admiration for Sontoku's doctrine.

The Toyoda Precepts remain alive and well at Toyota. Current president Katsuaki Watanabe secretly carries the Toyoda Precepts around with him, tucked into his business card holder. Whenever he is in a bind, he takes them out and reads them over a number of times, reaffirming the origins of the Toyota company.

Recently, Watanabe has been saying with a straight face: "I always set our goals high. I am asking our development team to design cars that clean up the air, cars in which you can cross the North American continent on a single charge of energy, cars that make people healthy."

Sakichi worked until the very end to invent a perpetual-motion machine, a device with unlimited power that, once given momentum, could run forever without stopping. While reading over the Toyoda Precepts, Watanabe is taking matters into his own hands and trying to turn Sakichi's world into a reality.

Chapter 2
What It Takes a Leader

IN ADDITION TO BUSINESS PRACTICES, "management" also refers to the managers themselves. A company's prospects depend entirely on the abilities of its leader. Business is combat, war. A president is the operation's high command and has only one job: to set forth the goals that the company aims to achieve. Waging war at the head of a large group called a company requires goals to be specified in a way that is comprehensible to its warriors on the ground; otherwise, the group crumbles into a mere herd of cattle.

In terms of setting targets, it is no different in the political world. Former Prime Minister Junichiro Koizumi set out to achieve the privatization of Japan's postal service and won two-thirds of the seats in the 2005 Lower House elections.

It is certainly true that no one knows what the future holds in the world of politics. Following in the wake of Koizumi, Shinzo Abe laid out highly ideological initiatives for building a "beautiful country" and "making a clean break from the postwar regime" in the run-up to the 2007 Upper House elections. But in the end, Abe's platform did not win the hearts and minds of the people, leading to a humiliating defeat. Despite having ignored the will of the people by high-handedly staying in office, he finally ceded control after making a policy speech at an extraordinary Diet session in the fall. Even more than their qualifications as politicians, the difference between the two prime ministers and what decided their outcomes was whether the goals they set out struck a chord among the people.

The leader must set goals

A company's performance hinges on economic trends. A company may also fall victim to natural disasters, such as an earthquake, and temporarily go into deficit as a result. However, the worst-case scenario—bankruptcy—is entirely the leader's responsibility. In the operation of a business, all disasters are essentially man-made and not natural. Decision-making at the top carries that much gravity.

Kiichiro Toyoda, Toyota's founder, set the visionary goal of "developing world-class compacts with the brains and skills of Japanese."

Faced with capital liberalization, the third president of Toyota, Taizo Ishida, the "re-founder" of the company, appealed to his employees to "defend your castle yourself." Ishida directed the manifesto not only to his employees but to the entire world, declaring, "Toyota will not capitulate to foreign companies."

Eiji Toyoda, Toyota's fifth president, realized Kiichiro's dream with the popular Corolla line of compact cars. He then set his sights on "Global Ten," capturing a 10 percent share of global sales. Initially, media and the company's staff reacted coolly to the proclamation, seeing it as one of "Eiji's fantasies," but employees gradually got down to business and achieved the objective in 2001.

Shoichiro, Kiichiro's eldest son and the sixth president of Toyota, was eager to join the ranks of international firms, a move for which Eiji had paved the way. Labeled relentlessly among media as the "backwoods daimyo of Mikawa," Shoichiro sought to reorient Toyota, which had immersed itself in a "Mikawa Monro Doctrine" closed to outsiders. He wanted to shift away from the company's introverted tendencies towards a more extroverted approach, thus building the foundation that would eventually vault Toyota into the position of world's top automaker.

Toyota's eighth president, Hiroshi Okuda, originally with Toyota Motor Sales, sensed an impending crisis in domestic sales, which had fallen below a 40 percent market share (new car sales excluding lightweight vehicles) while Toyota's attention was turned towards bolstering its international presence. Soon after being appointed president, he turned the company around with a policy to "recapture 40 percent," achieving the objective in a short period of time. The auto industry is constantly plagued with the fear of the abyss that lies in wait for those who sit back satisfied with the status quo.

Privately, Okuda had designs for "No. 1 in the World." While rebuilding Toyota's domestic sales, the cornerstone of the company's foundation, he spearheaded the development of new lines of cars including the Prius hybrid electric and the Lexus line of luxury vehicles. These moves utterly transformed the public's view of Toyota, a perception which had previously held that "Toyota's boring cars aimed for a B."

Concurrently, Toyota embarked aggressively on efforts to begin local production in the U.S. not only to avoid trade friction but to make Toyota less susceptible to exchange rate fluctuations. This series of strategies provided the momentum for Toyota's rise to the top.

Favorable sales in the U.S. market played a significant role in helping Toyota achieve the Global Ten mark first envisioned by Eiji. Fujio Cho, Toyota's ninth president, was the one responsible for the construction of a long-overdue plant in Kentucky and the one who planted the seeds to ensure that TPS took root in the U.S. In the spring of 2002, when achieving Global Ten appeared to be certain, Cho, along with Okuda, drafted "Global Vision 2010," aiming to raise Toyota's share of global sales from 10 to 15 percent. Toyota is already within range of achieving its goal. However, as he approaches his ninety-fifth birthday in September 2008, Eiji cautioned the younger generation of Toyota managers, who are as yet unschooled in the hardships of yesteryear, against letting this go to their head:

> Toyota's objective is to achieve a 15 percent share of global sales. Just because the company made it to number one in the world is no reason to get carried away. I dreamt that, after becoming number one in Japan, next would be number one in the world. The first step towards accomplishing this was Global Ten. But the target set five years ago by active management was 15 percent, and not world leader. If the goal were to achieve number one, the next objective could only be to maintain that status. Once on the defensive, a company can only go downhill. After reaching a target of 15 percent, Toyota must move on to a new goal.

Technological capability does not guarantee success

The history of the modern automotive industry extends for no more than 120 years at most. The auto business is a money-guzzler and, even more, it is difficult for new market entrants because it is so closely tied in with national industrial strategy. This alone has made the plight of emerging automakers a miserable one.

For the last successful example of this in the U.S., one must go all the way back to 1925 when Walter Chrysler formed the Chrysler Corporation. Established 13 years later in 1937, Toyota is still, comparatively speaking, an emerging force in the auto industry.

Former GM Vice President John DeLorean—the mind behind *On a Clear Day You Can See General Motors* (written by John Patrick Wright), which gives an insider's perspective on GM—solicited investors to finance the establishment of the DeLorean Motor Company (DMC) just prior to the first oil crisis in 1973. The "DMC-12," replete with butterfly doors designed by the celebrated Italian car designer Giorgetto Giugiaro, garnered enthusiastic support among some as the model for the time-traveling vehicle in the film *Back to the Future*.

DeLorean established a name for itself as a phenom of GM engineering, but was quickly branded as earning failing marks on the operational front. The reason for this, despite a breakthrough design that used stainless steel in the car's frame, is that the DMC-12's engine not only lacked the power of a sports car but had problems with quality due to a sloppy production process. A funding shortfall compounded this, leading the company to bankruptcy after having produced only 8,500 units. The cause of DeLorean's debacle was not so much poor managerial ability as an absence of it.

Now attracting attention in the U.S. is Tesla Motors, considered the "car company of Silicon Valley." The company sells the "Tesla Roadster," a sports car that runs on electricity. Despite retailing at a pricey $98,000, such environmentally concerned celebrities as California Governor Arnold Schwarzenegger, Google co-founders Sergey Brin and Larry Page, and actor George Clooney have added their names to the preorder list. The company's sales target for the Roadster is around 1,000 units per year, which they aim to increase to around 10,000 units with the release of their next sedan.

Judging by their plans, and to those who know the auto business well, Tesla appears to be little more than another quixotic company, similar to DMC. One does not succeed in the automotive business on high ideals alone. Even adding technological prowess to high ideals docs not guarantee success.

The differences between Toyota and Honda

Globally the last entrant into the auto industry, Honda pushed its way onto the scene as a dominant carmaker in a very brief time. Its secret was that the engineering genius Soichiro Honda and his sworn ally Takeo Fujisawa worked in tandem to propel the business forward. Fujisawa's tasks were finance and operations; namely, management. "In the beginning, we did everything we could except burglary and fraud," Fujisawa used to say of the extent to which they scrambled to raise funds. Meanwhile, they threw themselves wholeheartedly into an extensive marketing campaign dedicated to selling the products that Soichiro developed.

The truth is that Honda evolved from what at the time of its establishment basically consisted of two separate organizations: the Soichiro-led "Honda Industries," in charge of development and production, and the Fujisawa-led "Fujisawa Trading," which handled all other areas. Honda Motors thus crystallized as each man applied himself diligently to his own area of expertise. Soichiro and Fujisawa showed not just admiration but naked rivalry towards one another, but it was the dream they shared that opened the gate for Honda.

Soichiro loved to use the phrase "No. 1 in the world." He quickly delivered on his words by building a "world-renowned Honda" based on motorbike sales. His dream to become the global leader also in four-wheel vehicles was staked on Soichiro and Fujisawa's successors. Right after making the decision to begin production in the U.S. (in Ohio), which it accomplished before Toyota did, Honda's second president Kiyoshi Kawashima boasted to a crowd of newspaper reporters: "GM wasn't always the top automaker in the world. One day, we (Honda), too… Local production in the U.S. is the first step in this direction."

Even today, Honda is faring better than expected in the American market. After playing second fiddle to Honda in terms of on-site production, however, Toyota mounted a fierce comeback, overtaking Chrysler and then Ford in the U.S. market. Toyota achieved astonishing growth, eventually passing GM in passenger vehicle sales in July 2007.

Although Honda became the first automaker to design a low-emission vehicle to stamp out exhaust fumes and had a head start in local production in the U.S., it has been lagging behind Toyota. Other than sheer scale, this is due to the fact that its corporate image has become blurred, outstripped by Toyota for instance in the development of an eco-car to combat global warming. Takeo Fukui, Honda's current president, is rather abstract with the objectives that he outlines for the company: "We aim to become the world's most influential automaker on a technological and qualitative level."

Another difference between Toyota and Honda can be seen in how upper management is voted in. Although not stipulated in its bylaws, Honda customarily elects senior managers with technical expertise.

"Honda is a manufacturing company, so its future presidents should have an engineering background and have served as president of Honda R&D. Personnel from operations play exclusively a supporting role to the engineer president."

The person who first initiated this policy was not Soichiro but Fujisawa, the one responsible for all aspects of the company's business operations. From Soichiro to Fukui, Honda has turned out six different presidents. All of them have been engineers and, moreover, have served as president of R&D.

A continued succession of engineer presidents will allow Soichiro's ideas to be passed on, but Fujisawa's distinct management approach can be intoned by successors but not readily inherited. This once caused an in-house power struggle. Nobuhiko Kawamoto, Honda's fourth president, had a heated disagreement with the production department over Japan domestic sales, a conflict that was finally resolved with the absorption of "Fujisawa Trading" into "Honda Industries." "Honda Industries" executives thus gained full control on all aspects of management, including development, production and sales and marketing.

Toyota has chosen its leaders in a way that reflects the times and the company's standing. Of the ten presidents Toyota has turned out thus far, only three, all of whom hail from the Toyoda family— Kiichiro, Eiji and Shoichiro—can be referred to as engineer presidents.

All three individuals were brilliant engineers but were, at the same time, lauded as excellent business leaders.

While Toyota and Honda are neck-to-neck in their dedication to carmaking, their management styles are polar opposites. Since its inception, Toyota has upheld the Toyoda family name, while Honda has not hoisted its founding family's name quite in the same way, exemplified by the fact that neither Honda founder Soichiro nor Fujisawa ever had their children join the company. The relationship between the Honda company and the Honda family has waned over the years to the point that nowadays they no longer have any at all. Soichiro, who passed away in 1991, remains a symbol of Honda's legacy, while Fujisawa's existence has been forgotten.

In this respect, Toyota molds itself as a company whose existence owes solely to the Toyoda family. Okuda describes the role of the founding family: "Countries and organizations need a unifying symbol. Just like the emperor is a symbol of Japan, the Toyoda family is a symbol for Toyota, and this is something that we would like to hold on to."

To put it another way, the Toyoda family *is* the Toyoda Precepts. As long as Toyota's management does not deviate from the Toyoda Precepts, business operations will not lose their primary focus.

What enabled Toyota to become the world's leading automaker was the constant accession of well-qualified people to the top seat. When a poorly qualified individual accedes to leadership, it is usually because the top executive, who has the right to appoint a successor, wants to hold on to his or her status. Desiring to exert continued influence, salarymen CEO's have a tendency to appoint yes-men as successors. This dumbs down the corporate power structure, encouraging sycophancy and undercutting the organization's dynamism, and begins to lead the company into decline.

The Nissan saga

The picture of a misstep in leader selection, Nissan Motors capitulated to Renault. The de facto founder of Nissan was Yoshisuke Aikawa, Kiichiro's cousin-in-law (his wife's cousin). Aikawa presumed not to crown the company with his own name. Nissan is an abbreviation for Nihon Sangyo (Japan Industries). "The purpose of any company with which I am involved is to contribute to Japanese industry, so I never considered attaching my name to it," said Aikawa in his later years to describe his mindset towards business.

Aikawa's strategy was what is now referred to as M&A. His business grew immensely as he took public one after another the companies that he acquired until his firm was referred to as the "Nissan Konzern." He expanded into Manchuria (present-day northeast China) in accordance with national policy, but met with disaster when he conducted business together with the South Manchuria Railway, becoming a target for zaibatsu dissolution after the war and meeting with the miserable fate of being purged from public office as head of the zaibatsu. After being released, Aikawa cut ties with the business world and took up a new life in politics, never to return to Nissan.

After the war, Nissan twice fell victim to labor disputes. During the first labor dispute in 1949, the union backed down from its position and accepted the company's proposal to layoff workers. When the second dispute erupted in 1953, the union launched a protracted strike in an effort to regain lost ground. Nissan took on a hopeless battle by declaring a factory lockout, but finally brought the situation under control by making an agreement with a rival labor union. Taking the lead for the company was Katsuji Kawamata, who had joined Nissan after working at the Industrial Bank of Japan. He was then appointed president in recognition of his accomplishments. By this point, Aikawa's genetic imprint on Nissan had completely ceased to exist.

Kawamata forged a unique course for labor-management cooperation together with Ichiro Shioji, a close friend and the leader of Nissan Labor, and revived Nissan into a highly respectable firm on par with Toyota, over time earning himself an in-house reputation as a re-founder of the company. Pleased with his achievements, Kawamata built a bust of himself at the main entrance to Nissan's Oppama Plant in Yokosuka, Kanagawa Prefecture.

But the wheels of fortune kept turning. The situation turned around completely once Takashi Ishihara, coming from Aikawa connections, became president. Soon after assuming his post, Ishihara, declaring that "managers should act like managers and unions like unions," drew a clear line of demarcation between management and the union and renounced all previously established labor-management cooperation. He also railed fiercely against unions with regard to their implications for internationalization, escalating the issue into a family feud with Kawamata who, though then retired as chairman, had supported unions.

A company should basically be investing in "operations that will return a profit tomorrow," but Ishihara promoted "projects for the day after tomorrow" that offered little hope that invested capital would be recoverable in the future. As the company's top manager, Ishihara charged recklessly ahead hell-bent on international strategy under the slogan of "Pursuing Toyota."

Internationalization was one of the most pressing needs among Japanese companies in the 1980s. Considering rival Toyota's reluctance about going international, Ishihara's approach was not fundamentally wrong. But he pursued mostly dead-end projects with shaky prospects for profitability for which even amateur investors foresaw failure from the start. Ironically, Shioji, a union leader with experience having studied abroad, was possessed of international sensibilities. However, instead of enlisting its cooperation, Ishihara divided up the union and dismissed Shioji.

Ishihara ran the company from the outside even after retiring as chairman, continuing to push ahead with grab-bag tactics. By then the runaway train was out of control. Nissan personnel noticed that the quality of the company's management deteriorated every time there was a change in leadership, but no amount of grief on the part of salaried workers could put a stop to it.

The results spoke for themselves. Yoshifumi Tsuji, the second president after Ishihara, created a disgraceful legacy during his 4-year tenure as president, incurring losses all across the board. He was forced to step down amidst frustration and disappointment. His replacement, Yoshikazu Hanawa, dubbed the "Prince of Nissan," desperately sought to rectify his predecessor's hasty strategies but it was too late. He found that the countdown to bankruptcy had already begun.

As Hanawa struggled without success to rebuild Nissan, it suddenly became a central figure on the stage of the industry's international reorganization. After traversing a winding and arduous path, Nissan finally capitulated to France's Renault, inducing Ishihara to say: "When I was president, that company was no more than a target for a merger."

Nissan, now a foreign-affiliated company, underwent successful restructuring under the leadership of Carlos Ghosn, who was sent in by Renault. Many of Nissan's employees can no longer recall even the names of past presidents such as Aikawa, Nissan's founder, let alone Kawamata—deemed the company's re-founder—or Ishihara.

The god of sales: mixing business with the personal

To this day Toyota has consistently upheld the spirit of its founder in this regard. Toyota's success owes to the ever-watchful eye of Eiji who, still in good condition and fully cognizant of the long history of the Toyoda Automatic Loom Works automobile division, has ensured that individuals who lack the spirit and ability of the company's founders do not make top executive.

The most overshadowed of Toyota's past presidents were its third president, Fukio Nakagawa, who died suddenly from heart failure, and its seventh president, Tatsuro Toyoda, who suffered from high blood pressure. Both men either passed away or fell ill without having fulfilled their life's ambitions.

Toyota, too, once encountered a crisis. The stage was not the main arm of Toyota but, rather, the former Toyota Motor Sales. At the end of 1949, Toyota, unable to muster the ¥200 million needed to close out the year, was exposed to the threat of bankruptcy. Financial institutions were reluctant to extend Toyota financing and Toyota's main suppliers began to hold back their wares. Rumors on the street that the company was destined for bankruptcy started taking on a ring of truth. The person who saved the company was Takeo Takanashi, head of the Bank of Japan's Nagoya branch. Judging that the Nagoya region would be dealt a catastrophic blow if Toyota went under, he orchestrated a loan syndicate through the Bank of Japan to extend Toyota an emergency loan in the amount of ¥180 million at year's end. This was a substantial BOJ special loan. With this Toyota was just able to stave off the worst possible scenario. The loan came with one condition, however: the separation of production and sales. On this the BOJ's intentions were clear:

> Forcing production in the face of flagging sales bogged down Toyota's finances. It will be difficult for Toyota to fully restructure its operations no matter how much financing they

are provided until the company modifies such an unsound business approach. Consequently, Toyota Motor Company must split up production and sales and devote itself exclusively to the manufacturing side of automaking.

Toyota Motor Sales was thus established in April 1950. One of the conditions of the new company was to cut off relations with Toyota Motor Company, which also prohibited investment. Shotaro Kamiya, managing director of Toyota Motor Sales, scraped together ¥80 million of capital and straightaway assumed the presidency of the new company.

Both Kiichiro and Eiji understood the separation of Toyota Sales from Toyota Motor as a temporary measure to avert further disaster. After Toyota's restructuring was complete, Eiji proposed a merger several times to Kamiya, but the latter displayed no intention whatsoever to act on this proposal, saying only, "Give me some time— I'll think it over." When he considered Kamiya's meritorious service to the company, Eiji was forced with difficulty to abandon hope for a merger anytime while he was still around.

With the intensifying pace of motorization, Kamiya, stating categorically that "Toyota Motor and Toyota Motor Sales are two wheels on the same car," appealed to staff members that the two companies were on an equal footing with one another and further encouraged the self-reliance of Toyota Sales' employees. The more he appealed for self-reliance, however, the more he brought the two companies' differences into bold relief. Coordinating between the two companies was partly to blame for Toyota's delayed international expansion.

After becoming involved in the tourist industry and the oil business during his later years, Kamiya began to attract attention for business practices that mixed the public and the private. He invited frowns for constructing a bust of himself not only at Toyota Sales' Nagoya headquarters but also at its Tokyo office. A merger was the only option to break out of the vicious cycle. Toyota Motor, which had long since been buying up shares of Toyota Motor Sales, already owned a majority stake in the company. The rest was just a matter of timing.

Kamiya, who had been praised as the "god of sales," passed away on Christmas night in December 1980 without having left a declaration of intent. Then-president Teizo Yamamoto, who had looked up to Kamiya as a mentor, was beginning to show signs that he too had inherited Kamiya's practice of mixing business with the personal. Consequently, the next year Eiji exercised his authority as a major shareholder to forcibly remove Yamamoto from his post and set up Shoichiro, a direct descendant of the Toyoda family, as the new president, and had Shoichiro look into the possibility of a merger. After receiving word from Shoichiro to move quickly ahead, the two companies merged in July 1982.

Thus began Toyota's advance. This was also the time when Nissan's dead-end international strategies began to fall apart at the seams.

Chapter 3
A Founder's Dreams and Frustrations

T HE RELEASE OF THE TOYODA automatic loom invented by Sakichi coincided perfectly with a global financial crisis. Nonetheless, it sold like wild fire. This was because the loom's primary users in the textile industry, bracing for a price war, descended upon the automatic loom as a way to cut costs. However, the initial impact of the loom faded with time. As is the lot of capitalism, competition intensifies when there is perceived demand or a rapid succession of new market entrants.

In the final years of Sakichi's life, Kiichiro shouldered the engineering and product development of Toyoda Automatic Loom Works. He subsequently obtained 32 patents and utility model rights based on textile machines, leading to a rise in Kiichiro's fame as an inventor. It is worth mentioning that this also includes machines for producing synthetic textiles. Considering that synthetic textiles first started to take off only around 1941 when war in the Pacific was no longer avoidable, one can say that Kiichiro, like Sakichi, truly practiced the Toyoda Precept of being "at the vanguard of the times."

Yet Kiichiro felt that he could not hope for any further expansion as a manufacturer of textile machinery until he had developed new products to succeed the automatic loom. He thought it necessary to devise and productize a fine spinning machine that would stretch crude fibers into a thin thread, followed by a high-draft fine spinning machine which that draw out the thread even further. This was in 1929.

Kiichiro was vexed. Exuberant about their successful experiences with automatic looms despite the unprecedented worldwide recession, the company's workers hardly felt a sense of impending crisis. However much Kiichiro advocated for the improvement of manufacturing techniques, he failed to persuade employees to take it seriously. So he had no other option but to undertake the development of a high-draft spinning machine himself, something which up to that point was seen as a difficult thing to do, in order to convince his employees of the urgent situation that the company faced. Succeeding in doing so would lift Toyoda's level of technology through the roof, opening the door to new future fields based on this technology. Finding time on the side to develop a fine spinning machine, Kiichiro avidly sent away for and pored through machine technology research, as well as catalogues on the latest cutting and forging machines from machine makers in Europe and the United States.

From fine spinning machines to automobiles

As soon as he had determined to develop a high-draft spinning machine, Kiichiro vaguely envisioned moving into the automotive business. Before long he was sure of it. He realized that production techniques for textile parts and machinery—casting, forging, lathe turning—could all be applied to producing engines, the heart of automobiles.

Kiichiro obviously did not wander into the automotive business as a dilettantish pastime. He knew that branching out into automaking would require an exorbitant amount of money. On this basis, Kiichiro set out to build an automotive business from the perspective of a businessman.

The amazing thing about Kiichiro was that as an entrepreneur he carried out steady preparations for shifting towards automaking while also working on textile machinery as an inventor. It was in 1931 when he succeeded in the experimental production of a small 4-horsepower gasoline engine. Gaining confidence from this, in 1933 he built an automobile division within Toyoda Automatic Loom Works. He then revised the loom works' articles of incorporation to include the automotive business in 1934.

The question then is what made Kiichiro so confident of success as to make the decision to shift over to the automotive business entirely. Even if he had no doubt that automaking was a promising industry, he lived in an age when even large conglomerates like Mitsui, Mitsubishi and Sumitomo thought twice about moving into the industry because of the risk that it entailed.

With Toyoda Automatic Loom Works still little more than a provincial conglomerate, Kiichiro resolutely declared that he would try his hand in this unknown market. Everyone around him, including his brother-in-law Risaburo (the husband of Kiichiro's younger sister Aiko), as well as Ishida, his general manager, were vehemently and justifiably opposed to such a course of action. The public reacted tepidly, waiting to see him in action. Nevertheless, Kiichiro's will was unwavering.

Kiichiro used to his greatest possible advantage an episode that occurred in 1927. Sakichi, while sitting together at a small dinner party on the night he returned from Nagoya after having met alone with Emperor Hirohito, turned to Kiichiro and said: "I served my country by inventing Automatic Loom Works. You need to make cars. Serve your country by making cars." Bringing the episode to light several years after Sakichi's passing, Kiichiro interpreted Sakichi's words as a sort of "final testament" encouraging him to enter into the automaking business. This served to silence opposition not only from within but from outside the company as well, including financial institutions.

A bankruptcy crisis provoked by Toyota's founder

Toyota Motor's first president when it was established in 1937 was not its founder Kiichiro but his brother-in-law Risaburo. Prewar civil law stipulated that "the head of family members registered under the same household shall be the eldest son." Based on this law, after Sakichi passed away the head of the Toyoda family became not the eldest Toyoda son but its eldest son-in-law, Risaburo. Viewed against the institution of family prevalent in Japan at the time, it was natural for Risaburo to assume the top leadership position of the automotive company started as a Toyoda family business. However, Risaburo was not just an ornamental president.

The two men were completely different not only in terms of the environments in which they were born and raised but also in their personalities and sense of accountability. Regardless of Kiichiro's standing in the family registry hierarchy, he felt strongly that "everything down to the ashes in the Toyoda furnace belongs to the me, the eldest son." He was prepared to make a heroic sacrifice even if it meant losing everything, all the more because the automotive business that he was working so hard on was a legacy bequeathed to him by Sakichi.

On the other hand, Risaburo had none of the common reservations that a husband married into the family might have, since he knew that his own elder brother Ichizo Kodama had provided Sakichi support from the shadows on the business front. Moreover, Risaburo had gained a broader perspective on business owing to his involvement in global enterprise as an employee of the trading house Itochu Corporation before marrying into the family.

People, materials, money and time comprise the backbone of business. Partly because no one else at Toyoda Automatic Loom Works at the time was acquainted with automotive technology, Kiichiro had to take his employees by the hand and teach them everything step by step. He filled in the gaps of his engine development team by scouting out capable workers himself. Eiji—his double—was the first person to whom Kiichiro taught the ins and outs of Just-In-Time, which Kiichiro had devised himself. He then assigned Eiji the task of supervising employees when implementing the system at the field level. Kiichiro's skill at using people to their full advantage stems from a take-charge and caring disposition that made him a good person to work for.

As the company's founder, he worked out the issue of time at his own discretion. In fact, when producing trucks, he skipped prototypes altogether and muscled straight into production so as to assure his company's standing as an approved business under the Automobile Manufacturing Industry Law.

The problems were materials and money. Producing vehicles required machinery and other equipment. Outfitting the company with equipment required money. Risaburo was the one who single-handedly undertook financing. Kiichiro was able to relax and concentrate solely on developing cars precisely because he did not have to expend his energy on the same kind of funding issues that always pose such a significant burden on a company initially.

It was only in January 1941 that Kiichiro became Toyota's second president, once Risaburo retired from his post as chairman due to health problems. Kiichiro's accession to president had the profound effect of demonstrating to outsiders the Toyoda family's full-fledged commitment to the automotive business.

Kiichiro's tragic drama began to unfold as soon as he assumed the presidency. In a stroke of misfortune, the war in the Pacific broke out in December of that year. In contrast to Kiichiro's determination, the situation intensified the strain on operations. Vehicle development and eventually even the activities of private companies were restricted. The dream that Kiichiro envisioned for himself of "making world-class compacts with homegrown technology" was in jeopardy.

As Japan's defeat became increasingly imminent in December 1943, the Diet passed the much-dreaded Munitions Company Act, designating Toyota as a company to supply munitions. Kiichiro became despondent, hardly showing up at the office. He soon left Nagoya to resettle in Tokyo to begin a reclusive life absorbed in reading.

Kiichiro entrusted full powers over Toyota's operations to executive vice-president Hisayoshi Akai, whom he had scouted from Mitsui & Co to be his managerial deputy. Akai had long since earned a name for himself as a consummate professional of human resources and general affairs while at Mitsui & Co. However, while a managerial professional, he was out of his league with automotive technology, which had him completely dependent on Eiji for anything related to automaking.

The war came to an end in 1945. Although Kiichiro was excited to be able to get back to work developing his long-sought compact cars, Akai passed away suddenly in a traffic accident in December of that year. Kiichiro, who had lost his right arm, chose Kazuo Kumabe, a fellow classmate from the University of Tokyo and now an associate professor there, to replace Akai as his managerial deputy. Though a complete amateur at running a business, Kumabe, like Kiichiro, was a diehard engineer through and through. This raised a red flag for Eiji: "The Boss (Kiichiro) could do what he wanted in the distressing times during the war and its aftermath because Akai knew management inside and out. Will Kumabe, risen from the ranks of academia, have the managerial wit and power that it takes to brave the stormy seas?"

Eiji's misgivings were right on target and operations went from bad to worse. The company's finances were in shambles. At that point in 1949, the company's capitalization was ¥210 million against annual sales of over ¥4 billion. Retained earnings were next to nothing and had already started eating up capital. Short-term and long-term loans together were upwards of ¥1 billion, almost five times capital, which created substantial monthly interest payments. Naturally, the company was not paying dividends. With their backs against the wall, bankruptcy would no longer be preventable if the company did not go against Sakichi's will and testament and act decisively to reduce its workforce.

As we saw, Toyota managed to get by with joint financing from financial institutions led by the Bank of Japan. The loan syndicate demanded the separation of production and sales as well as a fundamental streamlining of operations as a means for restructuring the company. Toyota accomplished the former in 1950 by establishing Toyota Motor Sales; as for fundamental streamlining, which meant laying off workers, Kiichiro would not hear of it. He hesitated because firing personnel ran counter to the Toyoda Precepts, an embodiment of his father Sakichi's life. Kiichiro had drafted the precepts himself and he would be bound by them.

Post-Kiichiro selections

In Japan, it is routine for a main bank as turnaround manager to send in a president when a company runs into financial problems. But the Toyoda family wanted to avoid bringing in a president from an outside financial institution at all costs, because doing so might lead to the abolition of the Toyoda Precepts. Toyota needed to find someone to replace Kiichiro as president to forestall a move by the bank.

Before publicly announcing Kiichiro's resignation, former president Risaburo called Kiichiro and Eiji, as well as general managers Tojiro Okamato and Taizo Ishida, over to his house to discuss Kiichiro's successor. Confined to his bed, Risaburo faced an uphill battle to recover his health. At 37, Eiji was still young—still too young to carry Toyota.

Remaining were Okamoto and Ishida. At Sakichi's request, Okamoto had been sent in by Ichizo Kodama, Risaburo's older brother, to work as general manager for the Toyoda family. Before joining Toyota, he had worked at Toyo Cotton (later the Tomen Corporation; presently Toyota Tsusho Corporation), a spin-off of the trading house Mitsui & Co. Although Kiichiro had previously approached Okamoto to feel him out as the next in line for president, he was quickly turned down. As a former trading company employee, Okamoto was as acquainted with global business as Risaburo, but his main shortcoming lied in his extremely mild-mannered nature. Okamoto himself was aware that he was ill-suited as a turnaround manager for the chaotic postwar years.

That left Ishida. But there was a slight complication in that Ishida, along with Risaburo, had strongly objected to Kiichiro's moving into the automobile business. Ishida was not on Kiichiro's good side, but the latter could not afford to get hung up on an event from the past at such a critical juncture.

Ishida had a good track record managing Toyoda Automatic Loom Works at the Toyota family's behest. Loom Works became embroiled in a labor dispute during the turmoil of the postwar period, but Ishida sorted it out masterfully every time without exception. Ishida was also credited with negotiating with General Headquarters (GHQ, i.e. the U.S. postwar occupation forces) to resume loom exports. His managerial philosophy was solid as well.

Automatic looms at that time were pulling in positive earnings on the back of a "snap-up economic boom,"[3] a time when one could slam a loom into motion and snap up ten thousand yen. But Loom Works manufactured auto parts for Toyota alongside the looms, and in the off chance that Toyota collapsed, a chain-reaction would inevitably take down Loom Works as well. Implored by Risaburo and Kiichiro, Ishida assumed the mantle of Toyota's third president.

"Please train the younger staff," Kiichiro entreated, the only condition he placed on Ishida. "Please be sure to school them in the ABCs of management."

"I can't make cars," Ishida answered with a confident air, "but leave management to me. Starting with Eiji, I'll bring junior staff up to be magnificent managers."

Kiichiro candidly acknowledged that lack of management was what had led to the company's financial tumult. Ishida, too, knew all too well that the challenges facing him involved restructuring management.

Kiichiro expressed his intent to resign and Ishida informally accepted his commission as incoming president on June 5, 1950. Ishida would simultaneously double as president of Toyoda Automatic Loom Works. Financial institutions did not protest Ishida assuming an

3. *Gachaman keiki*

additional post with such a prosperous company. The best they could manage was to send in Fukio Nakagawa, head of the Osaka office of the Imperial Bank of Japan (later Mitsui, then Sakura; presently Mitsui-Sumitomo Bank), as watchdog.

Announcing Kiichiro's future reinstatement

A general shareholders' meeting was held on July 18 based on the premise that Ishida would assume the presidency. It was there that Ishida advocated for a transfer of power back to Toyota's founder.

> Toyota was founded on the diligence and hard work of Kiichiro Toyoda. In fact, such a modern industry probably would not have evolved if not for Kiichiro. President Toyoda's premature and unfortunate resignation was an acknowledgment of responsibility for the company's financial ailments and a sincere apology to Toyota's shareholders and creditors. I, Taizo Ishida, having been appointed his successor, will do my humble best to improve the company's performance. In the event that I am able to live up to your expectations, I sincerely hope you will agree in advance to have Kiichiro Toyoda, the true father of this company, as president once again.

By announcing before taking office that power would be restored to Kiichiro, Ishida sought to immobilize influential forces—mainly dealers—that opposed Ishida's instatement as president. Mentioning this transfer of power at the general shareholders' meeting served to quell opposition.

A special meeting for shareholders and the board of directors, at which Ishida's succession was formally decided, was held some two weeks later in the late afternoon on July 31. Right before the board of directors meeting began, Ishida received good news: "Mr. Ishida, this is major. We were contacted by Sales just before noon. Apparently Toyota has received a large order from the American military. Prepare yourself. The order is for 1,000 heavy-duty trucks. They also say that we can expect additional orders in the future."

The Korean War brought great demand to Japan. During the one-year period from when the war began, special procurement orders totaling ¥113.4 billion were placed with Japan's principal industries, including not only automobiles but steel, electronics and textiles. In the automotive industry alone, a total of approximately ¥8.2 billion's worth of special procurements were made, Toyota heading the list at ¥3.6 billion. As luck would have it, in October of the previous year all controls on automobiles had been lifted including regulations governing the production of compact cars—ushering in an age when none would complain that a company was making too much money.

Although the sorrows of a neighbor at war were painful to bear, the special procurements enabled the Japanese economy, which had been driven to death's door throughout the turmoil of the postwar period and by the subsequent ultra-contractionary fiscal policy adopted by the Dodge Line, to step forth from the ruins and fortify the foundations of the astonishing growth to come.

Chapter 4
Toyota Learned from Ford

G OOD FORTUNE AND ADVERSITY COME equally to people and businesses alike. Opportunities for further advancement await companies that maximize good fortune and overcome adversity.

No company has been toyed with by international developments quite like Toyota has. Prior to World War II, the Second Sino-Japanese War broke out before the paint had dried on the walls of the newly established Toyota. Just as founder Kiichiro Toyoda assumed the presidency, the War in the Pacific began.

Special procurements for Korea poured in suddenly the very evening of the day that Taizo Ishida became president, bringing life-giving rains to drought-afflicted Toyota. Once an order is received and a contract is officially signed, the agreement serves as a letter of credit and can be partially exchanged for actual money even before the goods are delivered. It eased Toyota's cash-flow issues in a single bound.

When he accepted the presidency, the public sympathized with Ishida as a man over sixty who ended up, of all places he could have gone, at a company that was counting down to total collapse. But as soon as the special procurements order came through, he was portrayed as the luckiest man in the world, a byword of good fortune. This was particularly true for financial institutions, which hoisted Ishida up as a "god of good fortune."

Whatever good fortune Ishida had was a combination of luck and skill. Without the productive capacity to fill the massive order, Toyota would not have been able to take advantage of its luck, Ishida or not. Ishida proved that it takes someone to bring good fortune to life.

How might Toyota have turned out if Kiichiro had remained

president throughout the Korean War? With the flood of special procurement orders, he probably would have withdrawn the plan to lay off personnel, thus resolving the labor dispute. But as production on special procurements wound down, the same chronic problem of excess productive capacity and personnel likely would have surfaced. At the same time, the more plants continued to modernize to increase competitiveness, the more redundant workers would have become. Kiichiro would have lapsed into contradiction.

In this respect, Ishida, who saw himself as the consummate managerial professional, was quick to make his move. At a board of directors meeting immediately after the special procurement orders came through, he swiftly outlined four policy measures, a Policy of Passive Activism: 1) increase monthly output capacity from 650 to 1,000 vehicles by October; 2) meet scaled-up production by reassigning personnel and having them work two hours of overtime per day rather than by hiring new staff; 3) continue research into new models, but delay implementation; 4) borrow an additional ¥380 million (approximately $1.05 million; the fixed exchange rate at the time was $1=¥360) from financial institutions based on anticipated earnings from special procurements, but appropriate all of it towards rationalizing production.

Ishida's managerial philosophy was clear-cut: "A manager's principal mission is to make sure that a company is profitable. A manager must first earn money. A company will then be able to contribute to society by paying taxes, to fulfill its duty to shareholders by paying dividends, and to make its employees happy in the bargain."

An enormous quantity of special procurements made for an extremely busy season at the Koromo Plant well into the summer, busy enough to make Toyota workers' head spin. Nevertheless, Ishida was adamant about not jacking up the number of personnel. Ishida was not an engineer, but he had studied rationalization policy in-depth during his time with Toyoda Boshoku and Toyoda Automatic Loom Works. He constantly reiterated his theory, "If you have the money, then mechanize," to the board of directors. To Ishida, mechanization (automation) meant laborsaving.

Ishida's monetary philosophy, which could be likened to "penny pinching," was tantamount to this: continuously improving the company's financial standing by striving to accumulate wealth, while skimping by on a bare minimum of resources. His template for waste reduction continues to survive at Toyota today.

Back to the drawing board on tie-up negotiations with Ford

While special military procurements for the Korean War showered Toyota with enough good fortune to help it pull through reorganization, it also brought hard luck. Tie-up negotiations with Ford went back to square one.

Picking up from his suggestion in 1939 to begin joint production of trucks, Kiichiro aimed to form a partnership with Ford in the second go-around of negotiations. Although the initial plans did not see the light of day due to opposition from the U.S military, Kiichiro continued to take a modest approach to technology, maintaining until his dying day that he would learn all that he could from Western manufacturers who were at the vanguard of the automobile industry.

While Toyota was caught up in the midst of a management crisis in April 1950, Kiichiro called in Shotaro Kamiya, president of the newly inaugurated Toyota Motor Sales, to tell him to begin searching for a partner.

"Kamiya," he said, "unfortunately Toyota does not currently have the means to make compact cars by itself. We therefore have no choice but to ask for help from overseas manufacturers. Can you find Toyota a suitable automaker as quickly as possible?"

"Sir, what are you saying?" Kamiya replied. "Toyota is now on the verge of collapse. There are so many things that you can do as Toyota's president before negotiating an alliance with a foreign company."

"I know, I know," Kiichiro said. "But no matter what happens to Toyota we absolutely cannot stop developing automobiles. The day will eventually come when every household in Japan will have a car. I'll work on settling the labor dispute while you look for a partnership."

Even as he faced down a tight predicament, Kiichiro could not tear himself away from carmaking for a single day. It had already been over 20 years since he had begun developing engines. During an interim that eventually stretched to ten years following the suspension of vehicle development due to the outbreak of war, the technological gap between the U.S. and Japan had widened rather than shrunk.

Kiichiro began feeling impatient as he heard tell of the postwar prosperity in Detroit. Sluggish sales of the SA compact passenger car, independently developed by Toyota in 1947, was the biggest factor that led Kiichiro to conclude that it would be hopeless to try to make world-class vehicles at Japan's then-current level of technology. While the car demonstrated to the world Toyota's determination to develop compact cars, in the automotive world, where sales are everything, it was branded as a flop.

Though he had entrusted Kamiya with landing a partnership, at heart Kiichiro felt a kinship with Ford. Toyota was founded from the very beginning with aspirations to become the "Ford of Japan." Kiichiro, however, did not yearn for a financial tie-up with Ford; the purpose of a joint venture would be to obtain technology.

Kamiya, on the other hand, had the sober judgment of a businessman. While GM announced a policy not to make the principal components of engines and so forth overseas after World War II, in contrast Ford adopted a type of localism that allowed for its main parts to be made by affiliated overseas manufacturers. In addition, most appealing was Ford's strategy to allow for the re-export of cars produced through technical cooperation.

Kamiya went to the U.S. as an advance representative to initiate negotiations. As founder Henry Ford had passed away, power lied with his grandson Henry Ford II who sat at the company's helm. After discussing the prewar negotiations to form a joint venture, Kamiya proposed establishing a new partnership based on technical cooperation.

Ford was enormously profitable in Japan prior to the war, so Ford II, wanting to keep the dream alive, was actively receptive to Kamiya's proposal as a first step towards forming a full-fledged partnership. Rather like mortal enemies placed by fate in the same boat, at Kamiya's suggestion they made an agreement along the lines that Ford would provide technical guidance in the initial stage, while Toyota would produce Ford's compact cars under license in the second stage of the accord.

Upon hearing the news from Kamiya who had returned to Japan bearing immense gifts, Kiichiro smiled broadly from ear to ear with a personal sense of satisfaction. Kiichiro had already retired as president and, as such, was not involved with Toyota's management, but he still exerted a definite tacit influence over its affairs as the company's founder.

Kamiya and Eiji set about drafting up the agreement. As soon as this was done, Kamiya made plans to go back to the U.S.; if all went well, Eiji would go to Ford's headquarters in Detroit to formally sign the agreement.

The second round of talks looked to be gliding along smoothly, but a new development in international affairs cast a dark shadow over the negotiations. The Korean War broke out on the morning of the very same day that Kamiya took off for the U.S. from Tokyo's Haneda International Airport. He found out about it in a newspaper he picked up at the airport in Los Angeles on a stopover to Detroit. Still, at this point, he hardly imagined that this might compromise the progress that had been made thus far on talks with Ford. It was only after arriving in Detroit that the full implications hit him.

In preparation for the war's expansion, on the very day the war erupted the American government passed measures to prohibit direct investment in foreign countries and to ban essential technical experts from traveling abroad. Unfortunately, this applied to a majority of Ford's technicians, including four engineers who had been slated to be dispatched to Toyota to provide technical guidance. This was tantamount to wiping the slate clean of everything that had been accomplished so far in the negotiations.

It was then that Kamiya showed his resilience.

"Given that a confinement order has been issued for Ford's engineers," he told them, "Toyota has no choice but to abandon the partnership. Due to the extenuating circumstances, neither party is at fault. Yet paragraph 2 of the draft states that 'Ford shall accept two engineers from Toyota for training.' Regardless of the success or failure of partnership negotiations, please allow at least this to happen."

Nothing totally unexpected to Ford's set-up

Kamiya chose Eiji Toyoda and Shoichi Saito, who had joined Toyoda Automatic Loom Works (Automobile Division) as a first-round university graduate, to train at Ford. Upon returning to Japan, the two would give full scope to what they learned through training. All the prototypical components of the Toyota Production System, including quality control and a suggestion system, originated with Ford. In this sense, Ford was undeniably Toyota's mentor.

The training period lasted just a month and a half. After visiting machine tool manufacturers around the U.S., Eiji returned to Japan in the beginning of October and headed straight to the Kiichiro Toyoda Research Institute,[4] which Kiichiro had set up in Tokyo's Toranomon district. Seeing Eiji, Kiichiro cut right to the chase.

"Eiji," he said, "tell me what Ford is all about exactly as you saw it with your own eyes."

"Ford's Rouge Factory produces 8,000 cars per day, while Toyota's Koromo Plant makes 40, so in terms of scale the two are as different as an ant and an elephant. But as for what they are actually doing, there really isn't much of a difference. If I were pressed to point out a difference, I would say maybe machine tool performance. Toyota would need to purchase a huge amount of American-made machine tools if it were to try to raise productivity. After completing the training, I visited a few machine tool manufacturers and picked out some that Toyota should purchase."

Kiichiro nodded along to everything that Eiji said, and then asked him about the one thing that most piqued his interest. "By the way, Eiji, about how many years apart do you feel Toyota and Ford are in terms of manufacturing technology?"

"There are a lot of things that Toyota pays more careful attention to: the detailed arrangement of plant operations and production control and so forth," he said. "This may sound extreme, but there was absolutely nothing at Ford's plant that blew me away. Toyota could do anything there that it set its mind to."

Slightly taken aback by such an unexpected answer, Kiichiro leaned forward and asked, "Are you saying that you learned nothing at Ford's plant that you didn't already know?"

"In so many words, that's exactly what I'm saying. My honest impression is that, other than scale, there is no substantial difference on a technical level. For that reason, if Toyota were to expand its production scale, we could easily handle an American-caliber production system."

Kiichiro's face flushed, listening attentively and nodding along to Eiji's account. Later on, Kiichiro apparently told Ishida the following:

"Although technical cooperation with Ford never materialized, I'm really glad that you sent Eiji to Ford for training. He wasn't

---

4. *Toyoda Kiichiro Kenkyujo*

dazzled at all by Ford's sheer scale. On the contrary, he observed the actual state of things at Ford in a calm and dispassionate manner. Eiji's biggest assets are his objective stance toward foreign capital and unwavering confidence in Toyota. He's the only one to whom we can entrust Toyota's future."

The next day, Eiji reported to Ishida the fruits of his training.

"Eiji," Ishida replied. "You can go ahead and buy whatever machine tools you want. Techies shouldn't have to worry about money. The way we're going now, we'll be able to eliminate the company's total deficit before the year is out. But waste is deplorable. Use pencils and erasers until they're gone. I'm not going to just throw money away. But we'll use however much we need to modernize the factory for the sake of the company's future."

Eiji was put in charge of plant modernization after returning to Japan, but he could not use money completely at his own discretion. When he was unsure whether to buy a particular piece of new machinery, his first priority would be the efficient allocation of personnel. Leaving the issue of equipment aside, he would cut down to three the number of people working on a job that previously required five, then down to two for the job that required three. Coming up with rationalization measures to this end was the job of Taichi Ohno, who worked under Eiji and who would later come to be known as the father of TPS. Kiichiro's Just-In-Time, along with the logical layout of machinery, which Eiji picked up from Ford, and the increased efficiency of material handling, as conceived by Saito, came to form the basis of TPS.

Toyota implemented a series of rationalization measures based on Ford's "suggestion system." Ford's aim in developing such a system was to gather ideas from all its employees on how to improve operations. At the time Eiji went for training, Ford made positive use of this system to increase morale and enhance work efficiency.

"Come to think of it," Eiji thought, "the Boss highly valued the opinions of on-site workers. Before the war he strove to improve performance and boost work incentives by sometimes calling for suggestions for improvement[5] and offering a bonus to people who produced results. This is a little different from Ford, but the intended result is the same." Eiji then sought out a way to adopt the system at Toyota.

---

5. *Kaizen teian*

"Creative ideas" for rationalizing labor

Investment for a 5-year plant modernization plan worked out to ¥4.6 billion ($12.78 million). Although Toyota was doing well as a result of Korean War special procurements, it was no easy matter for a recuperating company to raise such a significant amount of financing. Managing funds was the job of Masaya Hanai, deputy director of the accounting department. He made the rounds and bowed his head every day at financial institutions to come up with the money to cover the following day's payments.

Banks would rarely loan money to Toyota since extending loans to textile companies such as Toyoda Automatic Loom Works, in the midst of its heyday, yielded a more favorable return. Toyota thus had to prostrate itself to borrow money. If Toyota could obtain funds, it could recoup ground back to the time prior to the labor dispute. Financing was a constant high-wire act.

Knowing full well the difficult financial straits that Toyota was in, Eiji stirred up debate in discussions with junior colleagues, saying, "Toyota doesn't have any money. What should we do?" The direction that emerged was to pursue further rationalization and to reduce transportation costs. Both of these, incidentally, could be achieved through resourcefulness. Having seen it with his own eyes at Ford's factory, Eiji knew that a few creative ideas with regard to moving things around would lead to conserving manpower.

Eiji created an in-house "Creative Ideas Committee"[6] to ensure that Kiichiro's incentive scheme and Ford's suggestion system became firmly entrenched as part of Toyota's own system. Upon hearing Eiji's plan to adopt the new system, Ishida slapped his knees with both hands in a gesture of full approval:

"People pursue creative ideas most avidly in difficult times. To sum it up, one can resolve a shortage of manpower by hiring new workers. But what happens if one endeavors not to do that? In my experience, it doesn't hurt production. Why? Because the workers suffer if they don't do anything about it. People then think about what they can do to alleviate the burden. Rather than aimlessly perform the work given them, they think of ways to streamline the work flow, so that one person does the work of two or even three people. Otherwise they will never finish their work. This is in no way overworking labor;

6. *Soikufu-iinkai*

rather, it is rationalizing labor."

"Creative ideas," which was selected in-house from among a number of different candidates, became the catchphrase for Toyota's efforts to streamline operations. It was the motto that subsequently came to represent the entire company. Picking up on a cue from posters that proclaimed "Quality & Safety" which were tacked prominently to everything in sight in Ford's Rouge Factory, Toyota considered a range of options before deciding on "Good Thinking, Good Products." Toyota continues to uphold these two slogans as the company's mottos even today

Chapter 5
The Toyota Production System

THE JAPANESE WORDS FOR "LEARN" and "imitate" share the same etymology.[7] Confucius's *Analects* state that "learning without thought is labor lost." In other words, you can learn a lot, but you're wasting your time if you don't use your own head too.

Shakyo is the act of hand-copying Buddhist sutras. Although originally performed to promulgate Buddhist scriptures, it later came to be seen as a meritorious deed and was practiced during memorial services and prayers. The reason it became integrated into memorial services is that one naturally comes to understand—or "learn"—what is written in Buddhist sutras by copying—or "imitating"—the sutras.

Kiichiro Toyoda looked to American company Smith Motors' compact 4-horsepower engine to determine whether Toyoda Automatic Loom Works would be able to produce automobiles. He felt that if Toyota could make the small toy-like engines installed in their vehicles, it would be the first step towards branching out into the automotive industry.

Following in the footsteps of his father Sakichi, Kiichiro laid out a tatami mat in a corner of the factory and resolved to sleep there, immersed in his studies. He first disassembled the small engine into pieces and proceeded to sketch out a diagram of its structure and components. He thus learned the basic structure of the engine while rebuilding the Smith engine with his own hands.

---

7. *Manabu*; *maneru*.

Homework from Eiji

The starting point for Toyota's rationalization and quality improvement strategy was Eiji's training at Ford. Both "Creative Ideas" and "Good Thinking, Good Products" were learned and imitated from Ford.

The basis of Toyota's development is *sangen-shugi*, or The Three Actualities, which consists of the actual object, the actual site and the actual facts. Manufacturing with a mere emphasis on going to the actual site to observe the actual objects is not fully professional. One must also face the actual facts, that is to say reality, to get a business off the ground.

The Toyota Production System (TPS), which remains a byword for Toyota, was born from a direct engagement with the facts. In 1951 the company launched a five-year plant and equipment modernization plan, which entailed singling out existing aging equipment that could be repaired and reused, dismantling equipment which was no longer usable, and introducing new, state-of-the-art equipment that doubled monthly capacity. Soon after, in the fall of that year, Eiji Toyoda, who exercised control over Toyota's technology wing, strolled into the company's machinery plant without a definite purpose in mind and began speaking to Taichi Ohno, the machinery plant manager who later came to be recognized as the progenitor of *Kanban Hoshiki*.[8]

"Mr. Ohno," Eiji said, "the plant looks like a storeroom. Can you do something to take care of this? The Boss (Kiichiro) came up with a production system for Toyoda Automatic Loom Works before the war to 'make the right parts at the right time and in the right amount every day.' In other words, it should be on time, and don't make more than necessary. The old man called this production system *Just-In-Time*. Unfortunately it didn't take hold at the Koromo Plant since parts stopped coming in when the war with China expanded into the Pacific. I would like you to develop a Just-In-Time system updated for the times. Sooner or later, the big man's going to come back to Toyota. When he does, he'll be shocked to see that Just-In-Time is already in operation. Let's work together to surprise him."

Ohno joined Toyoda Boshoku in 1931 after graduating from

8. *Kanban hoshiki*; a system designed to minimize waste by which a labeled card is returned to the previous process to indicate which parts are required for the subsequent process.

Nagoya Higher Technical School,[9] automatically becoming a Toyota employee when Toyoda Boshoku merged with Toyota in 1943. He was given a title equivalent to section chief and assigned to the automobile assembly plant. In 1947, before the painful scars of war had time to heal, he assumed the post of machinery manager at the Koromo Plant.

Reviving the Just-In-Time System was one of the things that Eiji yearned most to accomplish. When constructing the Koromo Plant, Kiichiro had intended to adopt an assembly-line system similar to Ford's. Semi-finished components that were made from metal castings at the Kariya automotive plant in those days were stored at a warehouse and then trimmed down by machine. Orders for individual components dictating how many of each were to be made would be sent to the work site every morning; subsequently, the instructions for boring holes would arrive. This is so-called small lot production. Kiichiro did away with this, changing the process so that order slips sent each morning included that day's production numbers. If workers were able to produce the number of units designated for that day, they could go home early; if not, they worked overtime.

The problem was how to install this conception of an assembly-line system at the Koromo Plant. It was a groundbreaking new production system that would require the deprogramming of employees already accustomed to small lot production, especially those involved with control and supervision in whom the old production method was already engrained. Kiichiro drafted up a four-inch-thick, scrupulously detailed pamphlet to make sure the assembly-line production system that he had devised would take hold at the Koromo Plant. Eiji read through the pamphlet from cover to cover and hit the floor running, eager to instruct personnel in place of the busy Kiichiro.

Once the assembly plant had been converted to an assembly-line system, accumulated surplus ultimately disappeared, as did the need for a warehouse. Purchased materials would be sold before they were paid for. If this system were to take hold, working capital would naturally no longer be needed.

---

9. Founded in 1905, Nagoya Higher Technical School merged with three other institutions to form the Nagoya Institute of Technology in 1949.

An "army of ants" in New York

So how exactly did Kiichiro come up with Just-In-Time? For a hint one can look to the time when Kiichiro, shortly after joining Toyoda Boshoku, accompanied his brother-in-law Risaburo and sister Aiko on a tour of the European and American textile industries in July 1921.

When Kiichiro joined Toyoda Boshoku, his father Sakichi, who was also an inventor, told him to "get involved in the spinning business, not loom development." Sakichi thus encouraged his son to pursue a career as a businessman rather than to walk the arduous path of an inventor. Leaving the management of Toyoda Boshoku to Risaburo, Sakichi then shifted his research base to Shanghai, China.

High-quality cotton yarn would be crucial to rendering his invention of the automatic loom, then in its final phase, into a perfectly crafted product. Toyoda Boshoku consequently ventured into the cotton spinning business. However, Toyoda lacked engineers versed in cotton spinning, a catastrophic deficiency for an emerging company. By necessity, Sakichi picked out a plethora of engineers from major spinning companies like Kanegafuchi Cotton Spinning Co. (now Kanebo). Even so, these engineers were unwilling to teach Toyoda Boshoku employees the standardized processes to which they had been privy at the companies they had worked for.

The spinning business, which began with a 6,000-spindle spinning machine, pulled in positive earnings from the start on the back of a boom in cotton exports thanks to the World War I economic climate. Before long, the number of spindles on a spinning machine had increased to 30,000. But the plant's main department was still occupied by engineers culled from other companies.

For Toyoda Boshoku to become an established wing of the Toyoda family business, it needed to attain a certain level of technology. Sakichi's son Kiichiro was the only one who could serve as the company's standard-bearer. Kiichiro, who alas was just barely out of university, still had a limited understanding of spinning and would not be able to provide employees with direct instruction. Sure enough, on the very day that he joined the company, he met with stiff resistance from age-worn engineers pulled from other spinning companies for the very reason that he was the factory owner's son, which kept him from entering the factory grounds, let alone going anywhere near the equipment.

In the early days after joining the company, Kiichiro spent a great deal of time in mental anguish. Sakichi, of course, was fully aware of his son's unfortunate position. The question remained as to what could be done to make a full-fledged spinning engineer out of Kiichiro. Sakichi's conclusion was to send him to Platt Brothers, a worldwide textile machinery manufacturer based in Manchester, Lancashire, the birthplace of the industrial revolution, where for one to two years he would learn everything from the basics down to the operations of the spinning business.

Approached about accepting Kiichiro, Platt expressed reluctance for fear that any long-term stay could threaten the security of the company's technical know-how. Yet the two parties managed to come to an understanding for short-term training. As it happened, Risaburo and Aiko were due to set out on a tour of the European and American textile industries in late July, so Sakichi decided to have Kiichiro accompany them.

"Open the door. It's a wide world out there," Sakichi said to Kiichiro over drinks after deciding to move to Shanghai. He told his son that, based on his own experience, the world across the sea helds unlimited potential. Sakichi sent Kiichiro along with his daughter and son-in-law on their tour of the U.S. because he wanted his son to view of something that he himself had during his visit to the U.S. in the fall of 1910: a swarm of cars clamoring across the Manhattan Bridge, which spans East River.

Around that time, one came across a smattering of cars in Nagoya, but Sakichi showed only moderate interest in them, claiming that cars were a "product completely unrelated to the invention of the loom." But upon further consideration, although cars and looms didn't share even the slightest visible resemblance, they were similar in that they used power and were "machines that were put to work" and "that did the work for you." Sakichi's conception of cars changed once he had seen the ant-like armada in New York.

"America is an amazing country," he thought. "At some point in the future that ant-like army will land on Japan, too. But regrettably I'll be too old to see it happen."

The point that Sakichi was driving at was that automobiles were a pursuit for younger engineers. For a time when Japanese thought that they had lived a full life at the age of 50, Sakichi was in remarkable possession of his faculties. No matter how great an interest he might have harbored in automobiles as an inventor, he was awake that it would be impossible for an individual acting alone to develop them for practical use. He wanted to show Kiichiro the face of the new industry that was making a sudden rise to power in America.

Just-In-Time

The Risaburo couple and Kiichiro made it to England by the turn of the new year and then went their own ways in London. It was there in London that Kiichiro had the experience that would build the conceptual foundation of Just-In-Time, which itself formed the backbone of the Toyota Production System. When Kiichiro arrived at Saint Pancras Station to go on to receive training at Platt, the Manchester-bound train had already left the station. He missed his train courtesy of an out-of-date train schedule.

"So that's how it works," he thought. "If a train leaves on time, then you miss your train even if you're only a minute late. Now I have to wait a few hours until the next train comes. Trains leave on time. Literally just in time. I wonder if this idea can't be applied to plant operations."

Kiichiro could not stop turning this experience over in his mind. He conceived of the Just-In-Time system just after completing the Koromo Plant. He then hung up in the corner of the new factory a conceptual diagram for this English-derived Japanese phrase and explained it to workers on the floor, citing as an example the episode in London when he missed his train.

"I'll bet everyone here has missed a train before," he said. "If a train leaves on time, you'll miss it even if you're just a second late, let alone an entire minute. 'Just in time' does not refer only to being on time. It means 'supplying the right parts at the right time and in the right amount.'"

Applying the supermarket system

Even though Ohno, charged by Eiji with jump-starting the Just-In-Time system, had begun to transform the assembly line with the aid of the pamphlet put together by Kiichiro and that Eiji had given

Ohno, he was having trouble coming up with good ideas. Unsure how to proceed, he even contemplated visiting Kiichiro in Tokyo to seek enlightenment directly from the source. But soon thereafter, on March 27, 1952, Kiichiro passed away suddenly at the young age of 57.

Just as Ohno ran up against a brick wall, he came across some information that played a decisive role in reviving the Just-In-Time system. Supermarkets were springing up all over the U.S. The person who told him about this was a classmate who had been the first from the Nagoya Higher Technical School's machinery department to go the U.S. He returned to Japan with souvenir color projector slides and gathered his classmates for a reunion and a slide show of the photographs.

The classmate explained each of the photos as the latest from America flashed across the screen. Among them was a number of pictures of supermarkets.

"Hey, these stores don't have any employees, do they," Ohno asked when he saw the photos. "Isn't that kind of a bad idea?"

"In America there are these stores called supermarkets. They only have one female sales clerk on the way out," the puffed-up classmate proffered in explanation. "Customers push around this thing that looks like a stroller, put the items they want into the stroller, and pay for them at the register on the way out. Doing it this way, the store can get by with having just one girl at the checkout. This keeps the payroll down, allowing the store to sell goods for cheap. Being able to buy cheap goods is an immense benefit to customers."

Ohno gave this some thought. "In factory terms," he reasoned, "customers going shopping is a downstream process. Customers buy only what they want from a store. Isn't this exactly what Kiichiro called 'just in time'? Depending on the size of his refrigerator and the amount of money in his wallet, the buyer can live quite economically by buying things as necessary. Can't this supermarket system be successfully implemented at a factory as well?"

Ohno saw just how rational a form of sales the supermarket system was, but at the same time it also made him realize how irrational the Japanese distribution system was.

At first glance, the delivery and *goyokiki* systems unique to Japan[10] seem quite convenient for the customers. The drawback is

10. *Goyokiki* is a system by which a person comes by on a regular route to take orders for later delivery.

that it costs more.

The same is true for Japanese greengrocers' pre-ordered delivery system. Suppose one does not have enough Chinese cabbage for the night's menu. It is not very considerate to order only Chinese cabbage from the person making the delivery, so one goes ahead and orders green onions and radishes even though one does not know whether it will be needed for the next day's menu. It creates waste.

Something similar occurs with tofu vendors. Every morning, tofu vendors load freshly-made tofu onto their bicycles and peddle their wares while blowing a whistle, bringing tofu right to people's front doorsteps. Often, however, a customers want tofu to put in their miso soup, but the tofu has sold well that day and is gone by the time the vendor makes it to that person's door.

Both the delivery and *goyokiki* systems may seem superficially convenient in that they offer such attentive service, but in truth they are uneconomical. In this regard, supermarkets are the complete opposite. Customers get in their cars and go shopping. This may be anomalous from the standpoint of traditional Japanese business practices, but it actually makes a lot of sense.

Upon hearing about this newfangled system, Ohno was sold. "If privately owned cars come into widespread use in Japan," he determined, "then supermarkets are sure to take hold, too. Actually, it might be the other way around. If supermarkets become popular in Japan, they'll hasten the arrival of an era of personal cars."

The traditional factory was similar to the irrational Japanese distribution system. When ordering parts, if things were left to the parts manufacturer, there would be a bulk delivery; the assembly plant had to store the excess parts outside the factory until they were used. This caused inventory to accumulate. Ohno saw that systematizing delivery so that the necessary parts arrived just prior to use would double or even triple productivity.

While Ohno had the feeling that the supermarket system could be applied to Just-In-Time, he was having a hard time coming up with specific measures to implement it. As the agonizing days wore on, a newspaper article in the spring of 1954 sealed it for him. The article reported that "the American aircraft manufacturer Lockheed Corporation saved $250,000 in one year by adopting a supermarket system for integrating parts into jets."

The process of building a single automobile on an assembly line involved having the right amount of the right parts arrive at the production line at the right time. The ability to implement this would considerably reduce inventory—almost down to nothing. Inventory, of course, exerts significant financial pressure on a business.

Ohno's habit was to analyze everything inside and out. The flow of production was, simply, the movement of materials. What if they looked at it the other way around? The conventional approach was for upstream processes to supply materials to downstream processes. In the process of building a car, materials were shaped into parts on the production line and then combined to form unit parts. Lastly, they were conveyed down to the assembly line. In other words, the body of a car was built as parts moved down the line from upstream processes to downstream processes.

What if this production process were reversed? Downstream processes would pull the right parts at the right time and in the right amount. Seen in this way, the natural thing would be for upstream processes to make only what was pulled out by downstream processes. One could then use an order slip, indicating how much of what was needed, as a means for linking multiple processes together. This order slip would be the famous *kanban*.[11] Production output could easily be controlled by sending a *kanban* to each process.

Ohno tried a variety of things based on this approach and finally presented a production plan that began at the general assembly line, the very last point of the manufacturing process, to the person in charge of the assembly line. Ohno turned on its head the very process of conveying parts used on the assembly line: formerly, parts from upstream processes were sent to downstream processes, while now, "downstream processes pull the right parts at the right time and in the right amount from upstream processes, and upstream processes make only what is pulled out by downstream processes."

Automation with a human touch

Originally called the Ohno System, once supermarkets made it to Japan, this system came to be known as the Supermarket System. The name was then changed to the Toyota System in the 1960s, and subsequently changed again to the Toyota Production System after

---

11. Labeled card.

the first oil crisis.

In any case, the fundamental idea underlying the Toyota Production System is the complete elimination of waste. Substantiating this idea are "Just-In-Time" and *ninben no tsuita "jidoka,"* or automation with a human touch. This term was coined by adding the *ninben* (a component of the character for "person") to the character for "move." *Kanban Hoshiki* is no more than a means to facilitate the smooth operation of the Toyota Production System.

There are a lot of machines in the world today that work automatically with the flip of a switch. The precision of machinery has improved in recent years to the point where the equipment or its functions are easily damaged if even the slightest foreign matter penetrates a machine's interior. If a thread-cutting tap is damaged, a screw comes loose, leading to a mountain of defective goods. With this type of automated machinery, it becomes impossible to prevent mass production of faulty products unless devices are built into the machine to automatically detect a malfunction.

The most vocal advocate for "automation with a human touch" at Toyota was Ohno. Although he did not know Sakichi Toyoda directly, Ohno respected Sakichi through his inventions. Despite the economic downturn at the time, Ohno was fortunate to have had the opportunity to join Toyota's founding company, Toyoda Boshoku, which Sakichi raised from the ground up. Ohno had thoroughly studied Sakichi's power loom from around the middle of World War II until he transferred to Toyota.

Ohno believed wholeheartedly that automation with a human touch originated with this power loom. Sakichi's power loom was designed to stop immediately if even a single thread of the warp severed or a weft was missing. In short, the machine was equipped with a device to assess quality, which ensured that it did not produce defective goods.

Ohno first adopted this idea at the factory at which he was in charge. The Toyota concept of automation with a human touch comes down to "machinery with an automatic shutoff function." Whether new or old, every machine in every one of Toyota's plants is still equipped with a shutoff function. Ohno is the one who added this human touch to Toyota's machinery; in other words, he bestowed it with human wisdom.

As a result, the definition of "operating a machine" changed dramatically. No personnel is required when the machinery is running properly; it is only if something goes wrong and a machine stops that someone needs to check it out. One person can oversee a number of machines, which helps curtail man-hours and increases production efficiency exponentially.

In a situation where a worker is directly manning the machinery, a malfunction will not right itself just because a person takes over for the machine. In this respect, machines equipped with a shutoff function will stop automatically in the event of a malfunction. One can then look into equipment stoppage to uncover the culprit. Once the cause is known, *kaizen*[12] gets underway. Ohno further developed this idea by giving workers the ability to stop the production line by pressing a button when something goes awry.

As automobiles are potentially lethal products, safety must be given the utmost priority during the manufacturing process. It is absolutely vital to clearly distinguish between normal and abnormal functioning with every machine, production line and factory in order to prevent recurrences. Thus Ohno, at an early stage of the system's evolution, added another pillar of support to bolster the Toyota Production System by taking the idea of automation with a human touch and applying it to Just-In-Time methodology.

---

12. Ongoing or continuous incremental improvement.

Chapter 6
Conditional Reinstatement of the President

Taizo Ishida, virtually an amateur when it came to automotive technology, found time to inspect every last inch of the factory in implementing the five-year plant and equipment modernization plan. In so doing, something came to his attention. People working at the factory yearned for the days back when Kiichiro was still around.

"It was boiling hot that summer in 1938 when the plant moved from Kariya to Koromo," Ohno recalled. "Deciding where to install the machinery hauled from the old plant was Managing Director Toyoda's (Eiji) job. He was still relatively new to the company, and he was still a bachelor. He slept in his office and used paint to outline the locations where the machinery was to be installed.

"The Boss (Kiichiro) came every morning to inspect whether the locations were correct. Even after the plant was up and running, every morning he would talk not only to us but to the machinery, saying, 'Hey, are you working hard? Are you getting enough to eat (i.e., are you getting oiled)?' Every corner of the Koromo Plant was saturated with the man's vision."

As Ishida was still with Toyoda Boshoku around that time, he had no idea what Kiichiro and Eiji were going through. When he had time, he would call on Eiji to see how things were going. The more he heard, the more he realized just how much passion and labor Kiichiro invested in automobiles, and what great hopes he had for Eiji.

The Koromo Plant brought out the best of Kiichiro's spirit of technological innovation. His decision to switch from the imperial system of measurement to the metric system to display car dimensions epitomized this spirit.

Japan ratified the Convention du Mètre in 1886, but it was long in taking hold. This was because Japanese industry had begun by mimicking American standards, which employed the imperial system. Both GM and Ford labeled the dimensions of engine bores and strokes entirely in inches. Kiichiro made the bold decision to switch over to the global standard of the metric system at the Koromo Plant, directing Eiji to take care of the work involved.

The task seemed simple at first, but in fact turned out to be extraordinarily difficult. Tools displayed in inches had to be done away with even if they were still usable. All plans had to be redrawn. Since this also required a grace period, it was literally costing them time and money.

The Ministry of War approved of Toyota's switch to the metric system and recommended Nissan do the same. With Toyota on the metric system and Nissan still on the imperial system, parts incompatibility would prevent them from sharing components when necessity called for it. Out of touch with technology, however, Nissan's management passed on adopting the metric system.

Japanese market monopolized by foreign capital

After around half a year as president, Ishida began to feel that his role as chief executive was coming to an end. Ishida's role at the company was, in a word, what is now called "restructuring." What worked in Ishida's favor was that special procurements for the Korean War poured in soon after initiating personnel cutbacks. He borrowed Eiji's idea to streamline labor by not boosting the number of personnel to meet increased production. He also allotted capital brought in from military procurement orders to modernize Toyota's plants in preparation for the motorization to come.

A president's job is to lay out the company's objectives for its employees. When founding Toyota, Kiichiro set the goal to "develop world-class compact passenger vehicles using Japanese brains and skills." But before starting in on that, he was forced to retire without having fulfilled his life's ambition.

Even with Ishida as president, Kiichiro did not give up on his dream. Ishida, however, was not up to the task. Kiichiro was the only one who could do it. Ishida gradually realized that the assignment given him was to set the stage for Kiichiro to work his magic.

Plant management would be all right in the hands of Eiji and Saito. Administrative management was Ishida's area of expertise. Younger executives, such as accounting's Masaya Hanai, who ran around behind the scenes during the labor disputes, and human resources' Masao Yamamoto were well trained to lead the next generation for Toyota.

At the privately owned "Kiichiro Toyoda Research Institute" set up in Toranomon, Tokyo, Kiichiro was drawing up plans for a compact car, at the time thinking more about the future of Japan's automotive industry than Toyota itself.

The Japanese auto industry had profited from special procurement orders, but national income (GNP) was still nowhere near that of the U.S. Nevertheless, demand for automobiles had steadily begun to grow, and demand for cars from the taxi industry had also risen. Even so, the inability of domestic manufacturers to meet fierce consumer demand led many to give up on domestically produced cars in favor of government-surplus foreign cars.

In 1951, Toyota's monthly output of passenger cars finally reached 150 vehicles. However, vehicle performance was still not up to par. Although they took on the outward appearance of passenger cars, structurally they still did not represent a significant departure from trucks to the extent that they even shared many of the same parts.

Although Kiichiro, having been brought up-to-date on Eiji's training at Ford, determined that there was no need to turn to Ford for technical guidance, the fact of the matter was that higher-performance passenger cars from Europe and the United States were flooding the Japanese market.

"At this rate," he reasoned, "the Japanese auto market will become monopolized by foreign capital, just like before the war. To avoid this, there's no alternative but to tie-up with Ford and upgrade the level of technology in Japan as quickly as possible. Nissan was also brought into the tie-up negotiations before the war through administrative guidance from the Ministry of War. This time it would probably be beneficial to the development of the Japanese automotive industry as a whole if Nissan were brought in from the very beginning."

Kiichiro resolved to raise Japan's level of technology by bringing in rival Nissan to quickly make up for lagging technical development incurred during and after the war. This was a Copernican shift in thinking unique to Kiichiro, who was more concerned with advancing Japan's level of technology than Toyota's own development. What allowed him to think this way was his detachment from Toyota's business operations.

The next question was who to talk to at Nissan. Luckily, Genshichi Asahara, an old acquaintance of Kiichiro's, was with Nissan at the time. Although Asahara, who served as Nissan's president during the war, had met the unfortunate end of being purged from office along with Nissan's founder, Yoshisuke Aikawa, it had been informally decided that he would be reinstated as president in October 1951. Kiichiro's intention was to first sound out the idea with Asahara; if he found a pulse, he would then propose the idea to Ford.

Absentee president

Ishida knew nothing of Kiichiro's thinking. He also shied away from going into the Koromo office as much as possible, in order to encourage Eiji and other junior staff to be self-reliant. In the spring of 1951, Ishida put up a plate which read "Office of the President, Toyota Motor Corporation" in one of the rooms at Toyota's Nagoya branch, a two-storey wooden building across from Nagoya Station. The president's office though it was, he furnished it with only a modest work desk and a four-seater sofa for visitors. Unless there was a special event like a board of directors meeting, he took care of work for Automatic Loom Works in Kariya in the morning, then, circumnavigating Koromo, went straight to the president's office in front of Nagoya Station. When required to settle accounts, a secretary from headquarters would grab the necessary paperwork, suffer through a one-hour train ride, and bring the paperwork to the president's office.

Perhaps it was purely coincidental, but the head of Honda was doing something similar. Toyota's headquarters and factory were located in the same area, but Honda's headquarters were in Yaesu, in front of Tokyo Station, while its factory was in the outskirts of Tokyo in Saitama Prefecture. After riding out a management crisis in 1954, president and diehard engineer Soichiro Honda set up an office for the president at the company's Shirako Plant, home of the engineering division, the predecessor of Honda Technical Research Institute. He then used this as base camp for his activities. In a manner of speaking, Shirako was the seat of the Soichiro-led "Honda Industries," while "Fujisawa Trading," led by Takeo Fujisawa—the keeper of the presidential seal and the one charged with managing the company—was in Yaesu. This two-base system remained unchanged until the two men retired.

Fujisawa, however, did not show up at his office every day. For a time, he rented a room, coordinated all in black, in a building near the Matsuya Department Store in Tokyo's Ginza district. He brought with him a massive volume of books and business materials and proceeded to mull over Honda's future. Fujisawa lived an eccentric lifestyle. When tired, he would turn off the lights, lose himself in meditation, take a walk around the neighborhood and then return to his room. There were years during this period when the two leaders of the company would not see each other more than a handful of times. Even then they met not at the company but at a restaurant over drinks to report on their mutual states of affairs.

What Toyota and Honda had in common was that both companies could keep going whether their leaders were around or not.

The scenario behind Kiichiro's reinstatement

When summer came, Ishida paid a visit to Risaburo to inquire after his health and to bring up the topic of Kiichiro's reinstatement. "What I learned from being president is that Toyota belongs to Kiichiro," he said. "Every last bit of that plant is coated in his sweat and tears. The company's performance has straightened out thanks to Korean special procurements. So I thought we could see how things go and then ask him to come back as president."

Risaburo responded in a reserved manner that was rare for him. "Honestly, I, too, want Kiichiro back. But after saddling you with the task of reorganization, your role isn't going to just come to an end as soon as things start looking up."

"I'm already at the age when the big general (Sakichi) passed away," Ishida retorted undauntedly. "They could come for me at anytime. My home is not in Koromo (Toyota); it has always been in Kariya (Toyoda Automatic Loom Works)."

Even while doubling as president of Toyota, when Ishida said "my company" he was really referring to Automatic Loom Works.

He had always considered Toyota a company entrusted to him by someone else.

"Hearing you say that takes a load off my mind, Taizo," Risaburo said. "When Kiichiro told me that he was going to start an automotive business, I honestly felt that it was a reckless pursuit. When he stepped down from the front ranks of management, however, I took a step back and saw very clearly what potential cars have as a business. Then, just as I realized that, he was forced to retire. Even now, his passion for automobiles hasn't died down in the least. I want to channel that passion into Toyota by whatever means necessary."

"I feel the same way. The age of free competition in the automotive market is just around the corner. Toyota needs Kiichiro. Toyota will not survive, let alone aim for the top spot in Japan, unless Kiichiro comes back, bringing with him his burning drive for the autonomy of the Japanese auto industry. Toyota needs at the helm someone who is versed in cars. Let me talk to him. You won't regret it."

After repeated visits and entreaties, Ishida had Kiichiro take on the post of adviser for both Toyota and Toyoda Automatic Loom Works premised on his potential reinstatement. Despite this, Kiichiro revealed no interest in Toyota's operations and never once showed his face at Koromo.

Since becoming Toyota's president, Ishida worked with redoubled intensity, hardly giving his seat time to warm. From loan negotiations with financial institutions to talks with government officials to meetings with the automotive industry, he had his work cut out for him. On top of this, he also doubled as president of Automatic Loom Works. He was so busy that setting up a president's office in front of Nagoya Station made little difference.

Work required him to travel to the capital often, but no matter how busy he always made the time to meet with Kiichiro to report at length on how things stood at Toyota. He first brought up the idea of a comeback in autumn of 1951. "This should make you happy. With the help of Korean special procurements, Toyota's restructuring is nearly complete. Now that you seem to have recovered your health, won't you consider coming back?"

Kiichiro's response was blunt and to the point. "Ishida, I'm sorry but at the moment I'm completely absorbed in developing a small passenger car engine. Can you give me a little more time? I'll give it serious thought when I finish my research. How does that sound?"

Kiichiro wanted to avoid responding immediately because he was in the midst of arranging a three-company venture among Toyota, Nissan and Ford. He had already divulged his plan to Asahara, who had since returned as president of Nissan, and probed his interest regarding the matter but had yet to receive a response. Until he knew Nissan's intentions, he had to hold off on bringing the idea to Ford.

Automakers make passenger cars

After the turn of the new year, Ishida, who had gotten the feeling that Kiichiro would be willing to return to Toyota, used one emissary after another to try to persuade him. The first person he sent in was Eiji. In 1952, after wrapping up the customary New Year's visit to Hoko Jinja Shrine, Eiji took the overnight train bound for Tokyo. Upon arriving, Eiji got right down to business.

"Boss," he said, "President Ishida wants to enact your reinstatement as president at the general shareholders' meeting in July. I did not know about it because I was training with Ford, but apparently Ishida pledged at a shareholders' meeting to bring you in again once the company's full recovery was in sight. Ishida's feels that now is our chance."

"Eiji, what are you saying?" Kiichiro replied unexpectedly. "Don't get carried away just because profits are up a bit. After all, we're only talking about trucks selling well because of Korean military procurements. It's like restructuring by relying on others. Knock off the arrogance. What I want to make is a passenger vehicle, not trucks. You of all people should know this perfectly well. 'Automobile manufacturer' basically refers to a company that makes passenger cars. To put it in extreme terms, an automaker incapable of making a respectable passenger car has a tenuous existence in the world. An all-out passenger car needs to be able to race. You know why? Trucks carry baggage, but cars carry people, so we have to remove all possible risk of accidents. Racing is crucial to making a safe car. What's more, if we're shooting for a world-class compact passenger vehicle, then it has to be outfitted with a small engine with plenty of horsepower, the type one would use in a race. That's exactly the engine I'm developing now. Since it's you, I'll just come out and say it. Toyota as it stands now does not have the ability to develop a compact passenger car. I don't have the slightest intention of going back to such a company."

For Eiji, this amounted to an accusation that Toyota was not a respectable business. Astonished, he contested the point. "You say this, but we've already finished the specifications for the SF Toyopet, which is finally coming together."

"I went for a test drive in the SF," Kiichiro said, lashing out at Toyota's weak point as if he had been waiting for the moment all along. "The car definitely looks like a passenger car on the outside, but on the inside it's no more than a truck. That's not what a passenger car is. To me, it's a sham."

"I think so too, that's why..." Eiji pleaded desperately for the man's comeback.

Kiichiro would have nothing of it. "My vision is to make world-class compact passenger cars. It's too late to go all the way back to Koromo just to make trucks."

Considering all that was said, Eiji had little choice but to lay down his arms. When he went back to Koromo to tell Ishida how he had failed to persuade Kiichiro, Ishida roared with laughter, saying, "I figured as much. 'A rotting sea bream is still a sea bream,' and the scion is still the scion. We won't give up so easily."

The battle-hardened Ishida did not give up. To persuade Kiichiro he sent not only Risaburo but general manager Okamoto as well. As expected, Kiichiro responded politely as if he were considering the other's point of view for the very first time, but he never betrayed the same kind of passion for automobiles that he did when approached by Eiji.

He wanted to make a triumphant return to Toyota bearing the gift of a three-company venture, but Nissan still had not responded, arousing his impatience. If the three-company venture were to come together, he had even considered devoting himself exclusively to the new company without returning to Toyota. Kiichiro spoke his mind on what was happening at the time to Hanji Umehara, who had quit his position as associate professor at Tohoku University to join Toyota as technical director at Kiichiro's behest.

"I'm still ambivalent about returning to Toyota," Kiichiro said. "Toyota has Eiji. He's been right there beside me since he was young, taking care of so many of the difficult problems. Toyota's management will be fine as long as Eiji's around. That's what I brought Eiji up to do."

What Kiichiro was trying to say was that he had transplanted all his automaking genes to Eiji. Seiichi Yamanaka, who had been appointed auditor during the last year of the war, which was also the year that Eiji became a board member, felt the same way. "You always said in front of everyone that 'Eiji's still a kid,' but when you stepped down, weren't you wagering that Eiji would be able to take care of himself after Ishida leaves?"

I'd be delighted if you would have me back

Taking in the accounts of the emissaries he threw out there, Ishida quietly observed Kiichiro's vacillation. Then, in March of that year, when he deemed that the time was right, he hopped on an overnight train to Tokyo and dropped in on Kiichiro at his home in Setagaya, early in the morning and without any advance notice. Spring in name only, the morning was bone-chillingly cold. Ishida's sudden visit temporarily threw Kiichiro off-guard, but he could hardly turn Toyota's active president away. The two sat down to talk while sipping on rice porridge made by Kiichiro's wife, Hatako.

"I have a good knowledge of the textile industry," Ishida began, "but even now I don't know the first thing about automotive technology. But since Toyota's reorganization came off sooner than expected, my role there may as well be done. I'm not getting any younger, so I'm thinking about settling down to a quiet retirement."

Kiichiro sipped his porridge in silence. Waiting until the moment was right, Ishida brought up the subject of Kiichiro's reinstatement. "I would like you to come back and make compact cars to compete with those of foreign companies."

Donning a puzzled look, Kiichiro waited until Ishida had finished and voiced his biggest concern. "Is it true, Ishida, that Toyota will let me work on compact passenger cars? If this is true, I might reconsider."

"Men don't go back on their word," Ishida said. "From the very start, Toyota was the company that you founded to make world-class compact passenger cars. Unfortunately the war prevented you from following through with it. Not only that, but after getting wrapped up in the labor dispute you were forced to step down against your will. My job as the head of Toyoda was to rebuild Toyota. The restructuring went well and the company's back on its feet. On top of that, we now have some funding to work with to develop the cars."

"You mean to say that Toyota's that solid?" Kiichiro said half-jokingly, draped in a big smile but wanting to make doubly sure. "These cars are money-guzzlers, Ishida. But I'm sure you know that already."

His good humor then faded into an expression of all-seriousness. "Toyota absolutely must start working on passenger cars," he said. "I'm now developing a 1500cc engine. If Toyota starts working on these cars, young engineers alone won't cut it. In such a case, I'll take the younger engineers under my wing."

"Absolutely. You will have to take command in order to develop legitimate compact cars. The engineering team helmed by Eiji can hardly wait to get their hands dirty with full-scale development. The timing couldn't be better. I'll say it again: Toyota has always been your creation. It's all yours, so have at it."

"I know, I know," Kiichiro said. "Ishida, I'm sorry for having been so selfish. I'd be delighted if you would have me back. Then at long last I'll be able to realize my dream and prove that we can make world-class compact passenger cars."

Beaten down by Ishida's tenacious adjurations, Kiichiro finally consented to coming back as president.

"Thank you so much," said Ishida. "This will take a huge weight off my shoulders. My body and mind feel lighter already. Eiji and crew will be thrilled to hear it. I'll start taking care of the arrangements for your reinstatement. It's still early March, but I'll work on getting approval from our financial interests and shareholders as soon as possible. You can begin serving as de facto president without having to wait for the general shareholders' meeting in July. Which reminds me—I have an idea. We're holding a general shareholders' meeting on July 18, the date I was called upon to pinch hit. I publicly pledged at the same meeting two years ago that I would make sure you were reinstated as president, and now I'll finally deliver on my promise two years later. If this is how it pans out, you will be sure to be reinstated, so please be sure to take care of yourself. Above all, make sure you don't drink too much."

Chapter 7
Toyoda Family Tragedy

TAIZO ISHIDA CARRIED THE GOOD news of Kiichiro's return back to Kariya that day. The next day, he opted not to go in to Toyoda Automatic Loom Works and instead headed straight for Toyota's headquarters in Koromo to report to management that Kiichiro had accepted his request to return. Everyone was immensely excited. The engineering team, Eiji in particular, could hardly contain themselves.

"The five-year plant and equipment modernization plan is moving along well thanks to Ishida, who ran around tirelessly in search of funding to give the company the financial leeway to upgrade facilities," Eiji noted. "The big man's opportune return just as we gained the footing to pursue full-scale production of passenger cars gives us a distinct edge."

Formulated in the spring of 1951, the plan called for an investment of a total ¥5.8 billion into productive capacity upgrades, including ¥5.4 billion for machinery and equipment and another ¥400 million for equipment maintenance and repair. The plan was divided into three phases. Phase 1 would improve upon the basic conditions for establishing a system of mass production. Phase 2 would upgrade and expand plant facilities geared towards the production of passenger cars. Finally, phase 3 would expand production through automation. Kiichiro accepted the call to return to the company during Phase 2, something that was seen as a blessing for Toyota since this was the most intensive period of vehicle development.

Kiichiro collapses

At 57 a man is in the prime of his life. Perhaps a person's awareness of this makes one euphoric, but Kiichiro became so animated as to seem like a different person. The next day, starting off with the Ministry of International Trade and Industry (MITI), he made energetic visits to various financial institutions and business partners in preparation for his return.

The only problem was his health. With no hobbies outside of work, Kiichiro drank for pleasure. The Toyoda family were notoriously heavy drinkers. The one in the family who hit it the hardest was Heikichi, the second youngest brother of Eiji's father Sakichi. Heikichi was a boozer but never let it get the best of him. Kiichiro and Eiji were similarly fond of the bottle but kept it under control.

The Toyoda family lineage was rife with heavy drinkers and, worse still, high blood pressure. After the age of 40, Kiichiro began to suffer from hypertension. Compounded by the strains of the labor dispute, Kiichiro was ordered by the doctor to stop putting excessive stress on his body and subsequently confined himself to his country villa. In hindsight, his absence at the time ended up protracting the labor dispute longer than necessary, helping him dig himself into a deeper hole.

Along with his genealogy, changes in his environment had spurred Kiichiro to drink heavily. After extricating himself from Toyota out of necessity, he often spent his nights drinking and getting wound up about the future of the Japanese automotive industry. The bitter disappointment from having to quit the company that he himself had founded led him to drink more heavily than before.

Once Kiichiro's reinstatement as president had been fixed, he took a room in at the Yanagi Inn in Tokyo's Tsukiji district, an establishment run by the family of a friend from school. Kiichiro made versatile use of his new abode as a drawing room-cum-study-cum-lodging. In the four months left until his reinstatement, he had only two tasks that he needed to accomplish before time ran out.

One was to draw up the blueprint for the passenger cars that he would work on first after becoming president. The other was writing a manuscript in connection with having been selected as one of the "50 Outstanding Japanese Inventors"[13] by the Japan Society for

13. *Nihon hatsumeika goju kessen*

Publishing Books on Inventions.[14] He decided to confine the theme of the piece to his experiences in the textile industry in keeping with the book *Invention: a Personal Account*,[15] authored by Sakichi. He chose as his title "The Birth and Upbringing of the Automatic Loom: My Memories of the Automatic Loom."[16]

In between working on the blueprints and writing the manuscript, as incoming president Kiichiro went around to pay his respects to various concerned parties and at night dined at the Yanagi together with friends who had taken care of him over the years. As he could not afford to waste any time, once the dinner party had ended he would sleep right there in the same room. When he was not visiting Koromo, he used the Yanagi as his base of operations for both his personal life and for work.

On March 21, tragedy struck, less than two weeks after communicating to Ishida his desire to return. Feeling like he was coming down with a cold that day, Kiichiro was not at his physical best. Finishing breakfast as usual, he sequestered himself to his room and set to work on the technical drawings for the blueprint.

It is thought that he had an attack just before noon. Kurata, a Toyota engineering secretary who had brought cold medicine, discovered Kiichiro just after 2 o'clock in the afternoon lying unconscious in front of the blueprints splayed out on the floor. He was taken by ambulance to the main branch of the University of Tokyo Hospital and given urgent medical attention by Professor Kakinuma, the foremost authority in brain surgery. It was to no avail and Kiichiro remained comatose. Professor Kakinuma contacted Kiichiro's wife Hatako that evening to inform her that her husband's outlook was bleak, at which point Kiichiro was transported home to Setagaya.

Hearing that Kiichiro had collapsed, Ishida, Eiji and a number of others all jumped into a car and rushed over from Koromo in droves, but Kiichiro would not open his eyes again. The man's tempestuous life came to an end on March 27, 1952. The cause of death was hemorrhaging of the brain.

Ishida, eyes upcast, stood before Kiichiro's body in a stupor. "What an ill-fated man was he. Luck was never on his side when he needed it most. For better or worse, Kiichiro never outgrew the

---

14. *Hatsumei tosho kankokai*
15. *Hatsumei shiki*
16. *Jidoshokki oitachi no ki: jidoshokki no omoidebanashi*

temperament of a young man from a well-to-do family."

"The old man died of euphoria," Eiji, to whom Kiichiro had entrusted Toyota's future, said, giving vent to his unfocused anger. "I kept telling him not to drink so much, but he wouldn't listen to me."

The last will of Risaburo, Toyota's first president

When he received the tragic news, Risaburo was overcome with chagrin, beating a pillow on the hospital bed as Ishida, who had informed him of what had happened, looked on.

"He was almost twelve years younger than me," Risaburo lamented. "I was hoping he could have lived for at least another ten years to keep contributing to Toyota. He still had so much left in him... Hey, Taizo. Development of the compact car—what Kiichiro wanted more than anything—is finally on the right track, isn't it? Since he died without ever getting a chance to see it, his soul won't rest until we make it happen. If it's any consolation, the company has recovered in superb fashion because of your hard work. I, too, want to regain my health and do what I can to help Toyota."

Kiichiro was at his prime in his late fifties. Because of the wealth of knowledge and experience in automotive technology he had attained, Kiichiro's death was devastating not only for Toyota but was also a great loss for Japanese industry as such.

What with the sudden outbreak of the Second Sino-Japanese War right after the founding of Toyota, followed by the turmoil during and after the War in the Pacific, and his retirement just prior to receiving an order for special military procurements for the Korean War—and now his sudden death just before a presidential comeback—Kiichiro's luck had been against him all along. The war was not his doing, but Kiichiro's forced retirement and his death just prior to his comeback had come, in the words of Ishida, from a certain laxness.

In preparation for returning as president, Kiichiro had spent nearly every night recounting his dreams of a Japanese-produced passenger car to elicit the cooperation of concerned parties, but it had all been for naught. Perhaps he could have prevented tragedy from striking had he had the discipline required of a business leader and more thoroughly watched over his health.

Joint funeral services were held in Tokyo and Nagoya for both

Toyota Motor and Toyoda Automatic Loom Works. Overall, nearly 5,000 people attended.

But the family tragedy continued. On June 3, a mere two and a half months after Kiichiro's abrupt death, Risaburo followed Kiichiro into the land of no return, succumbing to a chest disease he had been fighting since summer of the previous year.

After having tentatively decided to return as president, Kiichiro had gone to inquire after Risaburo's health and to tell him the news. Putting the past behind him, Risaburo took Kiichiro's hand. "I am so glad to hear it," he told him tearfully. "Now that you've finally decided to go back to Toyota, I'll be able to greet my father-in-law (Sakichi) in the other world with pride. Now the future of the Toyoda family is in safe hands."

The episode intensified the shock of Kiichiro's sudden passing all the more for Risaburo, to the point that he felt too worn down to attend Kiichiro's funeral in Nagoya, while the one in Tokyo was out of the question. The day after the funeral in Nagoya, Eiji paid a visit to Risaburo to see how he was doing after receiving the bad news about Kiichiro. He had hardly set foot in the room when he realized that Risaburo's life, too, was drawing to a close.

"Listen, Eiji," Risaburo groaned from bed. "No matter what happens with Toyota, you absolutely must make a success of the passenger car under development. That's the only way to requite Kiichiro's death. You know this better than anyone. The future of Toyota and the Toyoda family rides on your shoulders."

The man who had opposed the Toyoda family's entry into the automotive business more strenuously than anyone else now exhorted from his sickbed: "Toyota can't cling desperately to trucks forever. Make these passenger cars happen if it's the last thing you do!"

"Please rest assured. We're making great strides with the cars under development," Eiji told the dying man. "You must witness our success in the place of Kiichiro, who has departed for the next world."

"In that's the case, I'm relieved."

Risaburo, whose illness grew steadily worse after Kiichiro's death, drew his last breath before ever seeing the concept car for the newly developed small passenger vehicle spearheaded by Eiji. Risaburo passed away at the age of 68. The nearly overlapping deaths of the two brothers-in-law, who served as Toyota's first and second presidents, projected to the public the image of a Toyoda family stricken by tragedy.

The circumstances that led Ishida to stay on

The unexpected death of Toyota's founder brought Ishida's ideal scenario crumbling to the ground. After giving over the president's seat to Kiichiro, instead of becoming chairman, Ishida intended to retire to a bucolic life at the home of his adoptive family in Omi, Shiga Prefecture. Losing Kiichiro, however, and soon after, Risaburo, whom Ishida loved like a brother, he could not just go back to Omi and lead a carefree life in seclusion.

Although Toyota had gone public in 1949, listing its shares on the market before the company's management crisis surfaced, Ishida could never escape from the mindset that Toyota Motor Corporation was a Toyoda family business. If the next in line for president were to be chosen from within the Toyoda family, Eiji was the only possible candidate. Ishida knew all too well that Kiichiro had told those close to him before he died that "Toyota will be fine as long as Eiji's around."

Even so, he hesitated to put Eiji in as the next president straightaway. Eiji was still only 39. Knowing very well the demands of operating a business through his experience in the ultra-competitive prewar textile industry, Ishida considered Eiji's managerial ability to be a question mark even if the younger man had proven to be a top-notch engineer. There would be no other veteran executives around to support him.

Ishida felt that Eiji, before becoming president, first needed to exercise leadership in not only modernizing the company's plant facilities but also in developing the compact car, which still remained Kiichiro and Risaburo's dying wish. The project to develop a new compact passenger vehicle was already underway but Toyota would not be able to expand, let alone survive in the global automotive industry, without seeing the project through to a successful conclusion. It all depended on Eiji whether the project came off as hoped.

Assuming that promoting Eiji was not a viable option, the company could call instead on Fukio Nakagawa, a director from the Imperial Bank of Japan who had been sent in as a quid pro quo for extending loans to Toyota. He would only fill the position until Eiji was ready, of course, but Ishida hesitated because a former bank official might prioritize financial standing over everything else, wiping out all of Kiichiro's manufacturing DNA from the company. Ishida knew better than anyone how difficult it would be to restore the DNA once it was lost.

Added to this was the presence of Toyota Motor Sales, which complicated the selection of successor presidents. Its main board members, led by president Shotaro Kamiya, had all been scouted by Kiichiro when he began the automotive business. The president of Toyota Motor would have to face off against the forces of Toyota Motor Sales. Neither Eiji nor Nakagawa were equipped to match up against Kamiya.

For the moment, Ishida could not do as he would have liked. If he forced his own retirement, he could be accused of being irresponsible. The only path left open to Ishida was to remain as president and initiate Eiji into the ways of leadership.

The general shareholders' meeting at which Kiichiro was supposed to have been welcomed as the new president was held according to schedule. At the meeting, 27-year-old Shoichiro, Kiichiro's eldest son, was appointed to the board of directors through the good offices of Ishida. After returning from Wakkanai, Hokkaido, Shoichiro had opted out of joining Toyota, spending some time at Toyoda Soken but going on to work for Aichi Kogyo (now Aisin Seiki). Kiichiro was not particularly insistent on bringing his son into the company that he had built.

The auto business picked up in a flurry around the time when Ishida's reappointment was confirmed. The Treaty of San Francisco came into effect on April 28, 1952, almost exactly one month after Kiichiro passed away, bringing an end to the American occupation and leaving Japan an independent nation both in name and substance.

Korean special procurements resuscitated the Japanese economy and, in turn, ignited consumer spending. The Japanese lifestyle had also shown signs of Westernization along American lines. The Japanese auto industry had made a clean break from the turbulent times and was now in the process of ushering in a new age.

Changes first began to occur in peripheral industries. With the 1951 deregulation of limitations on oil use in automobiles, gas stations were springing up all around the country. Along with this came a ban on the use of alternative fuels based on wood and charcoal. The

Temporary Materials Supply and Demand Control Law was abolished, and soon later, the regulations governing the transfer of foreign-produced cars as well. At that point, MITI, which had emphasized the protection and nurturing of domestically built automobiles, could no longer justify the indefinite imposition of a high 40 percent tariff on imported cars.

The complete elimination of tariffs, however, would likely bring an avalanche of foreign cars into the Japanese market, stripping Japanese manufacturers of any chance to produce automobiles. Foreign companies aimed to force open the market in the name of trade liberalization; it meant first penetrating the Japanese market with their own corporate brand of cars and then pursuing direct investment at some future stage after ground had been broken on capital liberalization.

The Ministry of Transport's initiatives ran counter to those of MITI. The Ministry of Transport's theory was that "protecting Nissan and Toyota is going too far since they have profited so handsomely from Korean special procurements as to be paying out dividends. The international division of labor dictates that Japanese manufacturers focus exclusively on trucks and for passenger cars to be imported from abroad." Importers concurred with this logic, drafting up a booklet entitled "On the Necessity of Passenger Cars Imports," which clearly outlined their direct opposition to MITI policy.

The Ministry of Transport, touting economic principles, stood on the side of importers and consumers. MITI supported the protection and nurturing of domestic manufacturers. The conflict between the two escalated with each passing day. Failing to find common ground, before long it became a political issue and was brought before the Diet.

The issue was debated in the Upper House Committee on Transport on July 26, eight days after Toyota's shareholders' meeting. Four people were summoned as witnesses to testify before the committee. Ishida did not know until that day who, other than himself, would attend. Knowing that he would be the first person ever on the stand to represent Japanese automakers filled him with a sense of foreboding.

Toyota is making money, but not raking it in

As anticipated, Ishida was subjected to a barrage of questions from carping lawmakers dead-set against domestically produced cars. He fielded questions like:

"Isn't it true that Japanese cars are expensive because Japanese automakers are only concerned about profits?"

"Consumers are annoyed at having to buy undependable domestically produced cars built with inferior technology. Shouldn't we therefore import more cars from abroad?"

"Manufacturers are dependent on MITI's protection of domestically built cars."

As if admonishing a child, Ishida responded to the simplistic and naive line of questioning by explaining at great length that these were all views based on misconceptions.

Not taking kindly to being treated like a child, however, one assembly member focused emotional attacks on Toyota, saying, "I hear that a certain company in the automotive industry is reaping landslide profits. Meanwhile, its vehicles' performance hasn't improved in the least."

"No, we (Toyota) are making surprising little, much less than assembly members might think. But our cars are getting better with time."

"Don't bullshit me! According to what I've heard, aren't you paying out a 100 percent dividend and rewarding your board members with million-yen bonuses? It's downright criminal that you're living it up while you go around peddling jalopies. You're making a mockery of the Japanese people."

But Ishida did not budge an inch despite such provocative questions. It only managed to stir his naturally rebellious spirit. Ishida's aptitude for putting up a good fight was undisputed.

"Gentlemen," he said, "maybe not right now, but I guarantee that one day every one of you will be a Toyota customer. As a businessman, I am not in the position to argue with valuable future customers. Please allow me to say one thing, however. To what manufacturer in what country does the 100 percent dividend mentioned by this assemblyman refer? At the very least, Toyota absolutely does not engage in such absurd behavior. I'm sure there is no one in this business that does such a thing. To be more specific, I am thinking about us humble domestic manufacturers—unfortunately, I don't know how it works overseas. As far as Toyota is concerned, we are finally just now able to distribute dividends. The idea of giving out large bonuses is unthinkable. How would we be able to make low-cost, high-performance vehicles that way? Every member of our company works hard day and night thinking about nothing but that."

But Ishida's best effort—what he was really made of—was yet to come.

"We are not in the business of making quality cars because we were asked by the government—much less you gentlemen—to do it. To survive in the auto business, Toyota is working without rest to produce high-performance cars that live up to international standards as soon as humanly possible. Somehow we're making money, but we aren't raking it in. We're trying to save money but we're not loaded. To ignore the facts and to have me come to a place like this (the Diet), and then for everyone here to reprimand me—this is just unacceptable no matter how you look at it."

So much for that. While saying he would not talk back, he met the lawmakers head-on with his own counterarguments. He then ended on a note of strong determination.

"I respectfully and gratefully accept your opinions," he said. "I consider today not merely a kangaroo court, but as a rousing call to battle. Toyota will most definitely demonstrate that it can make cars to everyone's liking. Please be patient for just a little longer."

The congressional debate lasted for six endless hours. Before long, Ishida, who had been seen as a temporary remedy when he first took office, became the face of the industry for having unequivocally announced Toyota's determination to the Diet.

At the time Ishida was summoned to the Diet, Toyota's annual (June 1952 to May 1953) sales were ¥12.9 billion, with operating income of ¥1.73 billion and before-tax income of ¥1.46 billion. The reason that Ishida spoke so fervently and defiantly before the Diet owed to his absolute faith in the new compact car that Eiji had just begun to work on.

Chapter 8
Electing for Independent Development

THE ONLY COMPANY IN THE automotive industry to declare that they would pursue independent development based on Japanese technology was Toyota. Meanwhile, Nissan led the group of manufacturers who had allied with foreign companies. Genshichi Asahara, who returned to Nissan as president in 1951, visited the American and European automotive industries not just before the war but whenever he had the chance. Asahara was an established player within the industry and was considered the one executive most familiar with American and European automobiles. It was his firm belief after being reinstated as president that the only option for Nissan's further development was affiliating with a foreign company and that such cooperation to obtain technology should be a top priority for the Japanese auto industry if it were to branch out of Japan itself.

This line of thinking was identical to Kiichiro's and the sole reason why Kiichiro posed to him the idea of a three-company venture with Ford. Yet in the end, Asahara did not take up Kiichiro's offer because, while Kiichiro was focused exclusively on Ford as a potential business partner, Asahara was mainly interested in European cars. The first to get wind of changes at the U.S. Big Three automakers, Asahara judged that American cars were not very well suited to the Japanese market.

American cars or European cars?

In the 1950s, the Big Three turned to enhancing vehicle equipment to improve ride quality and comfort. The whole premise behind bolstering such equipment was to increase engine displacement. Popular thinking at the time dictated that gas tanks should be made heavier for long-distance travel because gas was inexpensive, giving sway to full-sized engines such as the inline six-cylinder and V8 engines. The Big Three also sought to incorporate fashionable accoutrements divorced from utility, marking a transition to outsized vehicles. This trend continued to develop for over twenty years, lasting until the first oil shock in the fall of 1973.

The image of American cars changed dramatically after 1950. Though Japanese remained infatuated with American cars, the dinosaur-like autos lost their utility in Japan, where roads are comparatively narrow. Well-acquainted with the state of the American and European auto industries, Asahara saw a tie-up with any of the U.S. Big Three to be unrealistic. In this sense, European manufacturers were a more appealing option in that they specialized in making compact and practical cars while steering away from outsized vehicles.

Asahara chose to affiliate with Britain's Austin Motor Company. Austin's flagship model, the Austin Seven, was known as the most popular British car in Japan. As of March 1952, some 1,286 could be seen cruising around Japan.

Nissan was not the only Japanese company looking to tie up with a foreign automaker. Backroom negotiations for technical cooperation were underway between Japan's oldest carmaker, Isuzu Motor, and Britain's Rootes Motors, as well as between Hino Motor and France's Regie Nationale des Usines (Renault). In contrast to such moves, MITI wanted at all costs to forestall foreign companies from taking control of Japan's automotive industry, a strategic industry essential to national economic development, even as the ministry coveted advanced technology from foreign companies. Given this, in June 1952, MITI drafted the Basic Policy for the Introduction of Foreign Investment into Japan's Passenger Car Industry, which essentially allowed for technical cooperation with foreign companies based on the supposition that doing so would maintain Japanese manufacturers' independence.

Although both were in the same boat during the ten-year technological vacuum that followed the end of the war, Nissan and Toyota chose to traverse opposite paths. While Nissan chose to tie up with a foreign company, Toyota elected to develop independently. Toyota's preference for independent development was not completely unrelated to Kiichiro's death. The basis for this decision lay in a conversation that took place during the New Year's holidays in 1952 when Eiji went to Tokyo as Ishida's emissary to meet with Kiichiro.

Eiji was still unaware of Kiichiro's plan to form a three-company venture with Ford and Nissan. After tie-up negotiations with Ford fell through with the outbreak of the Korean War, Eiji slowly but surely moved forward with plant modernization on the premise that Toyota was to develop a passenger car with its own technology. He believed that Kiichiro would take the lead on development until Kiichiro told him otherwise during their meeting in Tokyo: he didn't intend to return to a company that seemed incapable of developing a passenger car.

Although this frustrated Eiji to the point of tears, he figured that it would take time for Kiichiro to come around.

Eiji chooses to forge his own path

When work started up again on the morning of January 4, Eiji broached the subject with Ishida while the latter was preparing to deliver his New Year's greeting as the company's president.

"Mr. Ishida," he said, "under my supervision, the engineering department is beginning full-scale development of the passenger car assuming that the Boss will return."

Ishida, smiling, gave an unqualified nod of approval. "I've been eagerly awaiting the day when you would come up from the floor to tell me this," Ishida replied. "Kiichiro's in for a surprise when he gets back."

Eiji's on-site executive suite stood in a small wooden building in the corner of the production wing away from the main administrative building. In the innermost part of the room were desks for Eiji and Shoichi Saito, managing director. Saito had accompanied Eiji to the U.S. to train with Ford and was considered one of Toyota's so-called elite. Ishida, himself non-conversant with automotive technology, left all aspects of automaking from technical development to production to Kiichiro's two prized protégés.

In front of the desk sat a shabby coffee table and a sofa. Sitting on the sofa, Eiji gave Saito a candid account of how he pleaded with Kiichiro over the holidays to return as president and how the tables turned when Kiichiro instead gave *him* a lecture.

"That was the deciding factor for me, Saito," Eiji said. "I'm planning to give the official order for personnel to commence development of a world-class compact passenger car as soon as tomorrow. I told Ishida this morning of my intent to do so. We're going to use the R-type engine currently under development."

Leaning forward, Saito replied, "Sooner or later, Nissan, Hino and Isuzu are going to partner with foreign companies and throw themselves into making their own full-fledged passenger cars. If Toyota gets going now, we shouldn't be far behind."

"No matter what the Boss says, he'll no doubt be back at some point in the future. We should rightfully have Kiichiro spearhead the project, but if we wait around for that to happen, we're going to be that much more behind in bringing the car to market. Are you with me on this, Saito?"

"Of course. I look forward to being a part of it. The problem is who to lay it on."

"We'll need a man who can demonstrate strong leadership to see this through to the end. Japan still doesn't have a legitimate passenger car to take on the high-performance cars imported from Europe and the U.S. Toyota's going to make just such a car. We'll rush headlong into uncharted territory—we'll forge our own path. The man in charge will have to lead the way himself and blaze a trail for the rest to follow. You know, the more I think about it, the more I realize that *that man* is the one for the job." Eiji could picture his face now.

"I feel the same way," Saito agreed. "Yes, *that man* is the only one who can do it."

Unable to come up with ¥200 million of funding, Toyota had been driven to the brink of bankruptcy just two years before. They could expect to have to invest billions if they were to move forward with full-scale development of a passenger car. Introducing foreign technology would require only a fraction of the time and money it would take to develop a car independently and would entail that much less risk.

As well as Toyota had done thanks to Korean special procurements, independent development was a make-or-break proposition of the first order from an executive standpoint. Should they fail, it would be another roller-coaster ride straight to the bottom. Eiji decided to risk it, electing for the more difficult of the two paths.

The man to whom Eiji and Saito referred was none other than Kenya Nakamura, assistant general manager of the Auto Body Plant. There were two reasons as to why they chose him over everyone else. The first was his career prior to joining Toyota; the second was his words and actions since joining the company. With his imposing physique, unusual blue eyes and close-cropped hair, he stood apart from most Japanese. In appearance, Nakamura bore a vague resemblance to General Dwight Eisenhower, the war hero who had become president of the U.S., and the Hollywood character actor Yul Brynner.

Toyota's Yul Brynner

Having been at the company for fourteen years by that time, Nakamura was known by everyone at the company as a real character. He loathed any kind of formal event, which naturally included attendance at the Hoko Jinja Shrine on New Year's and the stiff holiday greetings that went along with it.

After graduating from Nagaoka College of Technology, he joined Kioritz Corporation, which was established to handle knockdown production (KD) of Chrysler's Dodge and Plymouth lines in Japan. Although the company started out well, KD tapered off with the Second Sino-Japanese War. In an attempt to overcome this, the company audaciously launched the development of a car based on Japanese technology. Nakamura, who was in his fourth year at Kioritz, was put in charge of the car's design. However, just as the blueprint for the chassis and body had been completed and he was set to begin work on designing an engine, he had a falling out with the company.

The company's sales manager carelessly thought that the engine could be made by simply making the parts based on the drawings and then putting them together. Nakamura vehemently protested.

"You've got to be kidding," he bristled. "If you simply make the parts without thinking it through and then there's a defect of some kind, we'll have no way of knowing what went wrong. I won't hand over any more specifications until I draw up a detailed diagram that I'm totally confident with. This is what any engineer would do in good conscience. Because with cars, people's lives are at stake."

This prompted Nakamura to finish up the designs and leave the company sooner than he would have liked. Kioritz produced a prototype called the *Nikko* based on Nakamura's specifications, but the car never saw the light of day due to the Japanese government's issuance of an injunction barring the production of domestically-built passenger cars in favor of assuring the continued production of military trucks. Prior to this, however, the company had found flaws in the car in the preproduction stage, so it probably would have turned out to be lemon even if it had reached the market.

After Nakamura quit the company and was getting ready to check out apartments, he spotted an issue of a magazine called *Ryusenkei* (Streamline) that he had purchased but not yet read. The colophon read: Volume 1, Number 1, January 1, 1937. He had bought it because of its name and because it was the first issue but set it aside as he was occupied with other things. Flipping through the pages, he found himself drawn into "Kiichiro Toyoda's Hopes for the New Year,"[17] an article that discussed Kiichiro's ambitions to build a passenger car with Japanese ingenuity. Contained therein was Kiichiro's mantra: *with Japanese brains and skills.*

1937 was the year that Toyota Motor Corporation was established. Nakamura read Kiichiro's New Year's aspirations and thought, "This is a person I want to work for." That day he sent Toyota a letter requesting employment, with his résumé attached. A few days later he received a reply asking him to come to Toyoda Automatic Loom Works in Kariya. At the time, Toyota was seriously lacking in engineers, so Nakamura's letter came as a godsend. After Nakamura asked to work either in the design division or in research, the person with whom he spoke gave him an honest rundown of the situation at Toyota.

"To be quite honest," he said, "the Auto Body Plant is in a bit of a fix. We are planning to increase body production efficiency at the Koromo Plant, which is nearly finished, by adopting welding machinery and high-frequency electric tools, but unfortunately we can't handle all the work with our current level of manpower. Looking at your résumé, it appears that you have experience with auto body production. How about it? Won't you consider working for a

---

17. *Toyoda kiichiro no nentokan*

few years in the Auto Body Plant? Rather than jump right into design or research, you should first test the waters a bit in the Auto Body Plant to see exactly what kind of company Toyota is. After that, I will see to it personally that you are transferred to the department of your choice."

Kiichiro's spokesman

As it turned out, Nakamura's wish was never fulfilled. By the time Toyota's labor dispute reached a climax, Nakamura had been promoted to foreman and chosen to stand atop the rostrum at shop floor rallies as floor representative. Amidst the clamoring, Nakamura gave passionate voice to his thinking on the situation that the company found itself in.

"There's a huge rushing river," he implored. "There's a boat on the right bank, but it will capsize if left to its own devices. If you try to move it to the left bank, it will get caught in the rapids and drift away. The reconstruction plan has to be the solution that prevents the boat from both capsizing and drifting away."

"Nakamura!" a union member cried out from the crowd. "You're a corporate spy! We're gonna kick you outta the union!"

Toyota's labor union was on the union shop system, so anyone expelled from the union would also have to leave the company. Nakamura knew about the rule but, passing it off as a trifle, proceeded to criticize the union anyway.

"Pushing for the president's resignation and demanding higher wages is wrong. Toyota cannot survive without diverting money for a pay raise into plant and equipment upgrades."

Unable to ignore Nakamura's no-win situation with the union, Toyota solved his dilemma by promoting him to assistant general manager in the midst of the heated dispute, making him a non-unionized worker.

Even after the intense labor dispute subsided, the union was steeped in the sense that developing a passenger car was the indulgent pursuit of a faction in the technical division and that such an obsession would once again drag the company down into difficult financial straits. But for Nakamura, who had joined Toyota intoxicated with Kiichiro's idea of carmaking, nothing could shake the belief in the primacy of passenger cars. "Trucks are no more than vehicles derived from passenger cars," went his theory. "These cars have been the source of automobiles all along. Companies that do not pursue development of passenger cars can only follow others. That would take a company down. The development of a passenger car must take precedent over everything else."

He had talked about his theory not only with peers but with general manager Shuji Ohno in 1949 as the financial crisis was beginning to creep up on Toyota. Ohno followed along eagerly at first, perhaps because he was a bit intrigued.

"So, Nakamura, say Toyota were to begin full-scale development of a passenger car," Ohno said. "How much do you think it would cost?"

"Probably no less than ¥2.5 billion," Nakamura readily replied.

"It's an interesting idea," Ohno said with a look of astonishment. "But such talk isn't going to get us anywhere. At the moment Toyota doesn't have ¥500 million, let alone ¥2.5 billion just sitting around. No one's going to go along with a fantasy like that. We need to be a bit more realistic here..."

Without missing a beat, Nakamura further expounded his theory.

"An automaker that doesn't produce passenger cars is destined to go under at some point or another. Are you prepared for that, Mr. Ohno? You may not be familiar with cars since you are not an engineer, but surely you must be aware of which way the pendulum is swinging in the global automotive industry. Passenger cars constitute eighty percent of the vehicles produced by the Big Three of GM, Ford and Chrysler, and over half for major European manufacturers. Sooner or later, the same will happen in Japan, too. If Toyota is still fixed then on making trucks... Well, it makes me sick to think about it."

Just as Ishida became president and the company's reorganization got underway, the special procurement order for a large volume of trucks buried Nakamura from morning till night in nothing but trucks. Even then, rather than suffer a change of heart, Nakamura's drive for passenger cars intensified.

"Toyota's definitely doing well with trucks at the moment," he thought. "But this won't continue for long. Toyota should prioritize passenger cars as its main product without further delay. Auto companies that fail to do this will not survive in the future."

It sounded to Eiji as if Nakamura were the mouthpiece for Kiichiro's mantras. On the surface, Eiji pretended that Nakamura's words' went in one ear and out the other, but inwardly he applauded Nakamura. Eiji's choice of Nakamura was therefore due not just to the man's previous experience and his work at Toyota, but his strong personality and the fact that Eiji greatly appreciated his many years of leadership in the Auto Body Plant.

The compact car on which Toyota would soon begin working was intended for large-scale production. Consequently, productivity would be a crucial element of the operation. Toyota already had the knack for increasing productivity with regard to engine and chassis production through its experience making trucks. The problem would be how to go about boosting productivity when manufacturing the body. Speeding up body production would of course require streamlining the production site, and overhauling everything starting from the design phase. In reality, however, opinions rarely meshed between the design department and the production site. As is the case with not just Toyota but with most companies, design departments are comprised mostly of inexperienced university-educated engineers, while the production floor consists mainly of skilled workers trained as craftsmen. The chief complaint from the production floor can generally be summarized by the claim that technical drawings drafted by young design engineers often leave out productivity considerations.

In this sense, Nakamura, through his involvement with design for the Kioritz Corporation before the war, his long service in the Auto Body Plant for Toyota, and his leadership capability, had what it took to mediate between the design department and the work floor for the purpose of developing a car for large-scale production. Eiji felt that moving forward with a legitimate passenger car would require a commander who could effectively marshal the artillery, the infantry, and all other necessary units. This was what he expected to see from Nakamura.

Chapter 9
The Standard for Japanese Cars

TOPPED WITH A JAGGED-EDGED ROOF resembling the teeth of a saw, the Toyota Auto Body Plant stands at the west corner of the Koromo Plant. Iron plating materials lie everywhere within the high-ceilinged factory, which is packed back-to-back with large metal cutting, lathe turning and other smaller machines. Perhaps owing to meticulous management and control, however, the atmosphere is far from cluttered.

January 4—back to work. The factory that morning that day was quiet, as if still reveling in post-New Year's celebrations. Meanwhile, Auto Body Plant assistant general manager Kenya Nakamura, sporting a yellowish-green uniform, was at work silently inspecting the machines in preparation for full-scale operations to begin the next day. As he worked, he was approached by a young engineer, clad in a white collared shirt and necktie overlain by a work smock, who came to wish Nakamura a happy new year. Toyota's workmen and engineers could be differentiated from one another based on whether they wore a white shirt and tie underneath their uniforms.

"Happy New Year, Mr. Nakamura," proffered the young engineer. "I look forward to continuing working with you this year."

"Oh, right, thanks," Nakamura replied brusquely, focused on inspecting the machinery. There it was. Knowing Nakamura's rather curt nature, the engineer withdrew without further ado. Nakamura's trademark look throughout the year consisted of a work smock worn over a plain white long-sleeved shirt. The long sleeves stayed long even during the summer. When asked whether he wasn't hot, he'd explain coolly, "Bare skin absorbs too much heat. A white long-sleeved shirt reflects heat, so it's cooler this way."

Making a full-fledged passenger car

Upon finishing lunch and going back to the room where the Auto Body Plant's managers congregated, Nakamura found a note lying on his desk, saying: "Come ASAP."

One look at the worm-like writing snaking across the page and Nakamura knew that the person who had sent for him was the head of the engineering department, Eiji Toyoda. Nakamura headed at a trot for the small building in front of the administrative building across a two-land pathway from the Auto Body Plant. Inside was the on-site executive suite from where the executives supervised the engineering department. Nakamura often came into contact with engineering executives as part of his job, so he took the occasion lightly, figuring it was probably just an exchange of ideas on where the Auto Body Plant should be headed going into the new year.

Managing director and assistant general manager. Although their stations were dissimilar, Eiji and Nakamura were both born in 1913 and thus the same age. Since both men were engineers, Nakamura felt a kinship with Eiji, and often bounced ideas off of him without the usual sense of reserve.

Upon entering the room, Eiji and Saito were sitting at the coffee table away from their workstations.

"Kenya," Eiji said, getting things started. "Toyota finally decided to begin developing a full-fledged compact passenger car."

Nakamura jumped at the words *passenger car*, shooting off questions rapid-fire. Eiji answered with finesse. Once things settled down a bit, Eiji said something that caught Nakamura off-guard.

"So Kenya," he said, "we would like to put you in charge of everything from design to production of the new car. Your title will be Chief Engineer for Vehicle Development."

Nakamura had difficulty understanding what Eiji was saying. The process of making a car involved the engineering department's design division drawing up the technical specifications for the car under development, manufacturing parts based on this blueprint, and then having the prototype division build a test car. The experimental division would then run tests to refine and improve the quality of the prototype for production. In other words, there was a self-contained system for vehicle development operated by various divisions within the engineering department. Though it also employed engineers, the

Auto Body Plant to which Nakamura belonged was the production site, a department within the company unrelated to car design.

Eiji was proposing to put a manager of this unrelated department in charge of developing the vehicle that would bear the torch of Toyota's future. This was not to say that Nakamura would be transferred to the engineering department; he would merely be given the title *Chief Engineer of Vehicle Development*.

Toyota had been using the term *shusa*, or chief engineer.[18] It was a title used solely for general managerial posts affiliated with arms of the company other than the assembly line. This time, however, the post lined up for Nakamura would be project leader, which clearly differed from *shusa* posts of the past.

The personnel who would join the project would take part through their current departments. They would be brought in to help develop the new car as members of the project while continuing to perform their regular work duties. The chief engineer of development would have to make people from other departments work toward achieving the objectives laid out for them. Nakamura had never dreamed that he would be the person appointed to do this.

Appointment as Chief Engineer

In taking on the position of chief engineer, there were a number of things that Nakamura had to confirm with Eiji: for instance, whether Toyota had a serious desire to work toward developing a passenger car, or whether the company would begin the project for now but throw in the towel later on if it did not work out.

"Did Toyota's biggest shareholder (Kiichiro) consent to initiating this project?" Nakamura mustered up the courage to ask.

Although Kiichiro had left the company and decisions on all important matters pertaining to Toyota's future were made based on consultations between Eiji and Ishida, any plans could easily be overturned if Kiichiro, the company's largest shareholder, raised an objection. Even if they thought it hundred percent certain that

---

18. *Shusa*, also meaning project manager or product manager; Toyota adopted the English term *chief engineer* in 1989. Cited in Managing Multiple Projects: Planning, Scheduling and Allocating Resources; Pennypacker, James S. and Dye, Lowell D., CRC Press, 2002.

Kiichiro would not oppose the development of a passenger car, being sure of this in advance would change the way in which they went about the project.

"Kenya," Eiji smiled, sensing Nakamura's apprehensions. "Don't worry about such trivial matters. The Boss is up in arms about how we're just standing around twiddling our thumbs."

Nakamura thought but did not go so far as to say: "If Toyota is inclined to develop a passenger car all by itself, then shouldn't you, as head of the engineering department, be the one to lead the project?"

Eiji, for his part, wanted to take the reins himself as chief engineer to develop a car that would make Kiichiro proud. Given his position of responsibility, however, Eiji could not have it his way. Passionately explaining just how important this project would be for Toyota, Eiji closed by saying, "Don't be nervous, Kenya. It's not like you. I'll step in if there's ever a problem."

Hearing such words reassured Nakamura that he could rely on Eiji to do just that. The drawbacks to the *shusa* system became evident whenever the chief engineer and the engineering department directly involved with development found themselves at odds. One of the people at the time with the power to shuffle around the development team was engineering director Hanji Umehara, whom Kiichiro had implored to join Toyota and who'd given up his position as associate professor at Tohoku University. A chief engineer, on the other hand, did not have this power, nor did he manage subordinates as their boss. He therefore did not have the right to issue orders. The people recruited into the project team did not necessarily have to listen to the chief engineer. But if this were to occur, it would pose a major hindrance to development efforts.

Although the chief engineer would be accountable on all points pertaining to the car to be developed, from cost accounting to profit planning and market response, he would not be able to devote himself exclusively to the task. The more Nakamura thought about it, the more he realized what a lousy position it was. But while talking about it with Eiji, he gradually came to see the grand scheme behind Eiji's thinking.

"Eiji is seriously promoting this project," Nakamura thought. "Come to think of it, since the old man left Toyota, Eiji has been directing everything related to technology. He has been put in a position since he was young to advise on all aspects of the company.

Someone like that doesn't just order his staff around on a whim. He knows everything there is to know on how his decisions will impact the company overall. Eiji perhaps is the real chief engineer for this project and I am his deputy. But even a deputy is given considerable authority to act. It's time to gird up our loins and get down to work."

Nakamura ran through all the questions he could think of to ask, while Eiji and Saito explained everything in detail, assuming from the outset that Nakamura would not refuse the assignment. Having been seen straight through, it would have been proper for Nakamura to reply in such manner as: "I understand. I'll do it. Thank you for this opportunity." But those words escaped him. Instead he asked: "So where do I begin?"

"What we've decided on for now," Eiji said, "is to use a 1500cc engine currently in development to make the largest passenger car possible that fits within the standards of a compact car."

The reason that Eiji did not hazard to sketch out a specific image of the car to be developed was that most of the demand for passenger cars at the time was for professional use as taxis and such. Though the future would no doubt bring increased demand for family cars, at that point it was hard even to speculate when Japan would become motorized and what form that would take. Accordingly, in developing a new-model vehicle, Eiji did not want to make any careless remarks to discourage Nakamura from keeping an eye out for signs of impending motorization and thinking outside-the-box.

The meeting with Eiji and Saito lasted an entire hour. It was a few days later when the company officially announced Nakamura's appointment by issuing a proclamation that read: "Kenya Nakamura appointed Chief Engineer of Development." Few people understood what this position entailed, all the more because no office had been set aside for the project and Nakamura would continue to perform his routine work duties.

Results of market research

Nakamura used his spare moments from work to conduct preliminary research prior to beginning full-scale planning and design. The first thing he did was to conduct interviews during his days off with Toyota's major dealers and taxi companies located in major cities like Tokyo and Osaka. He had dialogues with businessmen, salesmen and repair shop personnel to gather information on what kind of car they would like to see. Basically, he did what is now called market research.

Leaving aside all preconceived notions and expectations, he first tried to evoke an image of the car to be developed based on the opinions of people who would market, sell, use and repair them. This approach was in line with Eiji's thinking, an approach that valued the actual facts, the actual site and the actual object over everything else.

What he then realized was that nearly everyone he talked to had high expectations of what would come from Toyota's efforts to independently develop a full-fledged passenger car. He was able to garner a whole host of specific requests.

First off, an overwhelming number of people would support an American-style car. Despite the fact that the Big Three had made a dash towards oversized cars, these had yet to be imported to Japan. Due to Ford's and GM's pursuing knockdown production in Japan before the war, hired cars and taxi services predominantly used American cars. Almost all imported cars were American. Even after the war, the impression remained strong that a passenger car was equivalent to an American car.

Where opinions diverged was on the specifications for front suspension. As commercial vehicles travel a minimum of 10,000 kilometers per month, more than anything they would need to be sturdy enough to withstand heavy-duty use. Even if it meant sacrificing the quality of the ride to a certain extent, the car would have to offer rigid suspension to provide durability. However, independent suspension made more sense to the extent that quality of life would continue to improve over the years.

As his market research progressed, Nakamura's vision of the car he would develop began to materialize. The car would the "Crown," Toyota's first mass-produced passenger vehicle. The car's eventual success would prompt Toyota to adhere to the good-luck charm of giving their cars names that begin with the letter "C," as with the Corona and Corolla models.

Eiji kept a very close watch on what Nakamura was doing, but soon began to grow impatient. By early February President Ishida had told Eiji, "When Kiichiro comes back, I want to share with him the concept of the car you're developing and bowl him over." If Kiichiro were really coming back, Eiji would have to accelerate the current pace of development. Consequently, after conferring with Engineering Director Umehara, Eiji decided to assign Tatsuo Hasegawa, assistant manager of body design, to be Nakamura's assistant.

Hasegawa, an engineer who would later become chief engineer for development of the Corolla, showed great promise at the time as a key figure in body design. Graduating from the University of Tokyo's Department of Aeronautics in 1939, Hasegawa was a renowned prodigy who, after joining Tachikawa Aircraft Company, was simultaneously invited to be a lecturer at the University of Tokyo. At the young age of 27, he was appointed chief engineer of the interceptor that would shoot down American B-29 strategic bombers during the war. When Tachikawa Aircraft was prohibited after the war from producing airplanes using the company's name, Hasegawa left the company. He joined Toyota in 1947. He thus set out on a new career, going from aeronautical engineer to "car guy."

In the corporate world, a company's notice of appointment is absolute. But the right combination of people is paramount for projects on which the company's future depends. Even if the appointment came from the best intentions, if Hasegawa was unable to work in tandem with chief engineer Nakamura then the entire project would be in danger of running aground. This was Eiji's principal concern. Nakamura's and Hasegawa's personalities were in marked contrast to each other. While Nakamura had defiantly flown in the face of the union during the labor dispute, Hasegawa had stood toe to toe with the company as the head of the engineering department's workplace dispute resolution committee, maintaining that he would accept a pay cut but would on no account stand for employee layoffs.

Before officially announcing Hasegawa's appointment, Eiji called Nakamura into his office.

"Kenya," he said, "I'd like to bring body design's Hasegawa in as your assistant. You two are quite different personality-wise, but..."

"Personality has nothing to do with work, sir," Nakamura replied. "If you can get Hasegawa involved, so much the better. It will speed up development."

"Hasegawa is an excellent engineer, so the design division will probably be averse to it. It's easy for a company to appoint someone to a position, but it'll do more harm than good if it leaves an unpleasant aftertaste. Before I make the appointment, if you would, go talk to the director of the design division, Hasegawa's immediate supervisor."

As expected, the head of the design division was vehemently against sending Hasegawa to join the project team. With Hasegawa's appointment threatening to sail off course but with no other option open to him to avoid a fallout, Nakamura, notorious for his revulsion for bowing to others, bowed deeply to the younger director of the design division in a rare display of humility.

"I know there's a lot going on," he said, "but please agree to just this one thing."

Seeing Nakamura bowing his head, Eiji issued his verdict. "Kenya, the proudest man at Toyota, is bowing his head," he said to the design director. "Send Hasegawa to the project development team."

The next day, Hasegawa switched desks to join Nakamura in the Auto Body Plant. After laying out the details of his own work duties, Nakamura issued Hasegawa explicit instructions.

"You are an auto body specialist," he said. "Please put together your own ideas on what we should do in terms of styling."

When he found out in March that Kiichiro would be returning to Toyota to take the lead in developing the new passenger car, Nakamura sprang to his feet in elation. In mid-March, Kiichiro made his triumphant return to the Koromo Plant for the first time in two years. Just as Nakamura was deciding whether to go report to him the news of his appointment as chief engineer of development, Kiichiro made a sudden appearance at the Auto Body Plant. Perhaps because he had already heard from Eiji that the project was underway, he came in beaming.

"I was extremely impressed with Eiji's good judgment of character when I heard that you were the chief engineer of development," Kiichiro told Nakamura. "Just as you have said since way back when, a company that's incapable of developing a decent passenger car should not be called an automaker. As for compact cars, I have a lot of ideas as well. After things settle down, let's sit down and go over it together."

Nakamura was overjoyed to be personally addressed by Kiichiro. The deep emotion that Nakamura felt at this time, however, soon turned into a short-lived dream with Kiichiro's collapse less than a week later.

Building a stylish car

Eiji appointed Nakamura chief engineer of development on the assumption that Kiichiro would come back to the company. It would take at least three years to work out the concept, get moving on design, build a test car, complete durability testing and productize the passenger car.

Even with Kiichiro back as president, pressures from the company's business would make it difficult for him to head development. But even if he could not take direct command of the project, his very presence would boost engineers' morale. Eiji had included this in his calculations. But Kiichiro's sudden death derailed such calculations and there was no turning back. Upon returning to the factory after Kiichiro's funerals in Tokyo and Nagoya, Eiji called Nakamura and Hasegawa into his office.

"Just because the Boss is gone doesn't mean that we're halting development of the new car," he told them. "We'll keep going according to schedule."

Nakamura accelerated his research. Compiling the perspectives of dealers and taxi companies, he first decided that passenger cars must be able to stand up to use as taxis and hired cars.

Japanese roads were narrow and bumpy and were not made to facilitate the passage of carriages as they were in the U.S. Moreover, many of the main roadways were still unpaved. Consequently, the ability to withstand rough roads would be a mandatory precondition. It was for this reason that up until that point Toyota made taxis that looked like passenger cars on the outside, but were really trucks on the inside, by mounting a car body onto a truck frame. Using a truck frame, however, raised the center of gravity, destabilizing the car body. On top of that, the interior was cramped and the ride uncomfortable. The challenge given to Nakamura would be to develop a sturdy vehicle able to withstand harsh road conditions but without these disadvantages.

Before considering what kind of mechanism to utilize to improve ride quality and maneuverability, he had to hammer out styling. Figuring that out would provide an image of the car.

What puzzled Nakamura was how the differences between his and Kiichiro's conceptions of the car gradually came into relief. Kiichiro's approach was simple: in making a passenger car for the

1

general public, functionality should be the chief concern.

Speaking from the viewpoint of the seller, Shotaro Kamiya, president of Toyota Motor Sales, always said, "Toyota has the SF and PH models, the Toyopet, which are specified for use as taxis. But what we want is a compact sedan made for individual drivers that also emphasizes functionality." Kiichiro and Kamiya had both envisioned a practical car, but their vision was unrealistic.

The image that Nakamura had of the car he would be developing differed radically from the cars that Kiichiro and Kamiya had imagined. "The car has to have stylistic elegance," ran Nakamura's reasoning. "If we're going to make it anyway, I want to come up with a car that looks stylish enough to become the standard for Japanese cars. This stylishness must be backed by functionality. As such, we should probably style the car more after European than American cars."

Making a stylish car was Nakamura's own philosophy. Covering up an unstylish car with features and other mechanisms required giving explanations. But if a car left a good first impression and came equipped with the appropriate features, it wouldn't have to come with lengthy explanations and would be much easier to sell.

When Nakamura shared with Eiji his honest feelings on how different his car would be from Kiichiro's, Eiji dependably replied, "The Boss envisaged a car for the masses, so it stressed the importance of only the most essential features. At the present stage, however, it's probably too soon for Toyota to be making that kind of car. The car we have to design first is, just as you say, one that will become the standard for Japanese cars. Don't be led astray by others people's opinions; show us a car with your ideal specifications."

After heated debate, the project team reached consensus on six basic design principles: 1) American styling and a light, sporty feel; 2) a body as large as possible within the specifications of a compact car, so that it will not look scanty; 3) superior handling and a comfortable ride; 4) low price point for use as taxis; 5) sturdiness to withstand poor road conditions; 6) maximum speed of 100 km/h.

Itemized this way, the project team seemed to be doing nothing more than enumerate the features of the ideal car. Apart from the first principle, however, the vision was almost identical to Nakamura's own. What Nakamura had in mind before setting to work on specific designs was a car that would ride comfortably and not rattle or come apart even on bad roads.

Designers, who studied American cars, felt that increasingly oversized American cars were not appropriate for Japan considering road conditions and the lower quality of life. Even then, the team added that item to the list. They simply could not give up on that certain vivacity that American cars possessed.

Chapter 10
Toyota, Its Own Worst Enemy

O UT OF ALL ASPECTS OF Toyota's operations, the company's most distinguishing feature is its pursuit of self-sufficiency. For instance, large businesses in Japan have proactively adopted the outside director system in recent years. The idea behind doing so was that an outside perspective is necessary for continually increasing the value of the company. Meanwhile, even today, Toyota remains adamant about retaining inside directors. This is derived from the belief that only those within the company can both understand and apply Toyota's managerial creed as it is set forth in the Toyoda Precepts. Honda is the same in terms of its persistent dedication to maintaining inside directors.

Toyota's top management likes to use the term *jikotei kanketsu*.[19] Simply put, *jikotei kanketsu* is an approach in which each department—including development, production, sales and so forth—resolves their own problems. This seems like sectionalism at first, but what flows at the bottom of it is Toyota's unspoken wisdom—the whole of its unarticulated know-how and undocumented corporate practices.

To borrow the words of current president Katsuaki Watanabe, "To ensure the implementation of *jikotei kanketsu*, the ones upstream from you must be doing the best work they can. At the same time, you have to ensure that your processes are well understood by those working downstream. If you don't closely coordinate between processes up and down the line and to the right and left, your own processes aren't going to be complete." Close coordination involves identifying not only your own problem areas but those of others as

19. Defect-free process completion to ensure that no defective product leaves any production process.

well. It is Watanabe's view that a robust internal system of checks and balances between colleagues, extending from the production site to administrative departments, obviates implementation of the outside director system.

In a New Year's speech during his tenure as president, former president Hiroshi Okuda used the phrase "Bring down Toyota!"[20] In other words, when Toyota performs well, rival companies analyze its success and compete accordingly, and Okuda wanted Toyota's staff to work as if they were employees of a rival company looking for ways to top Toyota.

Another phrase that Okuda used to warn personnel was "Toyota's worst enemy is Toyota itself."[21] Although at first glance similar to "Bring down Toyota," it actually refers to something else. Now that Toyota is vying to be the world's leading automaker, its enemy is not rival automakers like GM or trade friction but arrogant complacency.

Toyota employs 65,000 regular employees in Japan. Adding in short-term employees and contract staff, 80,000 people work directly for Toyota. Most of them joined the company after Toyota had risen through the ranks of international companies to become "the world-renowned Toyota."

The pitfall of an organization, in the case of corporations, is that its employees become conceited once the firm achieves high profitability and prefer to sit back to enjoy the ride. It just so happens that an enormous building went up across from Nagoya Station at the end of 2006; Toyota's headquarter functions are now concentrated in central Nagoya. This massive building stands on the site of what was once the structure that housed the presidential office of Taizo Ishida while he served as president. Some in Nagoya these days even say (alluding to what was said of the dominant Heike clan in feudal-era Kyoto) that "if you aren't Toyota, then you aren't human." What would happen if Toyota's employees just sat around doing nothing?

What Okuda meant by the second "Toyota" in the phrase "Toyota's worst enemy is Toyota itself" is the conceit of Toyota employees. In other words, the enemy within, and the arrogance that comes from such aplomb can already be seen in Nagoya. This was all the more reason for Okuda to exhort his employees to be humble.

---

20. *Dato, Toyotaî*
21. *"Toyota no teki wa toyota"*

It is, in a way, an enviable predicament that prompted the company's chief executive to cry "Bring down Toyota!" and "Toyota's worst enemy is Toyota itself." Still, Okuda has reiterated this time and time again because pride and arrogance are also the trap that ensnares a company once it grows to become a giant.

Toyota was not built in a day

Rome was not built in a day. Toyota, as we know it today, also was not built in a day. The engine of Toyota's race to the top was the Crown, a compact passenger car developed using Japanese technology. The level of automotive technology in Japan around 1952, when the company began developing the car, was more than ten years behind that of Europe and the U.S. This was something that every engineer knew. To fill the void, Nissan moved to establish technical cooperation with Britain's Austin Motor, while Isuzu paired up with Britain's Rootes Motors and Hino with France's Renault.

Until just before his passing, Toyota's founder Kiichiro Toyoda had sought a tie-up with Ford. Despite this, President Ishida and Eiji, head of the engineering department, opted for independent development. *A 20-Year History of Toyota*[22] describes the circumstances surrounding that decision, ascribing it to Toyota's attempt to "achieve long-term development by reaffirming the company's traditional spirit of self-dependence exhibited since the time of Sakichi Toyoda."

This explanation undergoes some subtle changes in Toyota's *30-Year History*: "Our company's engineers have naturally fostered a strong sense of confidence and enthusiasm towards automotive technology. This was a time when these engineers, boosted by such confidence, opted not to affiliate with a foreign company and instead boldly decided to strike out on the more difficult path in line with the spirit of Japanese innovation exhibited since the time of Sakichi Toyoda."

Although these are assuredly consistent with the company's history, they are both mere postscript explanations typical of a company history. Even if Toyota at the time had had the foundation for making a passenger car with Japanese technology, it is questionable whether the company had the confidence to independently develop a

22. *Toyota 20-nenshi*

passenger car that would take on those of foreign companies.

Eiji, not Ishida, was the one who decided to pursue independent development over affiliating with a foreign company. After the labor dispute had abated, the faction within Toyota in favor of independent development was still in the minority. The faction in favor of tying up with a foreign company was so deep-seated in the union that the issue was even brought up during collective bargaining. "Independent development will take too much time," the union's argument ran. "If foreign-affiliated rivals like Nissan get a jump on us, Toyota's going to screw up its own future. After all, Toyota's level of technology is insufficient to develop a car that matches up with those of developed countries."

Eiji, however, aware of the almost self-deprecating views coming from within the company, still elected to pursue independent development.

After MITI issued its basic policy on affiliating with foreign companies in October 1957, a number of foreign firms applied to tie-up with Toyota as well. The most enthusiastic of them all was Volkswagen. VW's poster car, the Beetle, was developed before WWII in 1933 by Dr. Ferdinand Porsche at the request of Adolf Hitler. Released in 1938, the Beetle was truly a German people's car. Dr. Porsche was the founder of the consulting firm *Dr. Ing. h.c. F. Porsche GmbH, Konstruktionen und Beratungen für Motoren und Fahrzeugbau*, the predecessor of sports car maker Porsche AG. The Beetle was a big success not only in Europe and the U.S. but around the world. With cumulative production exceeding one million vehicles in August 1950, Volkswagen sold 380,000 cars globally in 1952. Many considered it just a matter of time before the Beetle pulled ahead of the Ford Model-T as the most widely produced car in the world. Volkswagen would not make for a bad business partner at all.

It is not that Eiji did not give some thought to pursuing independent development while affiliated with a foreign company at the same time, but he rejected the idea flat out before it reached a negotiation table. Toyota had already completed development of the R engine for use in a compact car. The project to develop the Crown, the car in which this engine was to be installed, was underway. Its design concept had been firming up bit by bit as the project progressed. Although no longer the case, at the time there was only a limited number of engineers who could be funneled into the development department. It would have been indeed quite inefficient to add in new foreign investment projects just after beginning independent development. Eiji also had to consider the risk that the morale of staff involved with the project for which Nakamura was responsible might wear down. Taking everything into account, Eiji came to a decision. By rejecting the idea of partnering with a foreign company, he cut off his own escape route in a sense.

On the other hand there had been Kiichiro, tenaciously fixated on working together with Ford, and on the other hand Eiji, who opted for independent development. What led to two such dramatically different development philosophies was the discrepancy between the positions of the founder and the one who had inherited the founder's last will. There was a two-year vacancy between Kiichiro's retirement and his decision to make a comeback. He had sought to tie-up with Ford, judging that it would be too difficult for Toyota to compete with European and American automakers on its own, because he had not witnessed firsthand the many advances at the Koromo Plant that had occurred during his absence.

On the other hand, Eiji's realization while training at Ford, that there was nothing Ford could do that Toyota could not, had given him a boost of confidence, spurring him to work furiously to modernize Toyota's plants. He had conveyed his thoughts to Kiichiro and launched the development project under the belief that, upon Kiirchiro's return, they'd work independently on a passenger car.

During his presidential New Year's greeting in January 1953, exactly one year after inaugurating the project, Ishida officially announced to the company that Toyota would develop a passenger car independently.

"The Japanese automotive industry," he said, "is now divided into two groups: automakers who are making a break for the foreign car camp, and those who are holding their ground in the domestic car camp. Our company has chosen the path of creating a domestic car built with our own technology, which has been our policy since the company's inception. We have audaciously chosen this more arduous path. This is not to say that developing a Japanese car is easy. But it is an ordeal that we must face once. I feel that the very act of prevailing through the tribulations to come will forge a future of promise for Toyota. Therefore, I beseech you to be take careful note of the difficult situation we face and ask that everyone works together amiably and cooperatively in making a vigorous push to bring the Japanese automotive industry into being."

It was already an open secret at the company that Toyota had begun working towards developing a sedan. Afraid that employees might become unduly elated, Ishida had so far avoided making an official announcement. He'd finally made known the existence of the development project a year later after ascertaining for himself that development was on the right track.

Immediately following the announcement, Eiji, addressing the labor union at the collective bargaining table, spoke frankly about his reasons for choosing independent development.

"Although we're drawing on domestic technology to develop the car," he said, "the time may come when we have no choice but to affiliate with a foreign manufacturer. However, even if we do end up in just such a situation, we won't be able to tie-up under favorable terms if we don't do what we are all capable of and get some technology under our belt. Conversely, without our own technology, Toyota will probably be forced to affiliate in what would amount to a complete capitulation. Our engineers in the engineering department and elsewhere are working hard to prevent this from happening."

The styling of the first version of the car came together at the end of June 1952, the year that Kiichiro passed away. The final version, which added tailfins to the car to conjure the image of American cars, left a striking impression on the eye. At the same time, people never got tired of the car's rounded design, which gave this particular element a long seven-year lifespan.

The design process reached its peak in the period from the end of that year to the beginning of 1953—for which they had, of course, sacrificed their New Year's holidays. Prototype 1 was finished in August 1953, twenty months after Nakamura had been appointed chief engineer. The body was hammered out from a piece of sheet metal. Merely having built a prototype was no cause for celebration; nevertheless, Eiji was overcome with emotion, saying before the new prototype, "I wish we could have shown you to the Boss and Risaburo."

Nakamura, as the head of the production site, could hardly allow himself to succumb to such emotion. He was more concerned with whether the prototype would run and, if it did, what troubles lay ahead. It was a potentially inexhaustible source of anxiety. No car was completely hassle-free from the very start. In fact a test car was, in a way, an agglomeration of defects.

Using public roads as a test course

Prototype 1 was designed simply to run. Then, after building Prototypes 2 and 3, the cars would undergo endurance testing, conducted by a test driver from the prototype division, and engineering testing, conducted by members of the design division. The long-awaited Prototype 2, along with the preparations to run it through a 20,000-kilometer test, was completed in May 1954.

Nowadays there is a full-fledged course equipped with every possible road condition where tests can be conducted away from the public eye. In addition, high-speed test courses have also been built in Hokkaido and the state of Arizona in the U.S. to fully facilitate testing in both frigid and blazing-hot conditions. At the time, however, Japanese automakers, including Toyota, did not have their own test courses. Honda, no more than a motorbike manufacturer back in those days, used the Arakawa levee in place of a test course.

Toyota had a small course off in the corner of its factory but it could not be used as a proper road course. As they had no other options, they obtained a license plate limited for test-car use and took the vehicle out on the open road. This was still a time when roads outside the main urban areas were unpaved except for major roads. Some roads were so bumpy that the car would actually get into the air at higher speeds. The long and short of it was that Japan was rife with such rough roads. In terms of results, however, building the car to withstand the worst of roads would later work to Toyota's advantage.

Test runs continued for nearly a year. Although Nakamura had been involved in the automotive industry since before the war, it took him until after the development project had started to get his driver's license. He had put in plenty of time working for car companies, but the era of the family car was still a long way off.

The speed test, which verified whether the car could travel 100 km/h, was where the test runs got tricky. There were no courses specifically for this, so the team had to use public roads. It required a long straightaway and, fortunately, there happened to be a road near headquarters that had a 5km stretch suitable for running a maximum speed test.

By anyone's reckoning, pushing 100 km/h on a public road constituted a speeding violation. And as luck would have it, there was a police box right along the way. Nakamura had gone to the police station to explain what they would be doing, but the police, for their part, could not officially condone such activities. The police were not as hardheaded as they might seem. Quite a few members of the police had siblings and other relatives working for Toyota, which often gave them access to inside information. So the police offered Toyota some unofficial, roundabout advice: "There's a good chance there won't be any police officers in the area around the time Toyota runs its test. But we'll all be in for it if you cause any accidents."

Toyota decided that, in carrying out the speed test, they would take extra care to wait until all cars in the vicinity of the starting and ending points, along with any cars trying to cross any of the intersections along the way, were stopped, and Toyota staff had explained to everyone what was happening. The drivers of the cars made to wait were utterly astounded to see a prototype car race by at a full 100 km/h right before their very eyes. In modern terms, this would be the equivalent of holding a Formula 1 competition on public roads. Soon it became the talk of the town, and throngs of spectators, who knew through word of mouth the day on which the test would be conducted, intrusively converged on the scene.

In October 1953, while test runs for Prototype 2 were culminating, Toyota kicked off development of a car which would later come to be called the Toyopet Master. Tozo Yabuta, head of the design division, was named chief engineer of development. While Nakamura was the type of person who showed an interest in trying new things, Yabuta was the type to build up knowledge and refine it.

Why did Toyota initiate development of another car that used the same engine and was the same size as the Crown before completing development of the Crown itself, a car so vital to the company's future? The reason was that they had converted the Crown's front axle into an independent front suspension but that the taxi industry had reservations about the suspension type. The same went for dealers. Their concerns related to durability.

Their contention that Japanese automakers previously had never used independent suspension was a persuasive argument. Nakamura expended all possible means to address their arguments, including fitting the car with a suspension arm and coil springs that were even wider than those used in American cars, which had twice the engine displacement of the Crown, but this alone failed to convince dealers.

Toyota's decision making, in general, was so excessively cautious that the company was ridiculed for "knocking on a stone bridge before crossing it." Although Eiji had complete faith in Nakamura, he decided to develop another car with a rigid suspension, essentially an extension of a conventional suspension, as an insurance policy in case the Crown did not work out. This was what evolved into the Master.

The timing of the production and release of the Master, whose inception came a year and nine months later, was set to correspond with that of the Crown. As the development period was limited, the Master would share many of the same parts originally developed for the Crown, including the transmission, gears, clutch and brake—whatever parts fit the Master's concept.

Sharing parts not only helped to shorten the development period, but also served to curtail production costs. Prototype 1's chassis was completed at the end of January 1954, four months after the project was put into action. Even though the car shared a considerable number of parts with the Crown, going from design to prototype in a four-month period was extraordinarily fast.

In terms of styling, in contrast to the Crown, which was designed to invoke an image of the American car and to look even bigger than it appeared, the Master was slimmed down into a sleeker European design. The car boasted a roof as thick and solid as that of conventional passenger cars, along with a high waistline. Conversely, the hood was built low and the rear without a tailfin, creating a good balance between the rear and the front of the car. Mounted with the same frame as that used in trucks, however, ride comfort did not even hold a candle to the Crown. Consequently, Toyota decided to release the Master for use as taxicabs, while the Crown would be marketed as a family car.

The Crown is ready at last

After sorting out the glitches one by one, production drawings were eventually wrapped up in July 1954, and the car came off the line in September. Yet prototype production continued. Although vehicles that were coming off the line were slated for distribution and sale, Nakamura could not shrug off lingering concerns about whether they would hold up as commodities.

Thus, in December of that year, he decided to conduct a 10,000-kilometer driving test between a car picked at random from the production line—the twenty-second car built during full-scale production—and Prototype 16. Nakamura was certain that neither vehicle would pose any problems no matter how poor the roads. The issue was performance and whether a car off the production line would be able to perform as well as a prototype.

Though not completely satisfied with the results, Nakamura decided to hope for the best. A torrent of requests flooded in not only from dealers but also from maniacal fans beseeching Toyota for a ride in their newly-developed car at the earliest opportunity—and, if possible, could they get a hold for themselves of the first car produced?

Both ordinary consumers and fanatics knew full well that the very first car would not be perfect. Many were devoted fans of Toyota who wanted to provide moral support; should the cars they purchased have any kind of trouble, they would be more than happy to notify Toyota of what improvements needed to be made. To wit, they were sympathetic to Toyota's policy to develop cars using only Japanese technology.

Ishida and Eiji were getting tired of waiting. From the perspective of management, they needed to hurry up and get the word out that the Crown—built entirely with homegrown technology—was ready at last.

January 1, 1955—8:30 a.m. Once the customary visit to Hoko Jinja Shrine to pray for the company's prosperity had wound down, all the managing executives in attendance headed for the assembly plant instead of the gymnasium. Unlike the average year, the managing executives were in full tuxedos.

A low platform had been set up in the center of the assembly plant, on top of which stood the Crown and the Master side-by-side. Above the cars stretched an arched wreathe of flowers. At the appointed time, the two cars started up. Eiji, who had been promoted to senior managing director, gripped the wheel of the Crown, while managing director Saito piloted the Master. When the cars surged to life, a sudden burst of applause tore through the factory from people waiting near the exit who had been involved with the project. The ovation intensified the moment Eiji alighted from the Crown and shook Ishida firmly by the hand.

Nakamura was nowhere to be seen at the commemoration ceremony; he was at home spending time with his family. He had never been very fond of such occasions. Indeed, nobody expected Nakamura to show up at the ceremony in a tuxedo when it was known that just having to put on a suit and tie aggravated the man. Eiji himself, acknowledging Nakamura to be "a pretty odd character," did not seem to mind the chief engineer's absence. He knew that Nakamura was the diametric opposite of the attention-seeking type.

Chapter 11
Constructing the Motomachi Plant

THE CROWN, FORGING THE WAY to Toyota's future, drew a larger-than-expected response. One American journalist appraised it as "No new, no old."

Automotive dealers intentionally displayed nothing but the Crown family car in showrooms. Had taxi companies wanted to get a hold of the Crown instead of the Master, which had been developed for use as a taxi cab, it would take over a year before it would become available. Just as chief engineer of development Kenya Nakamura had planned in honing in on major cities, the Crown was received as a full-fledged passenger car, gradually earning a solid reputation as the car that would eclipse Nissan's Austin and Isuzu's Hillman.

Toyota's policy to pursue independent development without falling back on foreign capital was initially questioned by critics and the public alike. When the Crown, which Toyota had rolled out with intense care, proved to be of a high quality, all the skepticism turned to praise and admiration. Not long after its release, some even began claiming that foreign cars were no longer necessary considering how far Japanese cars had come.

New wine, new wineskins

The key to the Crown's success lied in President Taizo Ishida's announcing a policy to pursue independent development—Eiji's chosen course—as the company's main objective a year after commencing development. Considering the position Toyota was in at the time, lying low for a year took on great significance. If the company had elected to announce the development project at the time it was launched, it would have agitated voices of dissent emanating from the union, which maintained that Toyota would not be able to compete with foreign companies with its then-current level of technology.

A year into its development, however, the Crown had already begun to take form, making it possible to drown out trepidation towards the project. In fact, the notion of making the founder's dream a reality even kindled enthusiasm among employees, spurring on a full flowering of the know-how Toyota had accumulated since its establishment.

Nakamura, telling himself that "customers will buy at least the first 1,000 vehicles off the production line out of charity, but that shouldn't set us at ease," asked customers to report any troubles, big or small. Nakamura analyzed each one in turn to determine whether they were design flaws or defects in the production process, then retraced his steps back to the original designs to see if there was anything that needed improvement.

He received a spate of claims that wrinkles were showing in the interior and the roof was too rigid, though these did not lead to any accidents. These were all issues that could be resolved with a careful response from dealers, but Nakamura had them report these complaints with the same gravity as problems with steering or brakes. After modifying and improving each of the defects, Toyota launched the Crown Deluxe line of luxury vehicles one year after releasing the Crown.

With the arrival of the Crown Deluxe, the standard Crown came to be seen as a taxi model and the Deluxe as a private car. The Master, originally developed as a taxi, was dragged down by anemic sales, which propped up the Crown in comparison. Production of the Master was discontinued two years later.

Monthly production of the Crown started in the hundreds, but favorable sales quickly compelled Toyota to boost production. Parts companies received increasingly large orders from Toyota each month, seeding suspicions among some suppliers that Toyota would not be able to use all the parts they ordered. Parts manufacturers shared the added concern that they would have to throw in the towel if these orders ever suddenly stopped coming in.

Vehicle sales steadily continued to improve, exceeding 7,000 in its inaugural year of 1955. Since the Deluxe hit the market the next year,

6,000 vehicles sold in the first half of 1956, and by year-end Toyota had sold a total of 9,250 vehicles, just a step away from the 10,000 mark. That same year, Austin sales numbered 3,174, while Hillmans ran to 2,134. Organizations affiliated with foreign companies were subject to production restrictions due to a foreign exchange quota, but the Crown, having been developed with Japanese technology, had no such limitations. Even discounting for this disparity, Toyota felt that it had already charged ahead of the pack.

In July 1956, a year and a half after the Crown's release, Japan's Economic Planning Agency declared in its Economic Survey of Japan that "the postwar is no longer." On achieving such miraculous growth only ten years after the devastation that followed in the wake of Japan's defeat in WWII, the Economic Survey wrote, "There probably is not a single person who could have predicted this." As shown by the subheading of the Economic Survey, which read "Unsustainably Rapid Expansion and its Repercussions,"[23] the economic white paper was pointing to the end of a period of high growth facilitated by postwar reconstruction.

Anticipating changes in the economy, Toyota introduced the Corona, which was one size smaller than the Crown, as well as the Toyoace pickup truck. They also set out to develop the 800cc Publica. Toyota invested high hopes in the Publica, discussing the idea of constructing a dedicated assembly plant to produce 3,000 vehicles per month in the Koromo Plant.

However, Crown sales remained stronger than expected, leading Toyota to focus on meeting demand for the Crown and tabling the construction of a new assembly plant. Planning for a People's Car necessitated changes in the crucial Publica, and its release was postponed until 1961.

The five-year modernization plan that Eiji implemented shortly after repatriating to Japan from Detroit had as its main tenet the introduction of the latest equipment at the Koromo Plant to raise its monthly production capacity to 10,000 vehicles. In the latter half of 1955, when prospects for achieving this objective were looking up, discussion among board members turned towards instituting a five-year post-modernization plan. A heated debate of the issue ensued among the board of directors.

"The Koromo Plant should be devoted exclusively to the

23. *Keizai hakusho: hayasugita kakudai to sono hansei*; 1957.

Crown."

"Where would we make the other models, like the Toyoace?"

"We could build an assembly plant outside the Koromo Plant where the test course is now."

"Even if we move out the test course, where would we make the main components, like the engine and transmission, that are installed in the vehicles?"

Listening to the various arguments, Eiji began to think, "We're going to get clogged up at *some* point even if we expand the Koromo Plant to meet increased production of the Crown. What we need is 'new wineskin for new wine.' We should think long-term and construct a new plant exclusively for full-scale passenger cars."

By early spring of 1957, Eiji came to a decision. Ishida, too, had been considering the idea of building a new factory. It was just around then that someone from the plant burst into the Ishida office with good news.

"Mr. Ishida," he said, "we just beat last month's production figure of 6,000 cars. At this rate, we'll hit our long-awaited monthly production goal of 10,000 vehicles either by the end of this year or next spring at the latest."

"That reminds me that this year marks Toyota's twentieth anniversary," Ishida said. "It would be great to reach the 10,000 vehicle mark the year that we commemorate the company's twentieth, but no such luck. We swapped out everything in the Koromo Plant for state-of-the-art equipment rather than expand its scale."

"But even if the 10,000 mark is not possible for the time being, Toyota's 300,000[th] car will soon be rolling off the line."

"When will that be?"

"Going by our current pace, I'd say definitely sometime in May."

It was the height of the "Iwato economic boom" of 1958 to 1961. While cars were still considered luxury goods, they were selling as soon as they were turned out thanks to demand from the taxi industry and from people with means, who were jostling to own a car for private use. Toyota's long-sought 300,000[th] vehicle moved off the line on May 30.

"300,000 cars on the company's twentieth anniversary..." Ishida thought, swept up by emotion. "Should that seem like a lot or a little? It's hard to say, but coming as far as we have has been anything but easy. I have to go visit the graves of the big general (Sakichi), the scion (Kiichiro) and Brother Ri (Risaburo) to pass along the news. Let's get number 300,000 all fixed up and ready to go."

Shoichiro appointed chairman of the construction committee

After the celebration, the deputy mayor of Koromo City dropped in on Ishida to give him some welcome news. "Koromo City is considering a new urban development project centered around automobiles," he said. "The city is set to acquire 130,000 square meters of government-owned land, the site of the now-defunct Tokai Aircraft Company.[24] How would Toyota like to buy this land?"

Ishida immediately consulted the board of directors. "The city came to ask us to buy land," he said. "It's the site of Tokai Aircraft, the place they used to make aircraft engines before the war. Toyota invested money in the company and Kiichiro served as its president. It wouldn't be altogether inappropriate for Toyota."

Ishida sat in the middle of Toyota's board of directors, with executive vice-president Fukio Nakagawa to his right and Eiji to his left. When Ishida finished making his proposal, Eiji quickly asked to speak. "Why don't we build our new plant there?" he proposed. "Although 130,000 square meters is a bit limited in terms of space. If I may, I'll look into whether we can buy up some of the surrounding farmland and report back with a more concrete plan at the next board meeting."

This mirrored Ishida's thoughts exactly. Nakagawa, originally a banker, had punctuated his participation in past discussions with ever-cautious opinions. Aware of this, Ishida beat him to the chase.

"A plant dedicated exclusively to passenger cars, ay? That's a good idea. The surrounding area's probably mostly wasteland anyway, so we should be able to buy it up without much of a problem."

At the board meeting a month later, Eiji provided a brief overview of the passenger car plant to be used mainly for producing the Crown. He had already reported to Ishida beforehand that the neighboring land was available for purchase. Partly because Eiji had already made

---

24. Tokai Aircraft was founded by Kiichiro Toyoda in 1943, and changed its name to Aichi Kogyo before merging with Shinkawa Kogyo to form Aisin Seiki.

the rounds to build a consensus behind the scenes, Ishida was the first to express his approval when Eiji wrapped up his presentation.

"It's Eiji's feeling that we should be able to buy up the surrounding farmland. Let's expedite the procedure."

The president's prompt approval, preempting Nakagawa from voicing his opinion, settled the new plant construction issue on the spot. Before ending the meeting, Eiji made another proposal then and there. "The Boss did everything for the Koromo Plant, from choosing the location to constructing the plant," he said. "It's because he took the initiative to build the plant in Koromo that Toyota is here today. The new plant we'll build on the site of the former Tokai Aircraft Company will decide whether Toyota can branch out across the globe as an automaker. How about calling on the Boss's own scion to head the construction of a new plant that's so essential to Toyota's future?"

Ishida nodded in agreement. Both Eiji and Ishida were thinking of giving Shoichiro, the grandson of Sakichi, to whom they owed a great debt of gratitude, valuable management experience by assigning him a major role in the company. "That's a good idea," said Ishida. "Kiichiro's dream was to develop a compact car built with the brains and skills of Japanese that can compete in the world. I, for one, believe that the Crown will be just such a car. Maybe fate has a hand in our appointing Shoichiro chairman of the construction committee for the Crown's new plant."

Shoichiro was shocked. He had been selected and appointed a board member at the general shareholders' meeting in July 1952, the year Kiichiro passed away. That was a mere four years ago. He was still only 31. It was only natural for him to wonder whether he could perform in such a significant capacity. Inferring this to be the case, Ishida came to the rescue.

"We will be able to meet immediate increased demand for the Crown by expanding our main plant," Ishida said. "Shoichiro will chair the new plant construction committee, but Eiji will stand by to oversee things. Shoichiro, your job will be to go around and take an in-depth look at cutting-edge factories in Europe and the United States, and then confer with Eiji. You'll build an impressive plant that will still be up to date ten years from now."

Shoichiro left Japan to tour European and American plants from September to December 1957. Upon his return, he devised a plan based on the layouts of the just-completed Flins Plant, France's

Renault's new state-of-the-art factory, as well as those of Italy's Fiat and West Germany's VW, while taking into account Japan-specific requirements for high-mix, low-volume production. The scale of the U.S. Big Three's plants was too large to provide much useful information.

The construction plan for the new factory was approved by the board of directors in August 1958, and it was named the Motomachi Plant. Construction cost ¥2.5 billion. The only issue was the scale of the plant. Thinking ahead into the future, Eiji wanted to propose monthly output of 10,000 vehicles based on a day and night shift system, but it was fairly evident that executive vice-president Nakagawa would demur, so he instead halved his proposal to 5,000 vehicles. Had he even suggested 10,000 cars per month, Nakagawa, guardian of Toyota's coffers, most likely would have strongly objected and complicated matters among the board.

A production scale of 10,000 vehicles per month was madness on second thought. No matter how popular the Crown, monthly sales at the time were still around 2,000 vehicles. Without an increase in demand, the plant's capacity utilization rate would be a mere 20 percent. Even a monthly output of 5,000 cars was perilous and indeed a courageous proposition.

The Motomachi Plant reaches production of 10,000 cars per month

Plant construction commenced at the end of November 1959. The first stage was completed in July of the next year. The first large-scale plant of its kind in Japan—consisting of three plants, one each for body, paint and assembly—was completed in the short period of just eight months. The secret was the formation of an organization called the *Hoenkai*, or the Toyota Support Group, an assemblage of affiliated companies in charge of materials, machinery, construction and equipment that stayed in close contact with one another. Toyota would subsequently seize the occasion of the Motomachi Plant's construction to build a number of plants in the area, and *Hoenkai* later gave itself a facelift to form *Eihokai*, a more permanent organization.

The new plant was equipped to handle a monthly output of 5,000 vehicles. Assuming future expansion, however, Eiji had obtained

Ishida's approval to have the buildings themselves constructed at a 10,000-vehicle capacity. When the board members conducted a pre-inspection of the premises before the ceremony to mark the completion of the new plant, Nakagawa, with a dubious expression on his face, remarked to Eiji: "The buildings seems pretty big for the equipment..."

"The president decided to make the buildings big enough to handle a monthly capacity of 10,000 cars," Eiji replied straight-faced. "For the time being, we'll operate on day shifts only, but this construction will allow us to change to day and night shifts and expand production to 10,000 cars per month if there is increased demand. President Kamiya at Toyota Sales is also looking into exporting the Crown to the U.S. If that happens at some point down the line, even a monthly output of 10,000 cars will no longer be enough. President Ishida took this into consideration and directed us to make bigger buildings."

Repeatedly mentioning Ishida, Eiji made it difficult for Nakagawa to protest.

The first Crown to roll out of the newly completed Motomachi Plant moved off the line at 8:08 a.m. on the eighth of August, the eighth month of the year. Toyota chose a string of number 8s because, in Japan, the number 8 is seen as an auspicious number signifying prosperity.

Guests were invited to attend an unveiling ceremony on September 18 to celebrate the completion of the plant. Those in attendance made no attempt to conceal their amazement at the plant's magnitude and advanced equipment. While industry peers were stunned with what Toyota had "gone and done," dealers were in trepidation that Toyota, having raised up such a large-scale plant, would saddle them with all the cars it would allow them to produce.

Then, only a week later on September 26, Japan was battered by the Ise Bay Typhoon, the most destructive storm since the Meiji Restoration. It claimed 5,098 lives and damaged 570,000 homes. Damage to the Motomachi Plant was minimal, requiring around two weeks to get the plant up and running again, but factories in the Nagoya district were devastated. The subcontracted plants Toyota had in the area were rendered inoperable from high water levels and moved their machinery to available buildings in the Motomachi Plant and resumed operations there. The plant's massive structures were already paying off.

Operating on day and night shifts, the Motomachi Plant reached a monthly output of 10,000 vehicles in December of that year. The second stage of construction began the next year in 1960, during which time Toyota introduced a cutting-edge large press machine and finished work on a high-performance press line, cutting costs dramatically. Although the Motomachi Plant was built within the economic framework of the "Iwato boom" of 1958 to 1961, it served as the springboard that thrust Toyota to the position of Japan's top automaker.

From Koromo to Toyota

1959, the year the new plant went up, was a commemorative year for Toyota, but there was yet another reason to celebrate. On January 1 of that year, Koromo City changed its name to Toyota City.[25] The reason for this was that locals were the only who could pronounce the city's written name as *Koromo*. Once a name change was agreed upon, the city council began asking citizens for suggestions for a new name. In the end they settled on Toyota City, named after Toyota Motor Corporation, rather than on any local place names.

Changing one's surname is a serious matter for an individual, and the same holds true for a place, whose name is an intangible asset passed down from ancestors. The transition can be rife with reluctance and regrets.

"Why did we decide to change Koromo City to Toyota City?" the mayor began, making a fervent appeal to citizens at a public hearing held in connection with the decision. "Our biggest aim in doing so is to definitively mold the city's character as the productive center of Toyota Motor. Based on a vision to make this the largest automotive productive district in the East, we will continue to attract a multitude of affiliated plants to relocate to the area around the Toyota's plants. We will develop Toyota City into an automaking kingdom."

The address of Toyota Motor Corporation's headquarters thus became 1 Toyota-Cho, Toyota City. Toyota City evolved into a town where Toyota's plants and employees went about their daily business. Before long, the positions of mayor and city assembly came to be

---

25. Though pronounced "Toyota," like Toyota Motor, Toyota City is written with the same characters as the surname Toyoda.

filled by people affiliated with Toyota Motor. Moreover, taxes paid
by Toyota to the city soon accounted for over 70 percent of the city's
total tax income, a percentage that grows even higher when adding in
taxes paid by affiliated plants. With the new name change to Toyota
City, the city fortified the figurative ramparts of Toyota's own castle
town.

Chapter 12
Initiating Exports to the U.S.

K IICHIRO TOYODA ENTERED INTO THE automotive industry out of a desire to serve his country by putting Japanese brains and skills to work to design a Japanese compact car on a par with those of foreign automakers. Toyota Motor Sales' Shotaro Kamiya fully endorsed the idea, hastening to join the effort from his post at General Motors Japan. Since before the war, Kamiya maintained the firm belief that Japan would have no future unless it earned foreign currency through exports—in other words, that Japan's survival was contingent upon becoming a trading nation.

Kamiya visited the U.S. twice after the war ended, first in 1950, the year that the Korean War broke out, to negotiate a partnership with Ford. Taking advantage of the interim between negotiations to cruise the expressways, he noticed that every car passing by was outsized. Recalling all the compact European cars shooting past on the German autobahn, however, Kamiya suspected that the day would come when smaller cars would coast down American highways.

Five years later, in the spring of 1955, Kamiya visited the U.S. for the second time when the Crown was released. He felt in his bones that the dynamics of automobile demand in the U.S. market was undergoing a radical shift. Just as he had anticipated, compact cars produced by European automakers, nowhere to be seen five years earlier, scooted around as if they owned the streets. The VW Beetle, in particular, gallantly racing alongside full-sized vehicles, left a lasting impression on Kamiya. While the Big Three treaded a path to dinosaurization, America—the center of the automotive world—was beginning to witness an incontrovertible market for compact cars.

The Crown comes to America

At the time, restrictions on dollar holdings significantly limited traveling abroad even for business. When Chief Engineer of Development Kenya Nakamura and Taichi Ohno, the father of the Toyota Production System, left for a three-month tour of the U.S. in 1956, the year after the Crown was released, they possessed no foreign currency, as Toyota had yet to begin exporting their cars to overseas markets. Consequently, to finance their trip, Toyota asked its affiliate Aisin Seiki to advance to them U.S. dollars it had earned from exporting its sewing machines. At such a rate the Japanese economy could hardly be expected to develop.

Kamiya strengthened his resolve. "The American market is sizeable. Toyota can pull in dollars if it successfully exports cars to the U.S. Luckily, a market for compact cars is taking shape, giving Toyota a chance to make inroads into the market. Toyota has yet to develop a car for export to the U.S., but we'll definitely make our way there."

Kamiya finally came to a decision in the spring of 1957, two years after his second trip to the U.S. The American market for compact cars went from a whiff of promise to a full-blown trend. VW had been the first to set up some 400 dealerships across the United States, selling 60,000 Beetles in 1957. Outstripping the illustrious Studebaker, the Beetle rose to the thirteenth best-selling model in the U.S. Second to VW was France's Renault, which sold 22,000 vehicles that year. Year after year, the market for compact cars continued to expand. It was considered a matter of time before their share of the overall automobile market would reach 10 percent.

Analyzing the American market for compact cars, Kamiya made the following assessment: "Although Detroit reigns over the global automotive industry, they simply can't remain indifferent to the rapid increase in imported cars. In the not distant future, there'll be a movement against auto imports. With no export history, Toyota cars will never be able to enter the American market if U.S. automakers install hard-handed measures like import restrictions. We don't have any time to lose sitting around saying that we don't have any cars eligible for export. Even if it's premature, Toyota needs to build up its standing now and gain a foothold in preparation for penetrating the U.S. market."

At a Toyota Motor Sales board meeting held just after his return to Japan, Kamiya sought approval for a proposal to begin exporting the Crown to the U.S. in the fall of that year. Most of the board members looked as though they'd swallowed a pigeon. After all, the market Kamiya proposed to export to was the automotive empire called America. Japanese automakers and the U.S. Big Three did not even compare in technological level, corporate girth, sales power, or any other indicator. Not a single board member had even considered exporting to the U.S.

Most of the top brass held the rather pessimistic opinion that trying to sell the Crown in the United States was like going to battle with bamboo spears; it would not hurt to wait until Toyota was stronger and see how things unfolded. But Kamiya did not yield. Explaining what he had seen with his own eyes—the shifting trend in the American auto market, the well-faring European cars, and the possibility of import controls—he finished by saying, "In business, timing is paramount. All that we know for sure is that once a wall of import restrictions goes up, we won't be able to export anything to the U.S., not even quality cars." Such a strong declaration from Kamiya, who had already begun to earn for himself a reputation as the "god of sales," silenced any further objections.

Highways easier said than done

Naturally Kamiya had not shirked behind-the-scenes maneu-vering to build a consensus. A frequent visitor at Toyota headquarters, Kamiya made his pitch to chief engineer of development Kenya Nakamura directly, saying, "Nakamura, I have a serious proposal for you. I want to export the Crown to the U.S."

Nakamura, convinced that the Crown had about a zero percent chance to compete internationally, looked at Kamiya quizzically. Then he said outright, "Mr. Kamiya, we don't have a chance. Please give up on the idea. We originally developed the Crown to handle Japan's poor road conditions. It wasn't designed for highways."

Knowing full well that Nakamura would object, Kamiya turned on the guile. "You're absolutely right," he said. "I know that the Crown wasn't designed for export. But it's fine the way it is. I just want Toyota to have the experience of having exported its cars to the U.S. I'm only thinking to export a few hundred cars, even just a few dozen cars, per year. Couldn't you can give it your blessing without taking it so seriously?"

Kamiya had already obtained Ishida's stamp of approval. Ishida shared Kamiya's larger concern that Japan's foreign currency shortfall was a serious threat to the economy. Although Toyoda Automatic Loom Works, for which Ishida doubled as president, promptly began exporting after the end of the war, it was evident that looms would never bring in much foreign currency.

When the Crown first hit the market, the American consul in Nagoya spoke flatteringly of it as a great car that would go over well in America. In fact, he suggested exporting it. This, of course, was diplomatic lip service, but Ishida had taken it literally and was thus primed to jump on Kamiya's proposal.

If the heads of manufacturing and sales agreed, the issue would be as good as settled, and indeed, at that point, Eiji could not object. Though unable to veil his anxieties, he hoped that putting the Crown on the road in the U.S. would also lead to advances in technology.

Toyota exporting its Japanese passenger cars to America, where autos had originated—the dreamlike scenario became a reality on August 25, 1957. That day, two sample Crowns which had been loaded onto a ship in Yokohama Bay arrived in Los Angeles Harbor. Toyota Motor Sales' Seishi Kato had arrived in Los Angeles two days prior as an advance party to await the ship's arrival.

It was on a blistering hot day that the S.S. President Cleveland, carrying two Crowns, sailed into LA Harbor. Miss Japan, clad in a kimono, waited at the harbor and laid bouquets of flowers on the cars after they were unloaded. Locals gave the cars a warm welcome as the first Japanese passenger vehicles to make landfall in the U.S. The Crowns were transported the next day to a service station in Little Tokyo, given license plates, and prepared to be taken for a drive meant as both demonstration and test.

In the hotel where he was staying, Kato received a deluge of phone calls and directs visits from those who had read about the event in the npapers. Almost all of them were angling to become dealers.

While taking the cars for a test drive in downtown LA, they dropped by Big Three dealerships to ask their impressions of the Crown. The news was upbeat right from the get-go, as one dealer said that Toyota could probably sell five hundred vehicles per month, while another said they would take on four hundred themselves.

This was the sales volume for just one individual dealer. Kato went back to his hotel and, together with staff that had come as part of the advance team, began counting their chicks before they had hatched. "Judging by dealers' reactions, selling 10,000 Crowns per month is not far-fetched," they told themselves. "We're going to have to tell Toyota Motor to up their productive capacity."

It is the way of the world that sweet dreams are of short duration. When they took the car up to 80 miles per hour on the highway the next day, the engine suddenly began making a clanging noise and the car quickly lost power. The Crown was breaking down without even having traveled 2,000 miles. The problem was a lack of horsepower. Though someone had praised the car's outward appearance as a baby Cadillac's, without horsepower in the engine the Crown did not stand a chance. Just as Nakamura had said, it was not the car for American highways.

An uphill battle for Toyota Motor Sales USA

Kato promptly sent word to Tokyo to give up on the project. Kamiya's response caught him by surprise. "Let's sell a hundred vehicles, even fifty if we can. For what it's worth, I want to be able to say that we sold something. Establishing a presence in the U.S. would be a significant step forward. At any rate, start making arrangements on setting up a company. It'll serve as our bridgehead in the American market."

Kato and his team thus stayed on in Los Angeles and made arrangements to set up an importing firm. After establishing Toyota Motor Sales USA in the LA suburb of Torrance at the end of October, the team returned to Japan. But setting up a company did not guarantee that product would sell right away. Not only was sales in the U.S. a complicated business, but Toyota needed to perform necessary modifications to their cars to conform to American safety standards.

The Crown was forced onto the market the next year in July 1958, but just as Kato and his team had feared, the outcome was humiliating. Not only did the car come up short on highways, but it also encountered a whole host of other technical problems, such as overheating. Toyota had to discontinue shipments at the end of the year. After enjoying widespread popularity in Japan, the Crown, ill-prepared for highways, failed to cut it in the United States. Rather than pull out of the market completely, however, Toyota replaced the Crown with the four-wheel-drive Land Cruiser, barely continuing its business just to preserve its tentative foothold in the market. Although plans to export the Crown had foundered, for Kamiya it was worth it merely to establish a presence.

Toyota engineers' pride had been dashed. Seeking to avenge themselves, in 1960 they released the Corona, developed as a lower-class car than the Crown. However, the Corona, too, came with its own set of flaws. At speeds higher than 65 mph, the engine overheated and the brakes lost their effectiveness.

With such a disastrous start to its American strategy, Toyota was nearing bankruptcy in the U.S., and only a substantial reduction in personnel kept the company afloat. Eiji Toyoda had personally embarked for the U.S. to conduct the restructuring.

He yearned for a second chance. "The timing of the Crown's release was not bad at all," he reasoned, "but unfortunately the car wasn't made to U.S. specs. Automobiles are an international commodity, so Toyota won't ever develop until it builds a car that can sell in America, the world's largest market. My assignment is to figure out how to build a car that suits the U.S. market."

Rival Nissan began exporting its vehicles to the United States in 1960, sending over the new-and-improved Bluebird and Datsun Truck. In the end, Toyota, which had gotten the early jump on the domestic competition, took a back seat while latecomer Nissan raced out to an early lead.

Toyota attempted to forge a breakthrough with its exports to the U.S. by giving up on the Crown in favor of modifying and improving the Corona. In 1964, they finished work on the third-generation Corona, designed specifically for the United States. After it achieved some popularity in Australia where it was exported in 1965, Toyota finally shipped the Corona to the U.S. in 1966. This was followed in 1967 by the Corolla, into which Toyota put its heart and soul. These two models would carve out an epoch of Toyota exports.

Honda set out to export its vehicles to the U.S. a full fifteen years after Toyota and endured the same hardships that Toyota once did. Honda's first four-wheel vehicle was the light-duty N360 *k-car*;[26]

---

26. *K-car (Kei-car)* is a category of small automobiles, including passenger cars, vans and pickup trucks.

mounted with an air-cooled engine, which Soichiro Honda personally helped to design. Riding the wave of motorization rolling through Japan at the time, the car sold explosively in the domestic market, catapulting Honda overnight to the position of top lightweight passenger-vehicle manufacturer.

Soichiro, reveling in the company's success, began planning exports to the U.S. Specified for use in Japan, however, the car was not designed for it. With an engine displacement of 360cc, it could navigate narrow Japanese roads aplenty but would be precarious on American roads, let alone its highways.

Accordingly, Honda built a car up to American specifications by expanding the engine to 600cc. Having established a reputation as "the world-renowned Honda" for his motorbikes, Soichiro was brimming with confidence, but motorbike dealers flatly refused to carry any cars; the U.S. utilized different distribution channels and sales practices for motorbikes and four-wheel-vehicles. With nowhere else to turn to, Honda reluctantly asked GM and Ford dealers to display the N600 in the corner of their showrooms. Furthermore, sales were restricted to Hawaii and the three west coast states of California, Oregon and Washington, yielding limited sales. Seen as enlarged motorbikes or sidecars with a hood, Honda's cars were initially received without much enthusiasm.

Even as Toyota and Nissan steadily began to increase sales in the U.S., Honda had yet to be treated as a full-fledged automaker.

Chapter 13

People's Car or Mass-Market Car?

T HE AUTOMOTIVE INDUSTRY IS A tremendously high-risk business. Whether new models or variations of existing models, it takes four to five years after launching development for a car to hit the market. When developing a car, automakers must anticipate not only social conditions but also changes in consumer lifestyles prior to the product's release. At present, the cost of developing a single model is immense.

If a car is a hit, the company that developed it recovers not only its investment but reaps enormous profits. On the other hand, if it flops, a company's legs are taken out from right under it. As a result, automotive enterprises are constantly seeking out low-risk, high-return business models.

What irks auto companies is that what generally holds true in the world of business— inexpensive quality products are sure to sell—does not necessarily apply. Even with an inexpensive, high-performance car, receiving payment in monthly installments is backbreaking for a dealer without adequate financial resources. But if a car is to be sold only for cash, the customer base would be paltry. In this respect, Toyota's sales strategy was ingenious.

Toyota receives funding from dealers

Until the Crown appeared, Toyota sold all its vehicles at Toyota Dealers;[27] per-model production and sales scale had been small despite a fairly large number of models. Together with the Crown, Toyota

27. *Toyota-ten*

developed a forward-control pickup truck with a one-ton payload, releasing it in September 1954 under the name Toyopet Truck. Auto three-wheelers were still prevalent in the truck market at the time, but the Toyopet Truck sold remarkably well, quickly driving out the three-wheelers.

Meanwhile, development of the Corona, which was loaded with a 1000cc engine, one size smaller than that of the Crown, continued to progress. At that rate, a single channel[28] would not be able to handle all of Toyota's products. Kamiya therefore considered using multiple channels. For existing Toyota dealers, this meant being divested of their rights.

Before the war, Kamiya deliberately chose wealthy people and families as Toyota dealers. Their power was amply demonstrated with the SB Truck, developed under the direct supervision of Kiichiro. When the SB Truck was ready for mass production in the spring of 1947 during the chaotic postwar era, Toyota outlined the truck's specifications and production plans at a Dealers Association[29] board meeting held in Nagoya. Association executives quickly became excited when they heard the truck's specs. Yet, for some reason, they were kept in the dark about its release date.

Dealers Association board meetings were held every month. Asked every month by association board members—they knew nothing of Toyota's tight financial situation—when the truck would go on sale, Toyota executives gave ambiguous, neither-here-nor-there responses: "Well, we're having a little trouble getting things set up for large-scale production" or "The truck's nickname is going to be determined by a prize competition, so our hands are tied until that gets figured out."

But the verbal chicanery could not go on forever. Kamiya and Eiji Toyoda, who respectively oversaw sales and manufacturing, attended the board meeting in August.

"In all honesty, we're only making ten pickup trucks a month," Eiji confided to the association, frankly divulging the state of affairs at Toyota. "A lack of funds is keeping us from getting going with production. Given the current economic outlook, it's difficult for us to get new loans from the Reconstruction Finance Corporation."

---

28. *Keiretsu*

29. *Hanbaiten kumiai. Toyota jidosha hanbaiten kumiai* changed its name to *Toyota jidosha hanbaiten kyokai* in May 1948.

After Eiji explained why Toyota was unable to begin mass production, Kamiya marshaled the courage to make a proposition. "Toyota has a proposal," he began. "We intend to set the wholesale value of one pickup truck at 200,000 yen. I sincerely apologize for having to ask you this, but we could manage to get the production line up and running if you could forward us just half of the sum, 100,000 yen, for each vehicle to be ordered." Eiji nodded along at Kamiya's side.

He was basically saying that he wanted the dealers to pay for the cars up front before they went on sale. Moreover, the proposal came with the condition that they pay in the new yen currency rather than the old one, which was losing validity. Though automakers are known to fund ailing dealers, the reverse was unheard of.

Noting the agitated looks on the association executives' faces, Eiji commented with a confident air, "Toyota founder Kiichiro Toyoda was directly involved in the development of this pickup truck. As the one in charge of manufacturing, I have complete confidence in our product."

For the dealers, no product meant no business. Association board members asked Kamiya and Eiji to leave the room and discussed their best course of action. They then reached a unanimous decision to accept Toyota's offer. There were 47 Toyota dealers across Japan, but thanks to the leonine work of the association executives, every single dealer without exception sent in the money by the September 15 deadline. Dealerships provided Toyota with 4.7 million yen of financing during a time when everyone in the country was pressed for money. Thus did a uniting of destinies of automaker and dealer take root, in what was to become a Toyota tradition.

Given this past, Toyota's idea to form a network involving multiple channels ran the risk of opening up a fissure in a manufacturer-dealer relationship built on mutual trust. Consequently, Kamiya set out on a pilgrimage across the country to win over Toyota dealers. Most of the wealthy individuals with whom he talked were interested in forming a dealer network. Although motorization had yet to occur, the dealers may have been hearing its velvet-soled footsteps approaching.

Established in 1956, the second channel of dealers was christened *Toyopet-ten*, or Toyopet Dealers. Based on great hopes for it to become an ace for Toyota, the Toyopet Truck was renamed the Toyoace.

Starting around 1955, Toyota also became involved in the

development of diesel automobiles, releasing a diesel pickup truck in 1957. Though Isuzu had already released a line of its own, Toyota saw potential in diesel vehicles and decided to enter the market. But soon thereafter, Eiji was summoned by MITI. "The diesel-powered vehicle market isn't all that big," he was told. "How about we leave that area to Isuzu? We'd like for Toyota to stop selling its diesel vehicles immediately."

"The government has no business telling us to desist," Eiji demurred, resisting MITI's blatant administrative guidance. "Toyota will continue selling its vehicles regardless of MITI's objections."

Drawing on this background, Eiji made a strong case with Kamiya to open a third channel in the autumn of 1957, the Diesel Dealers.[30] On Eiji's insistence, nine new dealers were set up in metropolitan areas such as Tokyo, Osaka and Nagoya, but soon it became clear that there was less demand for diesel vehicles than expected. Although the third channel of dealers faded away, it laid the groundwork for the establishment of Publica Dealers (later to become Corolla Dealers).

In an ironic twist of fate, during the later storm of capital liberalization, Isuzu formed a capital alliance with GM, coming under the control of the world leader in 1971. When, 34 years later, the partnership was dissolved as GM's business continued to falter, Isuzu turned to Toyota and formed a capital tie-up in the autumn of 2006. Toyota's aim was to acquire Isuzu's diesel technology to advance eco-car development.

A $1,000 car

In the automotive industry, they speak of a "Silverstone Curve." In a nutshell, returns to scale taper off after two to three hundred thousand cars produced per platform model. Toyota has closely adhered to this concept, foregoing further mass production after 200,000 units per platform model and instead designing a new model to seek out new customers. This increases total sales and is more advantageous from an operational standpoint. It naturally led Toyota to move toward becoming a full-line automaker.

Taking its first step toward becoming a full-line automaker, Toyota followed up the Crown, its flagship car, with the Corona. But

30. *Di-zeru-ten*

the road to getting there was anything but smooth. As head of the engineering department, Eiji had at first visualized something other than the Corona.

"The Boss founded Toyota figuring that the age of mass-market cars would eventually come to Japan just like it did in the U.S.," Eiji confided to technical director Hanji Umehara. "The age he envisioned is already here. I want to realize his dream by following up the Crown with a passenger car for the general public."

"What kind of car are you thinking about?" Umehara replied. "Sales' Kamiya is asking us to develop something smaller than the Crown for use as a taxi."

"No, I'd rather focus on a car for private use over taxis."

"So you're thinking of a light-duty k-car in line with MITI's vision for a people's car?"

In 1955, MITI proposed a People's Car Plan to automakers. The vehicle category hewing closest to MITI's plan was the k-car, mounted with a 360cc engine and specified for use in Japan. Small and mid-sized carmakers began to develop light-duty k-cars in the early 1950s. Even as some badmouthed the k-car—driven by those who couldn't afford a compact—as the "thumb in mouth" auto, it gradually gained public recognition as a simple and convenient private vehicle.

Eiji's response was unexpected. "I'm interested in the People's Car Plan, but it calls for a retail price of 250,000 yen. The k-car would be better for such an enterprise, but it has its fair share of technical problems. There's no way it can reach a maximum speed of 100 km/h as stipulated by MITI guidelines. The next compact car that Toyota needs to develop is probably somewhere in between a Crown and a k-car. It would have a target retail price of 360,000 yen. Since the exchange rate is 360 yen per dollar, you might call it the $1,000 car. It wouldn't be at all impossible to make it at one-third the cost of the Crown."

At Eiji's suggestion, Toyota prioritized development of a small mass-market car intended for the general public, beginning the project in April 1955. Tozo Yabuta, who had taken charge of the Toyoace, was designated chief engineer of development. From that day on, Yabuta was given a daily dose of memos from Eiji. They outlined Eiji's thoughts on standards that would satisfy customers while keeping costs down; Yabuta got a sense of the direction in which the mass-market car's development was headed.

The Yabuta team swung into action to design a car based on Eij's memos, quickly coming up with a draft for the first prototype at the end of September. Eiji immediately issued an urgent directive to build a prototype as soon as possible. It was beyond Yabuta what Eiji's real intention was in rushing it, but orders were orders. As for Eiji, he naturally had a reason for directing Yabuta to hurry the prototype along.

Though automakers proper had mixed feelings about MITI's People's Car Plan, it led some other manufacturers to dabble in the industry for the first time. Among these, moves by Komatsu, a manufacturer of bulldozers and other large construction equipment, garnered particular attention.

Komatsu set off an awesome display of fireworks. Asking German sports car maker Porsche to come up with a basic design, Komatsu outlined an arresting new plan to build a people's car consistent with MITI's intentions and put it on the market for 300,000 yen each. The problem was who would sell it. Komatsu would not be able to sell a large number of cars with its construction-oriented network of dealers.

At a press conference marking the firm's entrance into the automotive industry, President Yoshinari Kawai announced that Komatsu was hoping to distribute and sell the new car through Toyota Motor Sales, suggesting that backroom talks were already underway. Toyota Motor was utterly agog. Toyota Sales selling any car other than Toyota's showed a lack of faith in Toyota Motor's development efforts. It was tantamount to a stinging indictment of Eiji as the head of development. The only way to forestall Toyota Motor Sales from going ahead was for Toyota to publicly announce that they were already developing a people's car.

Judging by the fact that Kamiya did not turn down Komatsu's proposal, Eiji felt that Toyota Motor and Toyota Sales had begun to strike a dissonant note. The two certainly had differing opinions at the time on just about everything involving development and sales policy. Toyota Sales wanted cars that sold. The Crown was the only passenger car left since production and sale was discontinued for the Master, the Crown's sister car. K-cars were now in the limelight because of MITI's People's Car Plan, but Toyota Motor was showing no interest in developing a light-duty vehicle.

Toyota Motor was painfully aware what Sales was looking for, but developing a car required a certain period of time. That Sales did not understand this was a source of frustration. The squabbles between the two companies were bound to leak at some point, and, once they did, rumors began to spread that Toyota Motor and Toyota Sales were always in a tussle.

Upon seeing the papers the day after Kawai's press conference, Yabuta finally understood where Eiji was coming from. Working at top speed, Yabuta's team managed to draft up the basic technical drawings two weeks behind schedule and build a prototype in August 1956, two months later than Eiji had asked for. In September, President Ishida held a press conference to announce that Toyota had developed a new compact passenger car hewing to the People's Car Plan and had already built a prototype. It was extremely anomalous for Toyota to hold an extravagant unveiling ceremony at the prototype stage. One of the reasons they hyped it up so ostentatiously was to keep Toyota Sales in check.

Be that as it may, the prototype was still no more than a prototype. They had kept the gross vehicle weight down to a value close to what they had originally planned, but the engine generated less power than their target and made a lot of noise. Moreover, its styling was less appealing than previous designs. In contrast to the Crown, which had been designed from the beginning as a commercial product, the prototype was created to be a prototype; it clearly needed major design changes and numerous minor adjustments before it could be brought to market.

Yabuta's team conducted a series of performance and durability tests aimed at building a second prototype, but the more the car ran, the more the flaws in the car's FF (front engine, front-wheel drive) layout became apparent. The team knew that it would take no small amount of time and money to overcome these flaws.

Given that existing automakers were less enthusiastic than expected about the People's Car Plan, and given also that the Ministry of Finance was none too positive about providing supplementary funding, MITI had to abandon plans to offer financial assistance to manufacturers developing a People's Car. Even Komatsu, which had made a grand display of their entrance into the auto industry, gave up on the project when Toyota Sales proved reluctant about selling their cars, as prompted by Toyota Motor's potent diversion.

Senior Chief Engineer and Special Advisor

Toyota faced the issue of whether to prioritize development of a
car based on the People's Car Plan or the Corona, which was a full
size larger. What was clear at the time was that Toyota did not
have the ability to develop both cars simultaneously. Even if they
managed to, they certainly could not bear the risk of producing them
concurrently.

The conclusion was obvious before any discussion took place. Not
only could they anticipate guaranteed demand for the Corona from the
taxi industry, but it also held promise as an export. Furthermore, the
compact mass-market car whose development was already underway
still required a considerable amount of time before completion since
the car employed an FF layout and incorporated a light metal alloy in
its construction. Toyota would also have to work to bring down costs.
For these reasons, the company was forced to put the compact mass-
market car project on the backburner after they had finished building
a second prototype.

With the Crown no longer needing constant monitoring, Kenya
Nakamura was appointed chief engineer of the first-generation
Corona, which was destined to be speedily developed for taxi use.
Released in July 1957, the Corona met with the same short-lived fate
as the Master.

Nakamura subsequently followed up his efforts by beginning
work on a second-generation Corona. Chastened by the failure of the
first Corona, Nakamura tried to incorporate advanced technology into
the second-generation car. But under pressure to redress complaints
about its first incarnation and simultaneously responsible for minor
changes to the Crown, he was unable to develop the kind of car he
had envisioned.

The second-generation Corona was set to go into production
at the new state-of-the-art Motomachi No. 2 Plant and was rushed
into production as a matter of necessity. Not surprisingly, due to
imperfections in the chassis and confusion on the production line,
complaints began to roll in right from the start. While the dealers'
adept service departments fended off any truly devastating blow, two
consecutive generations of the Corona had been branded a failure.

"Thanks to you, Nakamura, we achieved nowhere near the ¥3
billion in expected income," executive vice-president Fukio Nakagawa

snorted, taking a jab at the chief engineer.

Eiji, who was present, retorted, "That's one way of tallying it, but cars are all about luck." While nothing more came of it right then, the development of the Crown and the Corona brought Eiji to feel that while Nakamura excelled at new projects, he did not at putting together a commercially viable car in a specified period of time.

For the third-generation Corona, Toyota took its chances and did not appoint Nakamura as chief engineer, instead going with the younger Atsushi Tajima. This did the trick. In January 1965, during the fifth month of the new car's release, it pulled ahead of rival Nissan's Bluebird for the first time since the original Corona hit the market. An intense sales war for the two models ensued, which the media dubbed the "CB war." The Corona remained popular and maintained a firm lead over the pursuing Bluebird, eventually setting a record as the bestselling car for thirty-three consecutive months.

But Eiji had not written off Nakamura. The Crown enjoyed a good reputation since its release but consumers were also beginning to grow weary of it. Automotive technology made remarkable advances during the interim and it was evident that the Crown would be left behind unless new technology was incorporated.

The first-generation Crown had come up short as a U.S. export when it failed to run at a maximum speed of 100 km/h. If the car were to be sold in the American market, it had to operate at speeds of 130-140 km/h and quietly at that. In this case, Nakamura was the only one for the job. After being appointed chief engineer for the second-generation Crown, he got right down to development, keeping in mind what a world-class car is supposed to be. When he was just about done, he and Eiji took the prototype for a ride down the newly opened Meishin (Nagoya-Kobe) Expressway.

"Hey, Kenya," Eiji said. "This car doesn't vibrate strangely like the original, and it reaches a maximum speed of 140 km/h. It can definitely pass muster in the U.S."

The second-generation Crown, whose rectilinear styling contrasted markedly with the original's rounded exterior, hit the market in October 1962.

In 1964, the year of the Tokyo Olympics, Nakamura turned 51, a suitable age for promotion to executive. Naturally this turned into a major issue at Toyota. Considering his achievements, it was only right that he be made an executive. At the same time, however, there were persistent objections: Nakamura did not fit the Toyota mold, and things never went with him as the top executive intended.

He certainly wasn't an organization man. Whenever, for instance, some member of the development staff suggested being more economical, he always responded, "How could you say that to folks who're grinding their noses at it? The best way to economize is to finish the job we're working on as soon as possible."

Examples abounded of organization-defying Nakamura-speak: "It's ridiculous to base decisions on a person's rank or post" and "A chief engineer shouldn't get pats on the back from human resources or accounting. I'll never be that type."

Toyota was already one of Japan's leading automakers. If Nakamura were to be promoted to executive, he needed to learn how to compromise and to swim with the world. Yet he was not one to stomach impurities. Nakamura as executive would only sow confusion within the organization if he couldn't be dissuaded from making the remarks typical of him. In his heart, Eiji wanted to promote Nakamura, but he had to safeguard against upsetting the company as a whole.

The position arranged for Nakamura was that of *riji*, which would have to translate as "director." Executive vice-president Nakagawa informed him of this in Eiji's presence: "Nakamura, we've set up a new post of 'director' for you to fill. It has the same status as executive, so you need to enroll in the executive training workshop. Sound good?"

"You don't need to do this," Nakamura answered unexpectedly. "Nakamura is just Nakamura."

Although Eiji had half-feared such a response, with an uncommonly stern look he warned Nakamura as though he might a child. "Kenya, don't talk like that. Think of the ones who'll come after you. It's going to put us out if you turn this down."

Upon consideration, a special post of director, since it was equivalent to executive, granted unsupervised freedom of action and the authority to draw up one's own budgets. It was a cushy position, come to think about it. Though Nakamura had hesitated at first, he accepted it in the end. At a subsequent board meeting, however, Nakamura suggested, "*Riji* has the image of an official organization post. It would be more appropriate if I were granted a title given to an expert of some sort who is given an administrative position, like 'consultant.'" Nakamura thus became not only Toyota's first chief engineer of development but also its first *sanyo* or consultant.

Many others came to be appointed chief engineers and consultants as Toyota expanded in scale and its vehicles gained in popularity. At some point or another Nakamura came to be called Senior Chief Engineer and Senior Consultant (*Daishusa/Dainsanyo*) as a way of differentiating him from all the others who came to fill the same positions.

After being appointed consultant, of course, Nakamura did not just sit back on his past laurels and idle around. There was a mountain of things that only Nakamura could do. For example, he would become the chief engineer of development for the Century, a line of high-end luxury vehicles made in commemoration of Sakichi Toyoda's hundredth birthday and Toyota's thirtieth anniversary.

Nakamura, who basked in the novelty of new adventures, valued advanced technology and originality. The Century integrated both of these. While the engine itself appropriated the Crown 8's V8 engine out of time considerations, the Century adopted unprecedented new electronic technology such as an air suspension equipped with height adjustability.

What best demonstrated Nakamura's perspicacity and foresight into the future potential of products was styling. "This car won't sell thousands of times over every month," he reasoned, "but what I intend to do with the Century is to build a highly coveted car, a source of envy that will make people want to drive it at some point. We won't change models for at least another ten years, so I'll completely do away with faddish elements."

The Century's design took conservatively after mid-sixties American models, but in its outward appearance it had a calm Japanese depth. Toyota continued to carry the same model for the next thirty years.

After the Century, Nakamura became involved with the development of a gas-turbine engine. Even after retiring from the company into a special advisory role in 1980, he lived a leisurely, dignified life engaged in research. The tagline "environmentally-friendly Toyota" caught on as the Prius, equipped with a hybrid system that combines electricity with a gasoline engine, entered the spotlight. This system was modeled on the gas-turbine hybrid system that Nakamura worked on during his tenure as special advisor. After witnessing the success of the Prius, which debuted in Japan in 1997,

Nakamura passed on to his final resting place in November 1998, shortly after celebrating his golden wedding anniversary. He was 85.

Chapter 14
Protect Your Own Castle

IT WAS IN 1959, AFTER a hiatus of two years, that Toyota resumed development of the Publica, its new, mass-market car. Tatsuo Hasegawa, who had been involved in developing the Crown under Kenya Nakamura, succeeded Tozo Yabuta as chief engineer. While Yabuta was the cautious type, executing flawlessly in line with his superiors' wishes, Hasegawa was the type to throw in his own ideas. The two could not be any more different.

Hasegawa's first assignment was to scrap the FF (front engine, front-wheel drive) layout. The FF layout had yet to achieve much of a reputation in the global automotive industry. With no models to draw from, development was not only slow going but extremely costly. Hasegawa's decision, which went against Eiji's development policy, meant ditching all the work that Yabuta, his predecessor, had overseen.

Given Hasegawa's unconcealed stance on the matter, Eiji had braced himself mentally regarding the FF layout's fate. Fully aware of the likely outcome, he had appointed Hasegawa as chief engineer, judging that hurrying the Publica to market outweighed pursuing technological possibilities.

Ironically, the Austin Mini, designed by Alec Issigonis of British Leyland Motor Corporation and later the FF standard, was released the year that Hasegawa abandoned the FF layout. Aside from sports cars, nearly every compact passenger car model around the world currently employs the FF layout. Looking back on it now, the fact that Eiji endeavored to introduce the FF layout, with its emphasis on interior comfort, a full fifty years ago can be seen as a testament to his keen insight into auto development.

The fourth round of tie-up negotiations with Ford

Hasegawa had no intention of turning his new mass-market car, which he had converted to the FR (front engine, rear-wheel drive) layout, into the "thumb in mouth" likes of the k-car. Although one of the main selling points of Toyota's vehicles up to that point had been the kind of ride comfort one might find in American cars, Hasegawa conversely aimed to build a car with superior handling.

By the time development had entered the crucial stages, yet another major drama was underway: talks to begin joint production with Ford. Toyota was the one to propose cooperation. After adopting the slogan of independent development and succeeding wildly with the Crown, why would Toyota enter negotiations to affiliate with Ford right then of all times? It all had to do with the liberalization of trade and capital in automobiles.

In 1961 the Japanese government decided to deregulate trade in trucks, buses and two-wheel vehicles, followed by passenger cars in 1965. Even though they would continue to impose high tariffs on car imports for some time to come, the government had determined to lower import duties on passenger cars by 6.4 percent and on trucks by 8 percent by 1972. The liberalization of capital restrictions was expected to follow. If implemented, it would be a foregone conclusion that the U.S. Big Three would flood the Japanese market. Japanese media likened the Big Three's arrival to the "coming of the black ships" in the closing days of the Tokugawa shogunate, whereby American warships pressed Japan to open up to the outside world.

Toyota consequently worked out plans for a joint venture with Ford to co-produce a new line of family cars in Japan, seeking to kill two birds with one stone—on the one hand gaining new technology in compact cars and, on the other, placing brakes on the onslaught of foreign capital. The one who conceived the plan was Shotaro Kamiya, president of Toyota Motor Sales. Kamiya wanted to renew the negotiations that had suffered such a tremendous setback due to the Korean War.

Ever since the automaker temporarily set aside the Yabuta-led project two years earlier, Kamiya had harbored doubts about Toyota Motor's ability to develop and produce a mass-market car. This was precisely why Toyota Sales had shown an interest in the People's Car that Komatsu was preparing to manufacture with Porsche.

Affiliating with Ford was more advantageous for Toyota Sales than Toyota Motor. Mass production meant mass sales. Large-scale production would not be a problem since manufacturer Toyota Motor had finished building the technologically advanced Motomachi Plant and had plans to build more new plants in adjoining areas.

In keeping with this, Toyota Sales set out to establish a new dealer network specializing in the Publica. A line of mass-market cars called for a method of sales more appropriate for the general public than with existing models. It would be imperative to adopt an American-style dealership system; this involved a small-scale multi-store system, sales territory sharing, and cash transactions, among other things. The aim was to keep retail prices as low as possible by setting up a solid dealership operation even if only on a small scale. Toyota Sales at the time had yet to attain the know-how to carry this out. The idea was for Toyota Motor to produce the cars, while Toyota Sales would sell them in bulk.

Kamiya had another objective, too: selling Toyota's vehicles in the U.S. and other countries around the world through Ford's network of dealers. It was to find a solution to these issues that Kamiya considered cooperating with Ford.

The greatest obstacle in pushing ahead with a tie-up was persuading family, i.e., Toyota Motor, which had set out with aplomb on a steady course of self-reliance thanks to the success of the Crown. Based on this success, President Taizo Ishida exhorted his employees to "defend their own castle." As such, it would be a challenge for Kamiya to employ his sales-centric logic to persuade Toyota Motor to see it his way.

Pondering how to convince Ishida, Kamiya thought, "Allowing foreign investment in Toyota Motor is out of the question, but how about a joint venture? Come to think of it, until the day he passed away Kiichiro pushed the idea of a three-company venture involving Nissan. It would be easier to get Toyota Motor to go along with a joint venture if the enterprise were limited only to the Publica. Ishida probably wouldn't object to a capital structure by which Toyota Motor had a 40 percent stake, Toyota Sales 20 percent and Ford 40 percent, which would allow the Toyota Group to retain control."

Toyota had already negotiated with Ford three times, both before and after WWII, but the talks had panned out due to the impact of the Pacific and Korean wars. Kamiya had run the show at all the negotiations. He was confident that the companies could come to an agreement because he was under the optimistic belief that "Ford was favorably disposed to Toyota." Moreover he felt that the multinational Ford would be the first to make its way into Japan if the Japanese government were to move to liberalize capital markets; Ford should not have any objections teaming up with Toyota, Japan's top automaker.

In addition to the investment ratio, Kamiya had another trick up his sleeve, which he proposed to Ishida: "How about having Toyota Motor take over the joint venture once it gets on a solid footing? This isn't a very nice way of putting it, but after Toyota learns all that it can from Ford, just give 'em the boot."

Ishida was skeptical about tying-up with Ford, but if a joint venture would allow him to stem the tide of foreign capital, he thought, then he would be able to protect Toyota's main operations. He thus accepted Kamiya's proposal.

Anticipating a fierce sparring duel from the beginning over the joint venture's investment ratio, Toyota Motor sent in executive vice-president Fukio Nakagawa, a former banker, as its head negotiator. Eiji Toyoda's role would be to explain Toyota's technology to Ford's engineers when they arrived in Japan.

Board members limited to Japanese citizens

Although negotiations had already begun, the ever-suspicious Ishida had not taken Kamiya's proposal at face value. If Ford, which Toyota was supposed to kick to the curb once the joint venture got on track, capitalized on the deal by adding its name to the list of Toyota Motor's major shareholders, it was certain that Ford would, by right, insist on having a representative on Toyota's board of directors.

The question was how to avoid this. Ishida decided to consult his old friend Minoru Segawa, president of Nomura Securities. Since joining Nomura, Segawa, a wheeler-dealer who took Nomura to the top of the industry, demonstrated such strong leadership in the field of sales and marketing as to earn for himself the sobriquet of "the bulldozer."

Born in 1906, Segawa was eighteen years younger than Ishida. Although the relationship between Toyota and Nomura—Toyota's lead managing underwriter—had initially brought the two men together, they got along exceptionally well under the pretext of both being Tokyo Giants fans. As time passed, they were soon on friendly enough terms to talk about work, pleasure and everything in between.

"Toyota has come all this way under the motto of self-reliance," Ishida said. "Our current move to establish joint production with Ford is aimed at preserving this. Kamiya of Toyota Sales has the optimistic belief that Toyota can just take over the joint venture in the future, but I simply can't risk allowing foreign investment in Toyota's main operations under any circumstances."

"You definitely need to consider what Ford intends to do if it gets a hold of Toyota shares," Segawa replied.

"Not only Ford, but other foreign companies as well are using all sorts of channels—banks, commercial establishments, securities firms—to find a way to tie-up with Toyota. Their stance, how they don't view us on equal terms, is nothing but rude and disrespectful."

"So what do you intend to do?"

"I think the same way Kiichiro did. I don't intend to disallow cooperation with Ford if it is confined only to technology. But I'm not going to let anyone walk all over Toyota. Can you think of any way to tie-up with Ford that would prevent them from poking their noses in Toyota's management?"

Segawa came up with an idea commensurate of a securities professional. "Since Toyota is a public company, you cannot exactly stop foreign companies from buying shares in Toyota. And I doubt you, of all people, have neglected to institute strong shareholder protection. So as a precaution, or rather just to be doubly sure, how about stipulating that 'eligibility for the board of directors is limited to those with Japanese citizenship?'"

"That's a good idea," Ishida said. "There's no way of telling what will happen if capital is deregulated. I'm going to look into your idea to see if it might work."

Although Toyota nowadays is a global enterprise, back then Japanese companies were afraid of foreign investment. Ishida snapped up Segawa's unexpected idea.

Negotiations to establish joint production with Ford began just after spring in 1960. As the production site would be in Japan, talks were held in Nagoya and Toyota City. Eiji, who was not taking direct part in the negotiations, instead took Ford's engineers on a tour of the plant and accompanied them on test drives of the car under development. Eiji had known one of the members of Ford's negotiating team during his time training with Ford, so the occasion served as the perfect opportunity to renew old acquaintances.

Ford's purpose in touring the plant was to verify that the Publica was indeed a full-fledged car. They'd heard that an automaker in a Far Eastern island nation had developed a mass-market car but had yet to give the story any credence.

Although negotiations went on for a year, Toyota soon found out that Ford's real intention was to acquire shares in Toyota's main operations to use as a foothold to dominate the Japanese market. Toyota quickly caught on to Ford's objective and turned down investment in Toyota's main body. Meanwhile, because Toyota's proposal would not have allowed Ford to take control either in joint production or technical guidance, the joint venture itself was voted down by Ford's board.

Kamiya's calculations had been in vain. Receiving word from Ford, Ishida fumed with rage. "Toyota was definitely the party that proposed a tie-up, but Ford has no sense of civility. What a way to say no." In other words, pretending interest in a partnership, Ford had pried all manners of information out of Toyota and had summarily called off the whole thing once they were through. According to Ishida's folksy, old-fashioned way of thinking, this flaunted moral etiquette. Be that as it may, the fact of the matter is that he also breathed a sigh of relief.

It was at the general shareholders' meeting in 1968, just prior to capital liberalization, that Toyota modified its articles of incorporation to provide against foreign board members: "Eligibility for the Toyota Motor Corporation Board of Directors shall be limited to those with Japanese citizenship." Toyota thus asserted itself as a Japanese corporation in name and substance that would not form capital alliances with foreign companies. This tenet holds true even today. Meanwhile, the clause on board member eligibility was later rescinded.

Yet fate would bring the companies to the negotiating table again. Before the onset of the global compact-car wars of the 1980s and amidst mounting U.S.-Japan trade friction over autos, Toyota proposed to Ford a joint production of compact passenger cars in the U.S. In previous partnership talks, Toyota had wanted Ford "to show it how to make compact cars," but the chief provision of the proposal in June 1980 was that Toyota would "show Ford how to make compact cars." In only twenty years, Toyota and Ford had traded places; master and apprentice had completely switched positions. The details of this round of talks will be discussed below, but the end result was that negotiations collapsed. Toyota turned to GM to launch joint production, occasioning a dramatic revision of the global auto industry map.

A car is the dream of the people

After talks with Ford over joint production of the Publica broke off, Toyota had to grapple with manufacturing it on its own. The completion of the Motomachi No. 2 Plant, built just to the north of the main Motomachi plant, was just around the corner. With expected sales of 10,000 vehicles per month, Toyota would have to lower costs and set a price within the range of what the average consumer could afford. The company therefore implemented thoroughgoing cost-control measures and began preparing a system whereby every expense incurred through design, trial production and research would be processed with individual *denpyo*, or labeled cards.

Toyota looked into how much every single one of over 20,000 parts would cost to make and submitted delivery prices to affiliated companies. A number of parts suppliers disapproved of this practice, maintaining that it would be difficult to deliver the parts at the prices tendered by Toyota. Managing directors Shoichi Saito and Shuji Ohno methodically put them through the Toyota-style approach of thinking things through with parts suppliers and meting out a solution to "make it worthwhile for all of us."

Despite such moving efforts, the $1,000 car (¥360,000) that Eiji had first set out to build never came to be. Simply adding profit onto the original cost would put the price above ¥500,000. Disregarding the bottom line altogether, Toyota boldly dropped the price down to ¥389,000.

To make such a low price feasible, Toyota excluded the radio from the car's standard equipment, installed a cheap heater that admittedly did not work very well, and covered the seats with vinyl. Inevitably, the car had a seedy appearance and could hardly be termed desirable.

After inviting public participation in naming the car as part of a vigorous publicity campaign, Toyota received over a million replies, eventually deciding on "Public Car," which they then shortened to "Publica." Based on such a high level of public interest in the mass-market car, Toyota's top management had little doubt that the Publica would sell—and they quite badly wanted it to succeed particularly because talks with Ford had fizzled out.

Along with Kamiya, one of the people who came over to Toyota from GM Japan during the prewar years was [Seishi] Kato, who headed sales in the Osaka region as general manager of the Toyota Motor Sales Kansai office. "We in sales believed that the point of a mass-market car was affordability. We therefore asked Toyota Motor to design the car without any unnecessary embellishments and to price the car as low as possible. The result was a marvelously functional but conversely uninspiring car."

The emphasis on affordability backfired. Although the Publica was definitely priced to compete with the k-car, Toyota had failed to understand that salarymen, its intended consumers, craved real passenger cars.

As yet no one viewed cars as a "substitute for walking"—a car was still an asset rather than a durable consumer good. An asset had to be plush. For consumers, passenger cars were a lofty dream. If they were going to overreach for the fruit, it needed to embody their dreams.

Naturally, Toyota's mass-market car was not received as well as expected when it first went on sale. Sales began to improve rapidly when the deluxe version, which featured enhanced equipment, came out in July 1963. Until then, sales had stagnated at around 1,700 vehicles per month, but the number soon shot up to 3,000. This was in spite of the fact that the price had gone up to ¥420,000 per vehicle. By year's end, sales of the Publica series, including vans, exceeded 7,000 vehicles.

A job for the head of the Toyota Group

The last thing Ishida could do as partnership negotiations with Ford reached their climax was take it easy. Though he was doubling as president of both Toyota and Toyoda Automatic Loom Works, helming the Toyota Group was also his crucial task.

One of the things that concerned Ishida was the continuing decline of Aichi Steel Works, which Kiichiro had helped to establish to provide Toyota with specialized steel products. Beset by one misfortune after another, Aichi Steel's president passed away in January 1961 at the young age of 51. Ishida had planned to have Yahata Steel (now Nippon Steel) send over a successor, but they politely declined.

The first person that everyone thought of when they heard the word reorganization was Ishida, whose raison d'etre was to serve as a vassal to the Toyoda family. As Aichi Steel was directly affiliated with Toyota, Aichi figured that Ishida could undertake the job at the drop of a hat if there were no other suitable candidates. Ishida, however, was a tricky customer. Deciding whether to take up the assignment, he opined with characteristic venom, "I'll do it if you're suggesting that I may as well do the job while I'm at it because I'm already indentured to Toyota. But I'm getting old, so I won't do it unless you're all in consensus."

Despite this warning, the position could not remain vacant forever. He finally assumed the presidency at the February board of directors meeting. He jumped right into the reorganization, forgetting that only a month ago he had grumbled about his old age.

The first order of business after assuming the presidency was modernizing plant and equipment to get operations back on the right track. But something else had to come first: equipment funding. This was where Ishida demonstrated his tremendous money sense.

His tireless motto was: "Defend your own castle." The essence of this was taking responsibility for the management of one's own company and not depending on outside help. Ishida also liked to speak of "guts." For him, it referred to the spirit of self-reliance. He hated the "salaryman spirit" or the nine-to-five attitude more than anything else.

"Japanese after the war lack a spirit of self-reliancce," he liked to say. "When I say 'guts,' I mean something like *bushido* from the old days. If you're not familiar with that, then the kind of fierce independence seen in the Semba merchants of Osaka."

When reorganizing Aichi Steel Works, Ishida took the optimistic view that an infusion of around ¥10 billion would manage to be enough. Yet, although the steel company was a core member of the Toyota Group, financial institutions had cold feet about advancing loans to an ailing company. Aichi Steel Works, for its part, wanted to avoid bank loans as well since that would increase the burden of interest payments. Although this pointed to an increase in capitalization, Aichi Steel's share price was below par value, so they could not expect general shareholders to pay in. Even if it were pushed through, with its shares below par the company would not be able to avoid stock forfeiture. Ishida forced a capital increase anyway; when he made the rounds to various Toyoda companies to ask them to pay in to increase capitalization, he also requested them to assume forfeited stock.

"The automotive and loom businesses exist today precisely because we had access to specialized steel," Ishida cautioned the head of each group company. "In a way, Aichi Steel Works is the mother of all Toyota-affiliated enterprises. To raise a child right, the mother must be strong and nurse it with quality milk. I'm asking each company to support its mother."

Ishida, having taken on the duties of Aichi Steel's new president, gradually raised its capital from ¥1 billion to ¥4.7 billion by October 1962.

Ishida habitually divulged the details of his thinking to close associates. "The ideal situation for me would be for the ten Toyoda companies to have a total capital stock of ¥100 billion and to have an equivalent amount of reserve deposits. We still have a long way to go, eh? In due course the day will come when the companies have attained this. When they do, it'll be smooth sailing from there. The Toyota Group will not budge no matter how intense international competition becomes. My job is to build the foundation for that. Whether I'm around or not, neither Kariya (Automatic Loom Works) nor Koromo (Toyota) will ever go under. My concern is for underdeveloped companies like Aichi Steel. We'll have to make a collective effort to foster those companies."

The ten Toyota companies to which he referred are Toyoda Automatic Loom Works, Toyota Motor, Toyota Motor Sales, Nippon Denso (now Denso), Minsei Spinning (now Toyota Boshoku), Aichi Kogyo (now Aisin Seiki), Toyoda Machine Works (now JTEKT), Toyota Auto Body, Toyota Tsusho, and Kanto Auto Works. Sometimes it's "the *eleven* Toyota companies," adding in Towa Real Estate, which can be considered a Toyoda family holdings company.

Chapter 15

The Corolla: Realizing the Dream of Toyota's Founder

IT IS SURPRISINGLY DIFFICULT FOR a top leader to decide whether to resign or remain in office. Particularly those who have achieved a great deal during their tenure as president tend to cling to power even after giving up the president's seat. One way to do this is by installing a yes-man as a successor president to pave the way to running the company from the outside. This creates a dual power structure within the company, leading the firm down a path of decline.

One legend within the Japanese auto industry that is still discussed today concerns the breezy retirement of Honda founders Soichiro Honda and Takeo Fujisawa. The two men, who shared a mutual bond of respect, affection and rivalry, retired in unison as president and executive vice-president, respectively, in the fall of 1973 ahead of the company's 25th anniversary. Soichiro was 66, while Fujisawa was 62.

The two were saluted by the public for stepping down to become supreme advisors with no involvement whatsoever in the company's management. Soichiro set up a personal office in the Ginza district and then set out on a "National Tour of Thanksgiving."

Fujisawa, meanwhile, renovated his home in Roppongi and turned it into a shop. The signboard read: "Kokaido—General Store for the Modern Arts." *Kokaido* was a newly coined name denoting a meeting place for aesthetes. Leaving the conduct of the business to his wife and two children, he entered a quiet life of dignified leisure absorbed in music, literature and art. Both men seldom showed their faces at headquarters, let alone meddle in Honda's management.

The two founders were able to live as they pleased because

Fujisawa, to whom Soichiro had entrusted Honda's business side, spent time bringing up successors. They both knew that no one could imitate their unique management style. The solution that Fujisawa came up with was a collective leadership system. As is it often said, the founders' style could be "intoned but not inherited."

Ishida steps down but does not promote Eiji

As for Toyota's past leaders, none have attempted a cloistered reign after retirement, nor did any retire to lives of quiet and ease like Soichiro and Fujisawa.

Aichi Steel's reorganization and the launch of the long-awaited Publica eased president Taizo Ishida's lingering concerns for the future of the company. At long last, he decided to bid farewell to the presidency. The problem was whom to set up as president. Toyota had become a "public institution" when it went public in 1949—an entity that has been entrusted to management, as it were, by shareholders and society as a whole. Ishida, however, was still occupied by an old idea: "Toyota is the company that Kiichiro built. Therefore, it belongs to the Toyoda family."

If the auto enterprise was a Toyoda family business, then Eiji, Sakichi Toyoda's nephew and Kiichiro's cousin, was the only choice as successor. Eiji had been promoted to executive vice-president the year before, with the post's duties divided in such a way that the extant VP Fukio Nakagawa handled clerical work and Eiji engineering. But Ishida promptly chose as his successor Nakagawa, who had been sent in from the Imperial Bank of Japan (now Sumitomo Mitsui Banking Corporation). Ishida had not been pressured by the bank to do so.

Eiji was coming along well as a leader; now that he was 48 years old and the executive vice-president to boot, he could be bumped up to president at any time. Considering his many achievements, his promotion would have been almost too right. Rather than appoint Eiji, however, Ishida appointed executive vice-president Nakagawa to serve as president in the interim.

This was Ishida's own idea. First off, although Toyota now had three passenger cars, the Crown, the Corolla and the Publica, it was hard to say that any of them measured up in the world market. Eiji would have to develop a car that could compete across the globe, and this would be impossible if he had to serve his duties as president. Moreover, Eiji did not have a strategist who could serve as his right-hand man. Until such a person could be brought up, Ishida felt that he himself needed to keep an eye on business operations as a whole.

Furthermore, there was also the question of where Toyota would end up after the shakeup within the auto industry that would inevitably occur were capital to be deregulated. Ishida was more experienced than Eiji at negotiating things of this nature.

August 1961: Ishida amended Toyota's articles of incorporation to become chairman, giving him the right of representation; Nakagawa became the new president. Ishida would continue to serve as the chairman of the board of directors and general shareholders' meetings. In American terms, while Ishida had held until then the dual posts of CEO and COO, he was now to become a full-time CEO. It could be said that, with a capital deregulation imbroglio imminent, Ishida wanted to keep Eiji, the Toyoda family's ace card, safely in hand.

Ten months later, on June 14, 1962, Toyota's total vehicle output to date reached one million. The one-millionth car to be produced at the Motomachi Plant was none other than the Crown Deluxe. An "employee appreciation evening," to which celebrities were invited to attend, was held on June 25; the next day, a "commemorative ceremony for one million cars produced" was held at the newly refurbished Toyota Hall. Attending the ceremony were not only people connected to Toyota but Prime Minister Hayato Ikeda, who came running in to offer a few congratulatory words.

"Congratulations for producing one million cars," he said. "I would like to extend my sincere congratulations to the managers and employees of Toyota, which raised up an automotive industry in Japan that some said would never come as far as it has today. I believe that the robust growth of Japanese industry, including automobiles, is due to the tireless efforts and wisdom of our own Japanese people. On the verge of deregulation, the automotive industry is bracing for the trials to come, but will fight through it with the time-tested gritty determination of the Japanese people. I look forward to the bright, glorious future to come."

Toyota and Nissan clash

Interest in the auto industry around 1961 when Nakagawa became Toyota's fourth president was focused on when the wave of private car ownership would wash over Japan. In the West, car ownership rates skyrocketed once the hurdle was overcome.

Leaving no stone unturned, every company's research department was frantically trying to uncover the circumstances that accounted for the surge in demand for passenger cars in Europe and the United States—specifically, how it corresponded to ownership rates of telephones, televisions and pianos, how salaried workers' annual income related to vehicle prices, and so forth. What this revealed was that car ownership swelled rapidly at the point when national income (GDP) per capita was 1 to 1.4 times the price of a car. Japan's national per-capita income in 1962 was ¥230,000. In four to five years, once Hayato Ikeda's Income Doubling Plan got underway, this would no doubt surpass ¥400,000. In fact, Japan's GDP, riding the wave of high economic growth sweeping the country, increased to ¥330,000 by 1965 and then to ¥380,000 by 1966.

Japanese private car ownership started out with 360cc k-cars but gradually shifted to 700-800cc mass-market cars like the Publica. Even so, drivers were still not satisfied. It was clear that automakers would next need to develop a 1000cc-class car.

Looking back from the vantage point of the present, 1966, when the Toyota Corolla and Nissan Sunny were released, was the inaugural year of the personal car in Japan. With the Sunny hitting the market in April and the Corolla in November, Nissan preceded Toyota by over half a year. Just prior to this, the two companies had been battling it out with the Corona and the Bluebird in what the media publicized extensively as the "CB War."

For many years, the three companies of Toyota, Nissan and Isuzu had been referred to as *Gosanke*, or The Three Houses of Japan's automotive industry, but with the CB War, Toyota and Nissan came to be referred to as the two *yokozuna* or Grand (Sumo) Champions.

Although a rivalry progressively began to emerge between the two companies, neither was aware, until just before the release of their new lines of mass-market cars, that they were developing similar products. Toyota never would have dreamt that the Sunny would become a rival. Nissan, meanwhile, had not developed the Sunny with the Corolla in mind. But once the cat was out of the bag, the two companies belatedly realized that their cars were in competition over the same concept.

Toyota's aim was to develop a "world-class passenger vehicle." Having a clearly defined concept for the kind of car they wanted to develop gave Toyota a distinct advantage over Nissan. What Eiji envisioned was a luxury line of Publicas. He was confident that Toyota could find a way to harness the failures and successes of the Publica in developing a new model. It was already widely understood within the company that the car Toyota would develop next would be their strategic marque, and the most talented staff from all departments was unstintingly poured into the development team. The impressive roster gave all the executives a sense of Eiji's investment in the model.

The release date of the Corolla had been set early on for a traditionally auspicious day in November 1966. As the Sunny had been released a full half-year earlier, Toyota had plenty of time to hammer out tactics for taking the rival car by storm. Heaven, earth and people were all working to Toyota's advantage.

In contrast to how the entire Toyota company worked together to build the Corolla, Nissan's development of the Sunny began with a sharp prodding of the head of the company by the company's engineers. President Katsuji Kawamata, who had come to be dubbed the Emperor of Nissan, was consistently reluctant to develop a car smaller than the Bluebird. Once the People's Car Plan began making headlines and Toyota launched development of the Publica, Kawamata feared that the Bluebird, Nissan's flagship model, would be upstaged by mass-market cars. His thinking was that the "lower-income sector of the population could drive used Bluebirds." This was the same type of mindset for which Ikeda had been condemned while serving as Minister of Finance, when he'd said, "Let the poor eat barley."

"Please get President Kawamata to approve the development of a mass-market car. Otherwise, Nissan will be left behind," field engineers implored Managing Director Tadashi Igarashi, who doubled as manager of the Yokohama Plant. Utterly frustrated with Kawamata, who showed little understanding of mass-market cars, the engineers were pleading with Igarashi to talk to the man.

Igarashi somehow managed to persuade Kawamata. Starting out by building a light van, Nissan steadily gained ground in the development of a family car. Beginning in 1964, Nissan's development team set out to come up with a design for a mass-market car. Favorable sales numbers for Toyota's Publica and Toyo Kogyo's (now Mazda) Familia compelled Kawamata to acknowledge that a mass-market car would be essential if Nissan were to gradually capture a sector of the population distinct from the one that purchased the Bluebird. At this point, just as his engineers had requested him to do, the president had to consent to developing a mass-market car based on their light van.

Kawamata, originally a banker, gave his development team strict orders to keep costs down to ¥200,000 per vehicle, to use Nissan-affiliated Aichi Machine Industry's facilities and equipment to build engines, and to revamp the existing production line at the Oppama Plant to use in manufacturing the new car.

Even while restrictions were put in place to placate Kawamata, the team somehow pulled through to complete a prototype in July 1964 and began running tests. There were seven prototypes in all, five light vans and two sedans. They had only those to conduct all necessary testing, including engine tests. The staff had to fight over the prototypes.

Nissan placed an ad in the papers on New Year's Day, 1966, inviting the public to send in their choice of names for the new car. Out of a substantial 8.5 million replies received in response, the company chose the name "Sunny." Nissan founder Yoshisuke Aikawa also participated in the naming scheme, sending in the moniker "Minimax."

It is worth mentioning that after being exonerated from postwar restrictions preventing him from taking up a post at the company, Aikawa, rather than return to Nissan, formed the "Political Federation of Japanese Small and Medium Enterprises,"[31] for which he served as president, and was also elected a member of the Upper House. His second son, Kinjiro, also entered the world of politics, and served as an Upper House member alongside his father. Coming under scrutiny for alleged election fraud, however, father and son both resigned their posts. Having witnessed the coming of the Sunny, Aikawa passed away in February 1966. He was 87.

The Sunny line, consisting of a standard two-door sedan and a deluxe van, went on sale on April 7. The standard model retailed for ¥410,000, while the deluxe was priced at ¥460,000. Nissan's

---

31. *Chusho kigyo seiji renmei*

sales department proposed introducing it as the $1,000 car (at the then-current exchange rate of ¥360 to a dollar) to generate positive publicity, but Kawamata flatly rejected the proposal, figuring it would cut into the company's profit margin.

Making the Corolla trigger a wave of motorization

If we were to liken Toyota's development of passenger cars to a hop, skip and a jump, the Crown was the hop, the Corona and Publica the skip, and the Corolla the jump.

In its enthusiasm for the Corolla, Toyota proved to be the opposite of Nissan. Eiji wanted not just to fulfill Kiichiro's dream but to trigger Japan's motorization with the Corolla.

The chief engineer of development for the Publica, Tatsuo Hasegawa, had outlined a plan to painstakingly pursue affordability and roadworthiness given the still low national income. Due to an emphasis on cutting costs, the car that he came up with was haunted by a shoddy image and ended up coming across as a "thumb in mouth" car. Toyota subsequently devoted itself to the deluxe model, whose eventual release boosted Toyota's share of the family car market to 74 percent by 1962.

The company's share of the market then began to decline owing to the appearance of rival vehicles. In 1963, Hasegawa suggested to Eiji that they change models.

"We developed the Publica with emphases on functionality, affordability, and practicality," Eiji unexpectedly replied. "With the current engine displacement, it's simply not possible to respond to customers' demands for things like interior comfort. With the Crown and Corona too, we approached development from the perspective of what we could do to gain the support of those who'll be driving them. Europe and the U.S. have nothing on us there. We'll make the car we're going to develop in the days ahead the standard for all Japanese cars. To do that, we're going to have to move development forward with the understanding that 'technology is a servant of commoditization.' I'll make this car trigger an upsurge of private car ownership. We'll build a new assembly plant with a 20,000-vehicle monthly capacity as well as a plant exclusively for engines. We've already finished acquiring the land for the engine plant. It's looking good on the land for the assembly plant as well. Hasegawa, this is the mass-market car on which Toyota's staked its fate. That's why *you* are going to be chief engineer of development."

After hearing such a display of the enthusiasm, Hasegawa froze. Toyota production at the time—combining all models of passenger cars and trucks like the Crown, Corona, Publica, Toyoace—had finally just reached 40,000 vehicles per month. Once the new factory was up, Toyota's production capacity would jump by 50 percent. But if motorization were slow to come around, Toyota would become plagued by overcapacity.

Hasegawa began with a detailed analysis of the successes and failures of the Publica, and then quickly got to work on a concept for the ideal mass-market car. "Even if the Corolla gets nearly a perfect score on things like performance, interior comfort and impression," he reasoned, "it will be a washout as a mass-market car if it's inaccessible to the general public in terms of price and maintenance costs. We can't allow quality to suffer simply to lower the price, however. A mass-market car has to score a 'B' in all subjects. The rest is figuring out which aspect of the car to improve beyond a 'B,' say with some unique innovation. In a nutshell, the Corolla must be a car that the general public will feel comfortable driving, a car that doesn't feel inferior to others, a car that people will want to drive forever."

Hasegawa's "B-average" doctrine was a reaction to how the Publica had come off as an inferior automobile. The new car would need to score well on contradictory criteria to gain the widespread support of consumers—the essence of Toyota's "B-average" philosophy.

On February 26, 1966 Hasegawa received a memo from Eiji telling him to "add another 100cc to expand the Corolla's engine displacement to 1100cc." The memo also got down to some of the finer points, including building the engine with a 75mm bore, which would require paring down part of the cylinder to minimize changes to parts and equipment, and to put the finishing touches on all modifications within six months.

Eiji suddenly gave these orders to Hasegawa because Nissan had just announced the specifications of the Sunny on February 16. He had only found out that day that the Sunny, slated for release in April, was not only equipped with a 1000cc engine, the same as the Corolla, but that it was also very similar in size.

A monster hit surpassing the Ford Model T and the VW Beetle

Shotaro Kamiya of Toyota Sales forbade managers in its various sales and marketing departments from giving orders for product development directly to Toyota Motor's chief engineer of development, having them instead go through the product planning division for all their concerns. Ill-considered opinions would only confuse the chief engineer. The product planning division had worked out a plan to increase engine displacement by 100cc to differentiate the Corolla from the Sunny, an idea that Kamiya had discussed directly with Ishida. Eiji quickly saw through this 100cc increase as merely a form of publicity, but he did not let on to this in his memo to Hasegawa.

Hasegawa, knowing how Eiji staked Toyota's future on the Corolla, called the director of the engine development division, Masuo Amano, into his office. "This is an order from the executive vice-president," he said, showing Amano Eiji's memo. "Don't grumble or gripe," he ordered sternly. "Just do it."

"While I understand what you're saying," Amano retorted in spite of Hasegawa's warning, "I have complete confidence in the 1000cc engine I developed for the Corolla. It'll beat the Sunny. As the chief engineer, you too must know that expanding the engine by another 100cc won't affect performance. It'd be risky to change something like that at such a late stage."

"This isn't a technical issue," Hasegawa replied. "It's a high-grade political matter. Everything for us comes down to the Corolla."

With such an urgent entreaty on the part of the chief engineer, the one who bore full responsibility for development, Amano, had no choice but to back down.

Plant construction was moving along well. Construction on the Kamigo Plant, the first plant in Japan dedicated exclusively to engines and which set a monthly target of producing 50,000 units, began in October 1964 and was completed the next year in September 1965. Meanwhile, construction on the assembly-based Takaoka Plant, for which Toyota had acquired the land in May 1965, was already underway in a bid in hopes of winding up by September 1966.

The Corolla was released on November 5, over six months after the Sunny. At ¥432,000 for the standard model and ¥495,000 for the deluxe, the Corolla was tens of thousands of yen more expensive than the Sunny, but the highly-touted "extra 100cc" made it seem something of a bargain among consumers.

Although sales volume in 1966 was limited to 12,000 vehicles, partially due to the fact that production never fully got on the right track, it quickly chalked up sales of 160,000 vehicles in 1967 and continued to thrive thereafter until, by 1972, sales were accelerating by some 100,000 cars annually. After releasing a number of new models, total production reached five million vehicles in June 1976, then surpassed ten million in 1983. Eiji was jubilant: "Make no mistake about it. The Corolla was what ignited motorization in Japan. It will only get better from here on out. This is a world-class car. We've made Kiichiro's dream a reality."

The Corolla indeed continued to flourish. At present, it is being produced at sixteen plants around the world and marketed in 144 countries and regions worldwide. With total production of over 32 million vehicles, it is the monster hit that eclipsed the Ford Model T and VW Beetle. What makes it a monster among monsters is that the Corolla, after changing models nine times, continues to evolve even today.

It would not be an overstatement to say that the Corolla was the driving force that propelled Toyota to the top rungs of world automaking. If Toyota had not brought the Corolla to market at the crux of motorization, world-best would still be a dream within a dream.

Sakichi Toyoda (1867-1930)
Founder of Toyoda Automatic Loom Works
and father of the Toyota Group

The G-type automatic loom that
Sakichi invented in 1924

Rizaburo Toyoda (1884-1952)
Toyota Motor's first president.
Initially opposed to entering auto business;
Kiichiro's passion won him over.

Kiichiro Toyoda (1894-1952)
Founder of Toyota Motor.
It all began with him.

Taizo Ishida (1888-1979)

Third president. Steered Toyota out of financial crisis; his frugal management style ("wringing an already dry towel") proved foundational.

Eiji Toyoda (1913-)

Fifth president. Toyota's "second founder"; he remains a pillar of the company. Inducted into U.S. Automotive Hall of Fame, 1994.

Shoichiro Toyoda (1925-)

Sixth president. Successfully merged manufacturing and sales divisions in 1982. As first president of newly united Toyota, indicated route to internationalization. Inducted into U.S. Automotive Hall of Fame, 2007.

Hiroshi Okuda (1932-)

Eighth president. First helmsman in 28 years from outside the Toyoda family. Oversaw shift from "conservative" corporate style to "aggressive management"; driving force behind Toyota's global ascendance.

Fujio Cho (1937-)

Ninth president. "Evangelist of the Toyota Production System" put local production in U.S. on track. Continued Okuda's policies and contributed to expansion of business.

Katsuaki Watanabe (1942-)

Tenth and current president

Masaya Hanai (1912-1995)

Former chairman;
"President of the Bank of Toyota"

Shotaro Kamiya (1898-1980)

President of Toyota Motor Sales;
"the god of sales"

Taichi Ohno (1912-1990)
Father of the Toyota Production System

Kenya Nakamura (l) (1913-1998)
Supervised development of first-generation Crown; "Toyota's Yul Brynner"

Tatsuo Hasegawa (1916-2008)
Supervised development of first-generation Corolla

The AA Model; Kiichiro headed the development team (1936)

Construction of the Koromo Plant; it began operating in 1938

AA Model frame assembly line at Koromo Plant

AA Model displayed at first retail conference

Eiji Toyoda writes from Detroit about research stay at Ford for the Toyota Newspaper

During the labor dispute of 1950, Toyota laid off workers for the first time; the company has never done so since.

Commemoration ceremony: completion of the Toyopet Crown Master (1955)

Motomachi Plant after
first stage of construction

First vehicle comes off
assembly line at
Motomachi Plant (1959)

Toyota's millionth
vehicle total (1962)

The labor-management joint declaration is signed, confirming a policy of cooperation (February 1962)

Twentieth anniversary of the labor-management joint declaration (1982)

Staff of Toyota and GM's Californian joint venture NUMMI (1984)

First Camry (for quality control) comes off line at U.S. local production plant in Kentucky (1986)

First-generation Crown

Second-generation Crown

First-generation Corona

Third-generation Corona

First-generation Publica

Publica deluxe model

First-generation Corolla

Century

First-generation Lexus

First-generation Prius

Chapter 16
Victors in the Industrial Reorganization Drama

T RADE IN PASSENGER CARS AND trucks was liberalized in 1965. This meant only that companies no longer needed to get a foreign exchange license to import; the government continued to levy a high 40 percent tariff on overseas cars. Despite all the fuss within the auto industry, trade liberalization did not have that great an impact.

What the industry feared most was the liberalization of capital and auto parts such as engines. As long as parts were not deregulated, foreign companies could not initiate knockdown production in Japan and, as long as capital was not deregulated, they could not buy controlling shares.

Frustrated with Japanese automobile policy, the U.S. government pressured Tokyo whenever the two governments met at sporadically held U.S.-Japan auto talks. Japanese car exports to the U.S. were on the rise, forcing the Japanese government to make concessions during the negotiations. After a period of rough going, talks were concluded between 1968 and 1969.

Through a series of negotiations, the two sides agreed that Japan would liberalize capital in March 1971. At the same time, they also agreed that Japan would completely deregulate auto parts such as engines by 1972, while also lowering import duties to 36 percent in 1968, 20 percent in 1970, and then eliminating them entirely in 1978.

Momentum builds for an industrial shake-up

MITI's concerns for medium-sized automakers prior to capital liberalization created the momentum for reorganizing domestic industries. It had become apparent that a gap between companies in the industry had gradually begun to open in the run-up to motorization and that medium-sized and lower automakers would not be able to survive on their own.

Although Toyota, which had risen to the top spot among Japanese automakers, stood in favor of domestic reorganization, chairman Taizo Ishida had no plans to take active initiative in the reorganization drama that was about to unfold. No matter how often the Toyota management policy was criticized as "the Mikawa Monroe Doctrine," Ishida strove to protect his own castle.

With capital liberalization just around the corner, medium and small automakers facing reorganization were ready to make a move. They were under pressure to make one of two choices: either affiliate with a foreign company or come under the control of a domestic automaker. These companies much preferred to come under the control of a domestic automaker than a foreign company.

The first company to approach Toyota was Prince Motor Company, the third largest in the industry after Toyota and Nissan. Owner and chairman Shojiro Ishibashi dropped in on Ishida in the fall of 1964, the year that the Tokyo Olympics were held. At the time, Prince, a company descended from the defunct Nakajima Aircraft, was a subsidiary of the leading tire maker Bridgestone. Noted for its technology, Prince seized on its affiliation with Bridgestone to devote itself to a slew of new car models and, in the ensuing mania, produced hot-selling cars like the "Skyline GT," abbreviated as the "*Suka G*" in Japanese. Pleased by this, Prince built the Murayama Plant with a capacity of 10,000 vehicles per month in a suburb of Tokyo. But the hot-sellers did not last, barely reaching monthly sales of 7,000 vehicles. Worried that this would adversely affect the operations of core business Bridgestone, Ishibashi steeled himself to pull out of the automotive business.

"It'll be difficult for Prince to continue to survive on its own," Ishibashi told Ishida, cutting right to the chase. "I would very much appreciate if the industry leader Toyota would take in my company."

The general climate at the time of the auto industry shake-up was that mergers were only expected. As such, Ishida had a good idea this was what Ishibashi had come to discuss. "Well, there's the issue of whether we can afford to do it... And our company's a bit different, so we need to consider whether or not we're good for each other."

Ishida was looking for a roundabout way to turn down a merger proposal that smacked of a bail-out so that Ishibashi would not lose face. But Ishibashi, an unsentimental businessman, immediately picked up on what Ishida was driving at. So he dropped the bomb: "If it doesn't work out with Toyota, I'll have to take my proposal to another automaker. Please understand this."

Ishibashi had sounded out Toyo Kogyo (now Mazda) before approaching Toyota. As they both did the bulk of their banking with Sumitomo (now Sumitomo Mitsui Banking Corporation), Sumitomo president Shozo Hotta went to great lengths to act as intermediary on Ishibashi's behalf. Although Hotta and Toyo Kogyo's owner-president Tsuneji Matsuda got along extremely well, Matsuda, determined to take Mazda in the direction he had set out for it, viewed the merger with Prince in a negative light.

Nissan president Kawamata's ambitions

At this point, the only company that could take on Prince was Nissan. A major impediment to this pairing, however, was that the two companies used different main banks: while Prince was with Sumitomo, Nissan used the Industrial Bank of Japan (now Mizuho Bank). So Ishibashi, who had extensive personal connections among politicians, asked Mitsujiro Ishii, an old friend from the same hometown (Kurume, Fukuoka Prefecture) who had once been up for election as president of the ruling Liberal Democratic Party (LDP), to mediate. With Ishii's help, Ishibashi planned to enlist the services of the Minister of International Trade and Industry Yoshio Sakurauchi.

In March 1965 Sakurauchi called in Nissan president Katsuji Kawamata to discuss a merger with Prince. Kawamata, a proud man and an authoritarian, was pleased to be approached directly by the Minister and soon got down to the specifics of the merger. Kawamata naturally had his own calculations for doing so. Toyota was slowly inching away from Nissan. If Nissan were to merge with Prince, it would not only be able to compete against Toyota but feasibly usurp

Toyota's position at the top of the industry. Immediately after the merger was announced, those in the auto industry had no doubt that "Nissan would soon overtake Toyota."

Kawamata also had his eye on Prince's real estate, including its factory. With the Japanese economy right in the midst of a rapid expansion, land values were skyrocketing. Even if Prince's operations were deteriorating somewhat, considering its hidden assets the company would not be a terrible purchase at all. This was truly a banker's mindset.

One of Kawamata's ulterior motives for absorbing Prince in line with government wishes was to improve his social standing as a businessman and to broaden his scope of activities as a financier. After the merger with Prince, Nissan's headquarters would come to be called the "MITI of Ginza," while Kawamata himself became the first person from the automotive industry to take over as vice-chairman of *Keidanren*, or the Federation of Economic Organizations. Meanwhile, in contrast to the ambitious Kawamata, Ishida opined that "business-world socializing is for people with time on their hands," implicitly criticizing Kawamata's thirst for authority.

After five-party talks at the end of May 1965 between Sakurauchi, Ishibashi, Kawamata, Hotta and Sohei Nakayama, president of the Industrial Bank of Japan, the merger between Nissan and Prince was announced on June 1. The new company started up in August 1966, just after the release of the Sunny. With such a large-scale merger, Toyota and Nissan towered above the rest of the automotive industry.

Cursed with lax management some thirty years later, Nissan came under the control of France's Renault. It is ironic that the first thing on Carlos Ghosn's agenda after he was dispatched by Renault to reorganize Nissan was to sell off the defunct Prince's Murayama Plant.

Alliance with Hino and Daihatsu

In October, two months after the merger between Nissan and Prince, Toyota announced an operational and capital alliance with Hino Motors. Through technical cooperation with Renault, Hino produced the "Renault 4CV" and used this technology to develop the "Contessa" line of compact passenger cars built with a RR (rear engine, rear-wheel drive) layout. Given discouraging sales, however, there were whispers that Hino would discontinue production, but doing so would leave the plant idle. On the other hand, debt would only snowball if production were continued.

Hino and Toyota both banked with Mitsui, which was headquartered in Hibiya. As Toyota's Tokyo branch was located in the same building as Mitsui's main office, whenever he made it up to Tokyo Ishida looked forward to dropping in for a chat with chairman Kiichiro Sato, with whom he was on friendly terms. Although Mitsui was uncertain about Hino's future, without the confidence to take the lead in reorganizing Hino, the bank just blindly poured more money into the company. Just before Ishibashi approached Ishida about the merger, Sato came out and asked Ishida to help out Hino.

Ishida sent not president Fukio Nakagawa but executive vice-president Eiji Toyoda to negotiate a deal. His decision was based on the thinking that "Eiji is going to be president of Toyota at some point. He may have just began developing the Corolla, but this kind of experience (tie-up negotiations) will come in handy down the line."

Toyota was not interested in taking Hino completely under its wing. Holding back the progress of negotiations was the issue of how to handle the Contessa, which competed with Toyota's own vehicles. Eiji went ahead and proposed that Hino pull out of the passenger car market. Taking the hint, Hino president Masanobu Matsukata suddenly proposed the following to Eiji in the spring of 1965: "Hino will cut off production of the Contessa. What I'd like to ask in return is that you give us something comparable to do in its place."

Eiji panicked. If Hino accepted Toyota's proposal to pull out of making passenger cars, there would be no easy way to back out of negotiations.

There was more to Matsukata's decision than meets the eye. In January 1965, just as talks were gaining momentum, Hino senior advisor Shoji Okubo succumbed to acute bronchitis. During his tenure as president, Okuba was awarded the *Légion d'honneur* by the French government for bringing production of the Renault 4CV to Japan. Happy about this, he set out to develop the Contessa based on the 4CV's technology. If Okubo were still alive, Matsukata would not have been able to discontinue the Contessa.

Although Matsukata had decided to suspend the production of passenger cars with the intention of merging with Toyota, it would be a burden on Toyota. In addition, Eiji had figured that the deal would be difficult to pull off due to antitrust laws.

The grounds for believing so were Nissan's merger with Prince. The Japan Fair Trade Commission had concluded: "[The new company's] market share will not exceed that of Toyota even if the two companies are merged. We will therefore allow the merger to take place." Eiji thus suspected that Toyota would not be able to merge with any other automakers in the future.

After thinking it through, Eiji's conclusion was to form an operational and capital alliance with Hino. In so doing, he stated, "Toyota will meet Hino's demands while adhering firmly to its own position. We'll move forward with reorganization on this basis." Limiting its capital contribution to 5 percent, Toyota commissioned Hino to produce small trucks. Commissioned production using Hino's own plant and equipment would supply funds to Hino. Meanwhile, Toyota would get by without building a new plant.

Once the tie-up was arranged, Eiji laid out one condition for Matsukata. "In associating with the industry leader Toyota, Hino absolutely *must* rise to the top of the large truck field. Resigning yourself to number two or three will get you tangled up in future industry shake-ups."

Fulfilling its promise to Eiji, Hino became the leading large truck manufacturer in just a few years. Keeping a close watch on the tie-up negotiations between the two companies was Tadao Watanabe, president of Sanwa Bank (now the Bank of Tokyo-Mitsubishi UFJ), Daihatsu Motor's main bank. Just after Toyota and Hino had begun talks in October 1966, Watanabe presented to Ishida the idea of an alliance. Watanabe's proposal baffled Eiji from the outset. "From what I can see from its balance sheet, Daihatsu is an excellent company, the epitome of solid management. Why would they come to us?"

No matter how soundly a company is managed, it does not guarantee that the company will fare well in the future. It is not clear if Daihatsu president Yuji Koishi, judging that his firm's outlook was bleak, asked its main bank, Sanwa, to mediate a deal with Toyota, or if Sanwa's Watanabe was the one who persuaded Koishi, but in any case Daihatsu and Toyota entered talks to affiliate. The problem was that the vehicles produced and marketed by Daihatsu rivaled Toyota's even more than Hino's did.

Since Toyota was not involved in light-duty k-cars, Eiji tried to persuade Daihatsu to specialize in them. Koishi, who was not as unsentimental as Matsukata, however, intended to continue as many of the existing models as possible. In the end, Toyota backed off from its position and the two companies reached an agreement that Daihatsu would continue to produce and market its compact passenger vehicles while also focusing on the k-car. They announced the deal in November 1967.

As with Hino, Toyota would commission production with Daihatsu, and acquired a 6 percent stake in the company. Sanwa, which acted as a go-between, shrewdly burrowed into Toyota's folds, joining Mitsui and Tokai (now the Bank of Tokyo-Mitsubishi UFJ) as a main bank.

Although Toyota for long laid great store in the independence of its business partners' management, former president Hiroshi Okuda, seizing on the international realignment of industry players afforded by the merger between Daimler-Benz and Chrysler in 1998, snatched up a majority of Hino's and Daihatsu's shares, bringing them under Toyota's control as consolidated subsidiaries.

Medium and small automakers poised to make a move

One after another, Prince, Hino and Daihatsu found suitable bachelors to take them in. Looking on from the sidelines, the remaining automakers were primed to move. While Toyota and Nissan were the main players on the acquiring side, Isuzu was the main player on the other front. With some exaggeration, all existing automakers were cast as potential suitors, and Isuzu was teased by the media for its indecisiveness in a *senryu*[32] that read: "Where are you going/drifting freely in the waves/the Isuzu."[33] Thus did Isuzu's "courtship odyssey" begin.

Toyota played a supporting role in the drama. Toyota Sales president Shotaro Kamiya saw it differently than Ishida. "Though it won't be all that hard for Toyota to pull ahead of the Nissan-Prince bloc solo," he reasoned, "rather than go on the defensive in the

---

32. *Senryu*, similar to haiku, is a 17-syllable poem that often emphasizes irony, satire, humor, and human drama instead of nature.

33. *Doko e iku, nami ni tadayou isuzu maru.*

reorganization drama, Toyota needs to be more proactive to extend its reach in the global market." He was furtively trying to seize the initiative to do this as the industrial realignment continued to unfold. Then, at the Toyota Sales general shareholders meeting in November 1966, Kamiya stirred up controversy with a suggestive comment: "It probably won't be long before we witness another merger take place." Everyone predicted that the partner would be Isuzu.

In 1962 Isuzu constructed a plant exclusively for passenger cars in Fujisawa, Kanagawa Prefecture, but stagnant sales eroded profits, giving Sanwa Bank, Isuzu's associate main bank, cause for concern about Isuzu's future. It was rumored that Sanwa, the third largest lender to Toyota Sales after Tokai and Mitsui Banks, stepped in to mediate a deal with Isuzu.

Kamiya's sights were set on the Fujisawa Plant. Toyota was making progress on acquiring land in Gotemba, at the base of Mt. Fuji, on which to build a third assembly plant to bolster those in Motomachi and Takaoka, but was making less headway than expected. A real estate agency that had gotten wind of this proposed to Kamiya: "How about buying Isuzu's Fujisawa Plant? If it suits you, we can put a deal together for ¥20 billion."

Taking a hint from this, Kamiya fleshed out an alliance that would not be financially draining. "Isuzu would concentrate on its specialty in trucks, discontinue production of its own brand of passenger cars, and produce Toyota's cars on commission at the Fujisawa Plant," he rationalized. "From Toyota's perspective, this would be equivalent to constructing a new plant." But the whole plan went up in smoke before negotiations because Isuzu president Eikichi Ohashi clung tenaciously to his company's brand of passenger cars. Isuzu was already conducting stealth tie-up negotiations with Fuji Heavy Industries.

Fuji is the company that cashed in on its renowned k-car, the "Subaru 360." Also a descendant of the former Nakajima Aircraft like Prince, Fuji was known for its superlative technology. Playing off the VW Beetle, the Subaru 360 was called *koganemushi* or the "scarab beetle" in the mania that ensued after its release.

On December 15, one month after Kamiya hinted at an alliance with Isuzu at a Toyota Sales general shareholders meeting, Isuzu and Fuji Heavy Industries announced a tie-up almost out of nowhere. The deal between the two companies gelled in a relatively short period partly due to the fact that both companies feared they would not be able to survive at all without forming a partnership.

The coupling was badmouthed as "the little man with a big wife." The scale of Fuji's operations was a couple of orders smaller than Isuzu's, and locating the advantages of a pairing between a k-car maker and a manufacturer primarily of large trucks proved difficult. A year later, nothing concrete had yet come of the two companies' plans, which had been mood-driven from the beginning.

The sense of crisis among medium and smaller automakers rose to a peak after the turn of the new year in 1968, when MITI's Heavy Industries Bureau revealed in a New Year's press conference its vision that there ought to be two main parties in the automotive industry. None too excited about this, soon afterward Mitsubishi Heavy Industries approached Isuzu and Fuji Heavy Industries about a merger. Media called this the "IMF Alliance." Mitsubishi aimed to take control by establishing a third major force to countervail Toyota and Nissan.

Although Isuzu, uncognizant of Mitsubishi's true motives, welcomed this, Fuji Heavy Industries, which competed against Mitsubish in the aircraft business, sniffed out Mitsubishi's ambitions and strongly objected. As a result, the deal fell through. The incident created a divide between Isuzu and Fuji, however, who broke off their alliance in May 1968.

Meanwhile, there was no guarantee that Fuji Heavy Industries would be able to survive on its own. The company split into two factions: one that insisted on affiliating with Toyota and another that argued in favor of coming under the control of Nissan, with whom Fuji shared deep ties through its main bank, the Industrial Bank of Japan. In the end, Fuji accommodated the inclination of its main bank and came under the control of Nissan.

In a shock to everyone, the stranded Isuzu tied up with Mitsubishi Heavy Industries a month later. Isuzu and Mitsubishi both specialized in large trucks but also produced passenger vehicles, and the match seemed fitting enough. To Mitsubishi, however, the tie-up with Isuzu was nothing but camouflage for an alliance with foreign capital. Mitsubishi Heavy Industries vice-president Yoichiro Makita, slated as next in line to take over the presidential suite, was exceedingly self-confident about his company's prospects, saying, "Mitsubushi Heavy Industries is not merely a builder of ships, machinery and motors. It is the best manufacturer in Japan. We're reconciled to being in the lower tier of the auto industry for the time being, but we'll invariably overtake Toyota and Nissan at some point to become the top automaker in Japan."

Mitsubishi, Isuzu and Toyo Kogyo turn to foreign companies

Makita's ambition to become Japan's leading automaker culminated with a capital alliance with Chrysler. More specifically, the company's automotive division would split off and form the independent Mitsubishi Motors Corporation, with the new company taking in capital from Chrysler. Negotiations yielded a basic agreement in May 1969, the year that Makita would become president. Since Isuzu was not informed of the negotiations, it cannot be denied that Mitsubishi's affiliation with Isuzu was merely a diversionary tactic to make a deal with a foreign company. The agreement with Isuzu was naturally dissolved shortly thereafter.

Isuzu's courtship odyssey continued. In March 1970, it made a deal with Nissan. Ohashi, who had consistently pushed for a partnership with a Japanese automaker, made a big show of declaring that Isuzu "would not part ways with Nissan for a long time to come." But disaster struck within. Vice-president Torao Aramaki, leader of the foreign faction, was promoted to president instead of Ohashi, who represented the Japanese faction, while Aramaki's right-hand man, Toshio Okamoto, was appointed vice-president. The foreign company faction thus came to occupy the nerve center of Isuzu's management.

The foreign faction, which had secretly been in touch with GM through Itochu Corporation before the alliance with Nissan, finally announced a capital alliance in November. One could say that Isuzu, betrayed by the tie-up between Chrysler and Mitsubishi, accordingly played the role of spoiler to Nissan with its alliance with GM.

Toyo Kogyo, after turning down a merger with Prince, had continued talks since 1970 to tie-up with Ford, but negotiations reached a deadlock over the capital contribution ratio. Just as this was playing out, president Tsuneji Matsuda suddenly passed away and was succeeded by his eldest son Kohei. Negotiations were temporarily suspended, then resumed intermittently thereafter, but the two parties, never able to bridge the gap over the capital contribution ratio, called it quits in February 1972.

Kohei's true feeling was that he was not about to let the company that his grandfather (Jujiro) built and his father (Tsuneji) worked so hard to develop be pushed around by Ford right under his nose. Soon after setting out on the path to independence, Toyo Kogyo's sales in the U.S. market fell off sharply; during the oil crisis, the U.S. Environmental Protection Agency (EPA) labeled Toyo's treasured RE (rotary engine) vehicle a "gas guzzler"—leading the company into financial turmoil. Although its main bank, Sumitomo, helped Toyo Kogyo to restructure, Sumitomo judged that it would be difficult for the company to survive on its own, and made an overture to Ford to reopen talks. It was in the spring of 1979 that negotiations produced an agreement.

Just when it appeared as if the alliances and dissolutions within the auto industry, which had all begun with capital liberalization, were winding down with Ford-Mazda saga, the irony of fate would once again strike the industry.

Nissan had come out on top in the global car war of the 1980s, emerging triumphant on the acquiring side of the international realignment drama alongside GM, Ford, Toyota and VW. But when all was said and done, Nissan paid the price for an incoherent international strategy and eventually fell into the hands of Renault. Fuji Heavy Industries took the occasion to disengage itself from Nissan and affiliate with GM, but later tied up with Toyota when GM started to face difficulties. Toyota's intention was to commission the production of Toyota vehicles at Fuji's plant in Indiana to accommodate increased demand for its cars in the U.S. Fuji Heavy Industries and Isuzu collaborated to build the plant when the two revived their partnership in the late 1980s (Isuzu later backed out).

Isuzu, too, dissolved its capital alliance with GM, and partnered up with Toyota. Toyota had been the one to initially propose a tie-up, with the objective of acquiring Isuzu's diesel engine technology. In any event, Toyota first glimpsed the global automaking throne when Hino and Daihatsu, which it had taken under its wing during the industrial shake-up prior to capital liberalization, became its consolidated subsidiaries; by then bringing Fuji Heavy Industries and Isuzu under its corporate umbrella, Toyota poised itself to open up a lead over GM.

188

Mitsubushi broke ties with Chrysler when the latter lapsed into financial disarray. After a series of ups and downs, Mitsubishi then formed a capital alliance with DaimlerChrysler, but dissolved this agreement as well after problems with vehicle recalls. Large truck manufacturer Nissan Diesel was then acquired by Sweden's Volvo. Light-duty k-car specialist Suzuki, surmising that "if it had to lean, it should lean on a large tree," turned to GM for a capital alliance but ended up breaking off the agreement just as Fuji and Isuzu had.

The victors in the reorganization drama that swirled around capital liberalization were thus Toyota and—consistently the odd man out—Honda.

Chapter 17
Toyota's Cornerstone: Labor-Management Cooperation

CHIEF EXECUTIVES ARE CURSED TO hard labor. Day in and day out, they must not only check to make sure the company is following through with the goals they laid out, but must grasp what kind of progress is being made towards achieving each goal. The reality is that they are under constant pressure from company meetings and events; weddings and funerals often take up their days off. As there is no distinction between the public and private lives of chief executives at Japanese firms, failing to take vigilant care of their health can invite tragic consequences.

Toyota's founder Kiichiro Toyoda died twice as a businessman. The first time was when he resigned to take responsibility for the labor dispute in 1950; the second was his death immediately following his decision to return to the company. If Kiichiro had kept a closer eye on maintaining his health, he never would have been termed the "tragic businessman"[34] and Toyota's history surely would have played out much differently than it did.

I was chosen because I'm the best person for the job

Fukio Nakagawa, who, following in Taizo Ishida's footsteps, became the fourth president of Toyota, suddenly passed away on October 13, 1967, just as the Japanese auto industry had begun to ride the wave of motorization sweeping across Japan. He died of acute myocardial infarction.

---

34. *Higeki no keieisha*

That morning, Nakagawa received a business report upon his return from Tokyo to Toyota headquarters and attended a board of directors meeting at Toyoda Automatic Loom Works. At night, he became nauseous during a business dinner and passed away on the spot. Suffering from diabetes, Nakagawa was on a restricted diet and exercise routine. On the day he passed away, he had run full speed through Tokyo Station to the train platform to catch a bullet train that he was about to miss, barely managing to catch the train on which he had reserved a seat. This abrupt burst of exercise very well may have shortened his life.

Tatsuro, Shoichiro Toyoda's younger brother and Toyota's sixth president, inherited the Toyoda genes for high blood pressure. Both Eiji and Shoichiro have taken high blood pressure medication since they were young. Tatsuro, however, with his slim physique and no noticeable symptoms of high tension, did not take the same medication. At a party after a regular general meeting of the Japan Automobile Dealers Assocation in February 1996, he began feeling ill and was taken to the hospital. It was a stroke. Luckily they were able to save his life, but the after-effects remained. The attending physician determined that it would be too demanding for him to continue serving as president.

Infelicitously, four of Toyota's ten presidents, including Risaburo, its first, were taken by illness and forced to resign their posts. By whatever twist of fate, the trio of Taizo Ishida, Eiji Toyoda and Hiroshi Okuda, who followed on the heels of Toyota leaders who succumbed to health complications, worked wonders to vault Toyota through periods of transition, which they were all the more successful in doing perhaps owing to the fact that they took care of themselves.

On a national level, if a president or prime minister meets with an untimely death, the post cannot stay vacant for even a single day. In this respect, since businesses have executive officers other than the president who have the right of representation, the short-term absence of a president does not pose as dire a problem to a company's operations.

Out of consideration for Nakagawa, Ishida left the president's seat vacant until the company funeral service had been held. It was over two weeks later on October 30 that Eiji, now 54, was appointed successor president. It was only assumed that Eiji, as executive vice-president with the right of representation, would be bumped up if something happened to the president. Far from being deeply moved in anyway, nothing really changed much for Eiji in terms of his mindset as he moved up the ladder from managing director to senior managing director, then from executive vice-president to president.

What did change, however, was the way others saw him. Those around him perceived the president to be head and shoulders above the executive vice-president. Toyoda Automatic Loom Works, a small company run by the Toyoda family which Eiji had first joined, could hardly afford to employ any university graduates. At the time, the company had only two university-educated staff members other than Kiichiro: Eiji and Shoichi Saito. If these two did not take the initiative to get things done, the company came to a standstill. They worked like there was no tomorrow and, before they knew it, Toyoda Automatic Loom Works was an exemplary Japanese company in excellent standing.

Media outlets wrote of Eiji's accession to the presidency as *taisei hokan*, or the "restoration of power [to the Toyoda family]."[35] This surprised even Eiji. Seeing the term *taisei hokan* in big bold print made Eiji think, "Those newspaper reporters are really quite old-fashioned."

What really threw him off, however, was a question posed at the press conference immediately following his installment. "Were you chosen as the new president because you're a member of the Toyoda family?" he was asked. "I think I was chosen because I'm the best person for the job," Eiji retorted disconsolately.

Eiji was under no illusions. Ishida, after retiring to the position of chairman at an advanced age, had promoted executive vice-president Nakagawa and, when Nakagawa died suddenly, Eiji, as executive vice-president, was simply promoted to president. Knowing that his turn would eventually come, he had been preparing since Kiichiro resigned to take responsibility for the labor dispute. Ishida knew more than anyone that these were the circumstances behind the promotion and always responded in the following way in media interviews:

"I think Eiji is a superb president, period. Toyota suffered through a barrage of trials and tribulations from before until after the war, and Eiji was right there going through the whole thing during a time when it was said that Toyota could go under at any time. Our industry-

---

35. *Taisei hokan* is most often used in the context of restoring power to the imperial family.

leading productive capacity was Eiji's doing all the way. He's always casually slipping into his work garb and walking around keeping an eye on the plant. Take a look at the bottom of his leather shoes. They have shards of metal stuck in them. He knows everything there is to know about the factory, down to every last planted tree. There are no other executives at Toyota as intimately familiar with the company. That's precisely why he was able to make all the right decisions with capital investments as well. He's ahead of me as an expert in business, too, by now, and nothing makes me happier than to see this."

With Ishida sticking around as chairman, after Eiji's promotion to president senior managing director Saito was promoted to executive vice-president, while managing director Shoichiro was elevated to senior managing director. Shoichiro would now oversee the engineering department over which Eiji had previously had full authority. Ishida recognized the importance of the head of Toyota having a full grasp of everything from vehicle engineering to sales. Although neither Ishida nor Nakagawa were engineers, there was Eiji, whom everyone at the company perceived to be the president of the future. Ishida and Nakagawa had been in charge of the routine business affairs involved with running the company, while Eiji was actually the one who had always set Toyota's operations in motion.

At rival Nissan, however, the white-collar Katsuji Kawamata, since transferring over from the Industrial Bank of Japan, had studied ferociously to attain some degree of knowledge about cars, but with only a passing proficiency he was still nowhere near as well-grounded as Eiji in technological and engineering expertise.

A white-collar president would not be a problem if he were surrounded by top managers well-versed in the technical aspects of automaking. Yet, after Kawamata came to be referred to as emperor by his staff, it became a thorny issue for subordinate personnel to express opinions that went against Kawamata's own views. Before long, it became increasingly uncommon for engineering executives' objectives to be reflected in management policy.

The events leading up to the development of the aforementioned Sunny family car clearly demonstrate this. Be that as it may, that Nissan was able to contend for supremacy with Toyota during the motorization years was attributable to the fact that Nissan had the full support of the union led by Ichiro Shioji. There was also a time when the trust imbuing Nissan's labor-managemement relations, built on the personal relationship between Kawamata and Shioji, was celebrated as a symbol of Japanese-style management.

Even though engineers moved in to occupy the nucleus of Toyota management, since the break-out of the CB War between the Corona and the Bluebird, Nissan came be known in the public arena for its technology, while Toyota was noted for its sales. Toyota Motor Sales was pleased with this image. Lauding Toyota Sales for its marketing efforts, Eiji took the rather relaxed view that "cars don't sell well if they didn't have the technology."

Toyota was fortunate in that Eiji was not simply an engineering president. Before graduating from university, Eiji had been recommended by his supervisor to join Hitachi, but Kiichiro strong-armed Ejii into joining Toyoda Automatic Loom Works. Even if Eiji had joined Hitachi, he was planning to come to Toyota to work with automobiles sooner or later. But as it happened, Eiji got involved with automaking as Kiichiro's right-hand man right after joining the company, taking over the plant's operations for Kiichiro, who had developed an aversion to going to work during the Pacific War. Eiji had made many important decisions as a member of the management team during the arduous postwar years as well. Appointed to the board of directors at the age of 32, he had navigated through a minefield of potentially ugly scenes that he would not have had experience dealing with as a salaried businessman, emerging from the ruckus with a heightened sense of confidence.

A company must not deceive its employees

Famous for "squeezing water from a dry towel," a major component of Toyota's streamlining policy is a trusting labor-management relationship. No matter how much a company excogitates on the subject, without cooperation from the union, successful streamlining is a castle in the sky.

Far from stretching labor, "squeezing water from a dry towel" in Toyota's case denotes the rationalization of labor. In simple terms, it refers to when both a company and its employees pool their ideas together to dramatically cut down costs and eliminate all forms of waste.

Automobiles are assembled with over 20,000 parts. Therefore, the production process is massive. Eliminating losses incurred from wasteful or slow-moving work on each production line directly contributes that much more to the bottom line.

Eiji likens this to priming the well. "Squeezing water from a dry towel first requires squeezing your own wits dry," he says. "The towel will produce water if you wet if first. A well pump needs prime. By putting a little water in the pump, you get more water."

"The towel will produce water if you wet if first" means a company and its employees can cut down waste with frequent communication and by using their wits. The elimination of waste allows the company to accumulate profit, which is then returned to employees in the near future. Squeezing the towel (using your wits) produces water (ideas). The origin of this "priming the well" is the slogan "creative ideas," which Eiji came up with thanks to his studies at Ford.

In any case, cooperation from the union is imperative for squeezing that dry towel. Having experienced this first-hand, Eiji spent time building trust with the union. In 1962, the year after Nakagawa became president, mainly through Eiji's efforts Toyota drafted and signed a labor-management joint declaration. The declaration concluded:

"We, the company and the union, aware of the public nature of our mission in the automobile industry, vow to work together to take effective and appropriate measures to overcome imminent liberalization, to cooperate towards the generative development of Japanese industry and the national economy, and to contribute to the successful transition from Toyota Japan to World Toyota."

Having released the Publica the previous year, 1962 was the year that Eiji secretly told himself that he would make Kiichiro's dream a reality with the car he would develop next. He then came up with the concept for the Corolla. The labor-management declaration slipped in the term "World Toyota" to express Kiichiro's dream of "making a world-class compact passenger vehicle."

Eiji's mantra is that "a company must not deceive its employees." Father and son Sakichi and Kiichiro put family-like human relationships above all else. Eiji is the same when it comes to extended familism. Toyota's good traditions took a beating, however, with the prolonged economic downturn and devastation of spirit after the war.

When some Toyota executives found that the provisional

deposition filed in court to reach a settlement between labor and management during the strike of 1950 was incomplete, they jumped for joy, thinking that it would allow the company to win the case. But Eiji, overhearing this, reprimanded them for their misguided joy.

"Regardless of the law, we must honor the spirit of the memorandum Toyota once signed stating that it 'will not lay off personnel as a means for overcoming a crisis.' Sure, we're at the crossroads of winning or losing this dispute, but ignoring the memorandum just because it isn't a signed document and what not would be a grave act of betrayal against our company's union members and employees. It's nothing but deceit. Doing such a thing, even if the company wins the legal battle, will shake our employees' faith in the company and will create the possibility of trouble in the future."

Although the landmark labor dispute led Kiichiro to resign the presidency so that the union would accept personnel cutbacks, in the end neither labor nor management emerged with a victory. It was a painful draw. In the company history, Eiji describes his distress at the time: "People that I had worked together with all that time left one after another, while I stayed. It was more than enough that management and personnel had to go through it once. We have to make sure that the company never lays a hand on its employees again."

A labor-management council[36] was set up once the labor dispute came to a close, but this did not completely eliminate the struggles between labor and management. With the enactment of the Anti-Subversive Activities Law following the 1952 "Bloody May Day" incident, the political leaders of Japan's labor movement, headed by the Japanese Communist Party, went underground.

The labor movement turned from a political battle to an economic one. The automotive industry at the time was dominated by Nissan's labor union. For one thing, the leader of their union, overstating the case—"even if companies go under, the union will remain"—pushed ahead with a whole succession of demands that companies would never even begin to go for. Sabotage was rampant, and the public sneered that "they lived out a year in ten months."

Keeping pace with Nissan, Toyota's labor union also turned their demands into an economic battle. Meanwhile, since social order had been restored, Toyota management was looking into shifting from

36. *Roshi kyogikai*

a cost-of-living-based compensation pay system during inflationary periods to a skill-based pay system. Unwilling to accept the change over to a new pay system, negotiations with the union broke off without reaching an accord.

The labor dispute, which had evolved from a work stoppage at the assembly plant on June 11, 1953, escalated into a walk-out and the denouncement of the department head and plant manager. The company, however, upholding the principle of "no work, no pay" with regard to union activities during scheduled work hours, docked the wages of union members for the period of time they were absent from the workplace.

A feeling of war-weariness began to set in among embattled union members, giving rise to a feeling that nothing would be gained from extreme progressivism. Little by little, with increasing calls "not to repeat the major dispute of 1950 that claimed so many victims," labor-management negotiations started up on August 5, reaching a deal to end the 55-day stand-off.

After concluding the labor-management joint declaration, Toyota erected a monument to commemorate the statement that both sides had collaborated to draft. Kenya Nakamura, chief engineer of the Crown, later stated with deep emotion, "It's not easy to restore trust between labor and management once it has collapsed. Eiji spent ten whole years trying to rebuild the relationship. The relationship of mutual trust between labor and management was the mainspring that spurred Toyota's subsequent development."

This relationship of trust with respect to every facet of labor-management interaction indeed serves as the foundation of Toyota's development. It is precisely because these bonds of trust were in place that Taichi Ohno was able to create *kanban*, revive the Just-In-Time approach devised by Kiichiro, and then use it to establish the Toyota Production System.

Nissan's labor-management relations, on the other hand, departed significantly from the Shioji-led labor union early on during the tenure of Takashi Ishihara, who became president after Kawamata's successor retired. Ishihara's policy was that the "union should act like a union," but those years were incidentally the beginning of Nissan's descent.

Toyota transcends Japan's borders

Concerns about the delayed effects of Japan's bubble economy developed into a full-blown financial crisis in November 1998. U.S. credit rating agency Moody's downgraded Japan's yen-denominated domestic bonds one notch from "Aaa"—the rate with the highest certainty of making scheduled principal and interest payments—to "Aa1."

Of course, these ratings were not requested by the Japanese government but were an unsolicited credit rating. The Japanese government was indignant. Just the previous year, however, the failing Yamaichi Securities, one of the four largest securities firms in Japan, had voluntarily gone out of business, suggesting that a downgrade would be inevitable.

In conjunction with lowering Japanese government bonds, Moody's downgraded Toyota's long-term bonds from Aaa to Aa1. As with government bonds, of course, Toyota had not enlisted to be rated. Moody's operates with a tacit understanding that "a company's credit rating should not go beyond the credit rating of its country." The premise seems to be that "not even a well-performing company can transcend its national trappings," a thinking that comes perhaps from the U.S. itself being such an economic behemoth. The logic may be accepted in the U.S., but it can hardly be applied to companies that have transcended their national boundaries and risen to become international corporations.

Moody's, which rates another party's credit without the latter's consent, must offer a rationale that is acceptable not just to the company but to the public at large. Regarding Toyota's lowered rating, the explanation that Moody's offered was this: "Toyota is fixated on lifetime employment. Maintaining this system poses a risk to the future operations of the company."

This enraged then-president Hiroshi Okuda. Failing to subside with merely lodging a protest, Okuda's anger took him directly to Moody's main offices, where he demanded a convincing explanation.

The financial impact on Toyota from the credit downgrade was less than a billion yen per annum, even after including its overseas subsidiaries. It wasn't a serious blow, but Okuda was adamant. "A corporate bond rating is the ability to repay borrowed money, isn't it? Toyota can pay it all back tomorrow. In the short-term, we keep excess cash on hand rather than turn to money management techniques so we'll have liquidity just in case. If we can repay everything tomorrow, it goes without saying that we are triple-A."

What really set off Okuda was Moody's reason for the downgrade. Toyota's managerial ethos is to practice with an almost simple fidelity a Japanese style of management—respect for employees, obsession with product quality—put in place by Kiichiro and Eiji.

Lifetime employment—or long-term employment that continues until the mandatory retirement age—forms the very basis of TPS, which has become a byword in the world of manufacturing. Long-term employment is a basic precondition of the company's career development program that allows TPS to take root and figures prominently in Toyota's ability to train employees in the advanced technology necessary for making high-quality cars.

The term *anmokuchi* ("silent knowledge") is often used in Japanese business circles. It refers to the practices within a company that can't be found in written form, the totality of wisdom that hasn't been put into words. As Okuda puts it, "the hunches and knacks." No amount of reading can teach someone how to master this. Every day, Toyota's veteran skilled workers convey the essence of manufacturing to their younger counterparts, the company's next generation ("convey" often taking the form of yelling). Over time it all turns into production muscle.

In Japan as well, the prevailing social climate at the peak of the bubble economy in the early 90s nearly eroded respect for manufacturing. The misguided idea that "thanks to information technology (IT), formalized knowledge (*keishikichi*) can replace silent knowledge—hunches and knacks don't count for as much" began to run rampant.

Toyota takes full advantage of IT and makes active efforts to convert its implicit knowledge into explicit knowledge. But the rub for those who want to devalue the implicit is that unless there's a constant groundswell of it coming from the work floor, there won't be much to make explicit.

Manufacturing is such that it necessarily involves a remainder that cannot be subsumed by formalized knowledge. Renowned scholars at Harvard University and MIT have praised TPS as the "world's preeminent system" since before the bubble economy inflated across Japan. Inspired by this, engineers from the world's most influential automakers visited Toyota to see, listen and learn about TPS at the field level. They then happily took their lessons, along with a detailed TPS manual handed to them at the end, back to their home countries.

Each company clamored to adopt TPS expertise, but most were unable to master it. They failed to see that there's a world of silent knowledge on the floor that cannot be converted into IT. One cannot possibly gain an understanding of that world of hunches and skills, formed through years of experience, just by visiting a plant or carefully reading through a manual.

Take the final inspection line, for example: whether car bodies are distorted slightly, whether body curvature came out according to specifications. It's undetectable via IT. Veteran technicians at the work site can nonetheless determine whether something is "off" by feeling and caressing the body, then examining how it reflects light. Technicians cannot have the hunches and knacks for this without receiving intensive training through long-term employment.

In 1995, the year that Okuda became president, the Japanese economy reached a recessionary nadir as the bubble economy neared an end. A "no growth without restructuring (i.e., layoffs)" mindset pervaded Japan's automotive industry. During this time, Okuda didn't hesitate to give everyone a piece of his own mind.

"I'm against the thinking that says fewer people means more money."

"If you're happy that your company's share price firmed up thanks to laying people off, you're not qualified to manage a business."

"First of all, did the executives drive themselves till they puked to protect their employees' jobs?"

"If your business isn't doing well, don't fire your *employees*. Take responsibility, and the axe."

Okuda, who originally hailed from the former Toyota Motor Sales, showed with these comments that he'd inherited the DNA of the original Toyota entity with all its tribulations. Okuda interpreted Ishida's "protect your own castle" to mean "a chief executive should not trouble other people." These "other people" naturally includes employees.

In August 2003, five years after the downgrading, Moody's raised the long-term bonds of Toyota and its subsidiaries back up to the highest possible Aaa. There were two reasons for this. One was that the recessionary impact on fluctuations in Toyota's earnings and cash flow was minimal due to the fact that Toyota's operations were geographically dispersed. The other was that Toyota's financials were flexible and that the debt protection measures it kept in place allowed for continual cost-cutting. Moody's, however, had already been aware of these two factors when it downgraded Toyota.

Moody's clearly made a misevaluation. They did not understand that a globalized corporation transcends its nation of origin.

The U.S. Big Three, about which former Prime Minister Kiichi Miyazawa, who passed away in the summer of 2007, once said "the U.S. auto industry is the Stars and Stripes itself," have only continued to decline in the 21st century. The Chrysler division of DaimlerChrysler was sold off to American investment fund Cerberus.

What Cerberus saw in acquiring Chrysler is unclear. Temporarily regaining footing through plants closures and layoffs is one thing, but that alone would never allow it to pose much of a threat to Toyota.

Chapter 18
Waving the Presidential Flag

THE MANAGERIAL SYSTEM DURING THE presidential tenures of Taizo Ishida and Fukio Nakagawa employed a dualistic structure where the president handled practical business affairs, while Eiji Toyoda handled production and technology. But Toyota management harmonized once Eiji assumed control of everything after his promotion to president. A system evolved in which Toyota developed cars, invested in plant and equipment, selected the company's top brass, and moved forward based on the course Eiji had mapped out for the company.

Eiji's term as president lasted a full fifteen years until Toyota Motor Corporation and Toyota Motor Sales merged into a single company in July 1982. Toyota's decision-making system, in which important matters were not decided until Eiji gave his nod of approval, remained unchanged even after he gave up the presidency for the chairmanship.

Eiji, better acquainted with Toyota's struggles than anyone else at the company, and having served at the top for upwards of a half-century including his tenure as chairman and as advisor, may be liable to be seen as some kind of super-autocrat; yet, curiously, he hasn't acquired such an image.

Eiji's executive talent came down to this: he never imposed his own ideas and decisions on subordinates and yet was able to conduce things to go according to his plans. It was a skill he acquired gradually after he became a board member at the young age of 32 and needed to manage employees older than himself. The trick to skillfully employ older staff is humility. Eiji retained the trait throughout his career.

Ishida, Toyota's go-to man

A company's fate can hinge on a wave of the presidential flag—that is to say, an executive order. A company in which employees do not heed that banner will not develop. The burden of being at the top is that decisions must be made even in the absence of material upon which to base them. Inevitably, it's lonely at the top.

Eiji's stint as banner-waver of Toyota technology covered the development of the Crown and the Corolla. He laid solid foundations for auto manufacture by building the Motomachi Plant for the Crown. This was less than five years since Toyota's recovery from the brink of collapse; the company was still only pulling in ¥16 billion in annual sales. It was at such a time that they went ahead with a new plant capable of producing 5,000 passenger vehicles a month.

It was Eiji, too, who came up with the Corolla concept to fulfill the founder's dream, constructing two plants, for assembly and engines, with a monthly capacity of 20,000 cars. In retrospect, both projects were high-stakes wagers. As the man in charge, of course, Eiji spent countless sleepless nights, but the wager hit the jackpot and Toyota rode the Corolla onto the world stage.

Ishida allowed Eiji to wield such bold command because he understood his own role at the company: "My job is to make money. To make money, so Eiji can do something big."

The Crown and Corolla succeeded because Ishida supported Eiji's command and, rather than just follow along, pointed the way for Toyota, hollering at the head of the ranks that they needed to defend their own castle.

Ishida stayed on as chairman and continued chairing general shareholders meetings even after Eiji became president, but, unlike during Fukio Nakagawa's tenure, he hardly ever inserted himself into the company's management. Although he put in daily appearances at Toyoda Automatic Loom Works, the firm he claimed to be "my company," except for urgent business such as board of directors meetings he never went in to Toyota, the company he said was "entrusted to me by the Toyoda family." He took care of work for the Toyota Group from the "President's Office" in the Toyota Building across from Nagoya Station, but in effect he was enjoying a sort of easy retirement, no longer running around to secure funds.

Then came New Year's Day, 1971, three years and two months

after Eiji became president. At the annual New Year's press conference held in Akasaka, Tokyo, Ishida dropped a bomb on the journalists in attendance: "I've decided to resign the chairmanship and step down from day-to-day management at the general shareholders meeting on July 18."

The next day's newspapers proclaimed, "Toyota's savior to retire." But those who knew Ishida best did not believe the news and chose to speculate, "That was Ishida-san holding forth in his usual manner, I'm sure the July retirement was an inadvertent remark," or "There he goes, Ishida-san playing the funny man," or even, "It was probably a slip of the tongue engineered by a cross-examining press."

Yet, asked by a journalist at the after-party if he intended to begin a period of "cloister rule" as advisor, Ishida had quizzically replied, "Even during my own presidency, Toyota management was in Eiji's hands. My job was the scarecrow's, just chasing away the crows. Now that all the crows have been scared away, I think I'm taking a trip around the world." Ishida's resignation was approved at the June account settlement board of directors meeting. The very next day, he was gone—off on his trip around the world.

Within Toyota, Eiji was becoming the all-important presence, but chairman Ishida was still Toyota's face to the world. The general shareholders meeting at which Ishida's resignation from the board of directors became official was held on July 18, a significant date for Toyota. Ishida, out of character from his normally loquacious self, delivered an impassive greeting and handed over chairing duties to Eiji.

Eiji was asked by shareholders what Ishida's role would be from then on. He answered, "He will be chief advisor, like the go-to man of wisdom Okubo Hikozaemon, the samurai," prompting a round of thunderous applause. The vacant post of chairman would be filled by Eiji's close friend Shoichi Saito, who single-handedly took over the banquet duties and so forth that Eiji was never any good at.

Responding to the Nixon Shock

Ishida stepped down during a *Kanotoi* year (it leaves a remainder of 51 when the year on the Western calendar is divided by 60), traditionally synonymous with turbulent times. The Chinese revolution of 1911, led by Sun Yat-Sen to bring down the Manchu Dynasty and form the Republic of China, was coined the *Kanotoi* Revolution because it fell on such a year.

The year Ishida retired played host to a seismic event that shook not only Japan but the entire world. After the World Table Tennis Championships held in Nagoya in April of that year, the Chinese team invited the American team to visit China. The ensuing "ping pong diplomacy" served as the occasion for U.S. President Nixon to pay an unexpected visit to China on July 15, sending reverberations to every corner of the world.

One month later, on August 15, President Nixon announced an emergency new economic policy, the chief provisions of which were an across-the-board ten-percent import surcharge and the suspension of the dollar's convertibility to gold. This policy was referred to as the "Nixon Shock" in Japan, where the blow fell hardest.

Perhaps Ishida was lucky, or his intuitions were particularly sharp, but the Nixon Shock came just a month after his retirement. He had had no way of knowing that this would happen, of course, but he definitely got out while the getting was good.

Pincered by import surcharges and a de facto floating currency, the Japanese economy was expected to sustain major casualties. Toyota's exports to the U.S., a triad consisting of the Corona, the Hiace pickup and the Corolla, had attained monthly sales of 30,000 vehicles in the American market. Toyota was naturally concerned about the adverse effects of Nixon's policy, but Eiji took it in stride. Indeed, right after Nixon announced his policy, Eiji jumped his board of directors with a lecture on currency.

"Fixed exchange rates have been sustainable because the dollar was so incredibly strong," he said. "But if the dollar weakens, of course, the system will no longer hold up. What was strange was maintaining fixed exchange rates in the first place. At some point the yen is probably going to be converted to a floating system. That's the way it should be. Toyota must adapt to a floating exchange system and continue to make competitive cars."

Toyota's board members, rattled by the game-changing Nixon Shock, thus learned the essence of exchange courtesy of Eiji and came to realize that he was not just an engineer president but conversant in finance. A president au fait with both technology and economics was like "an ogre equipped with a metal bludgeon" as the Japanese expression goes—a potent combination. Eiji had made a point to talk foreign exchange to both reassure and rouse his staff, in a light hoisting of the presidential banner.

Just as Eiji had anticipated, the Smithsonian Agreement went into effect at year's end and the dollar depreciated against gold, and the era of the 360-yen dollar, which had persisted for half a century, came to an end. The yen rate was set at ¥308 per dollar, but this did not last long, either. Two years later, in 1973, dollar instability resurfaced and the Smithsonian Agreement came apart completely; the international currency regime entered an age of fluctuating exchange rates.

A grade school student interested in currency exchange

Eiji's familiarity with the top was not completely unrelated to his upbringing. His father Heikichi, Sakichi Toyoda's younger brother, had helped Sakichi with his work from a young age, and when Sakichi began producing looms Heikichi started a woven fabric and spinning mill in Nagoya that used them.

What sparked Eiji's interest in currency exchange was an experience he had when Heikichi took him to Shanghai over summer break during his second year in elementary school. At the time, Sakichi was busy building a factory for Toyoda Spinning and Weaving Works in Shanghai. In circulation were 10 sen silver coins, 1 sen copper coins, and 1 yen silver coins. The latter, about the same size as a U.S. silver dollar, was referred to locally as "one dollar."

The day Eiji arrived in Shanghai, he received 10 yen in pocket money from Sakichi. Upon exchanging the bill for 1 yen coins and putting them in his pocket, he found that they were nearly heavy enough to rip a hole in his pocket, making the sum seem all the more valuable. What Eiji found odd was that there were days in Shanghai when one 10 sen silver coin could be exchanged for eleven 1 sen copper coins, as well as days when it was worth only nine. In any case, it was strange that the rate would change every day.

He asked Sakichi, "Couldn't you make money if you got 1 sen copper coins on the days you get eleven, and 10 sen silver coins on days you need just nine?"

"That's exactly right. Eiji, unlike me, you've got a knack for business," Sakichi said in praise of his nephew. But when Eiji asked why it was that way, the prolific inventor could not come up with a convincing answer. With the unadorned thinking of a child, Eiji came up with his own interpretation: "1 sen coins cost more when a lot of people want them, and 10 sen coins cost more when that's what even more people want." This odd phenomenon in Shanghai left a lasting impression in the boy. He later learned that it was called currency exchange.

To run the spinning mill, Heikichi had to know the daily market rates for textiles. Eiji helped out at the mill once he reached the upper elementary grade levels. When the phone rang to inform them of the day's going rates, Eiji would often take the call if no one else was around.

Regardless of who had picked up the phone, the person on the other end of the line would rattle off the day's rates in rapid succession. Eiji had to jot it all down on paper. Not knowing what the figures meant in the beginning, he persistently asked office staff what they referred to. Annoyed by Eiji's tenacity, the clerks grudgingly told the youngster what it was all about. Having seen it all take place, one day Heikichi gave Eiji a problem to solve just for kicks. "The rate for cotton on the New York market is X cents," he said. "We are going to use the cotton to make thread, turn it into fabric, and then sell it to our neighbor China. Will we make a profit or not?"

To solve the problem, one had to know the exchange rate for dollars. The silver rate also came into play since China, the buyer, was on a silver standard. The silver rate was determined on London's silver bullion market. Since the rates in London were in pounds, one needed the cross-rate for pounds and dollars. Next, one had to calculate the whole thing taking into account the dollar-yen rate. This was taxing arithmetic even for an adult, but Eiji was solving worldly word problems like these since his last couple years of elementary school.

Eiji had taken the Nixon Shock in stride, but by September the impact from both the import surcharge and yen depreciation was all-pervasive. Sales volume dropped sharply, falling below the 17,000-vehicle mark in December. The number of cars exported to the U.S. in 1972 slid to 293,000, a year-on-year drop of 110,000 vehicles.

Despite this, Toyota's overall performance was relatively unaffected. Toyota recorded increased earnings and profits during both the period ending November 1971, just after the Nixon Shock, and the period ending May 1972 (both accounted semi-annually). Eiji kept his composure because the percentage of cars that Toyota exported to the U.S. was still not all that high. He knew that domestic sales would be able to absorb the shock.

Struggles over emissions regulations

One of the things that gave Eiji cause for concern at the time was meeting emissions standards. In the automotive empire of America, smog in the California area was already becoming a serious social issue around 1940, but action to prevent the problem from becoming more widespread was put off with the start of World War II.

Once the war ended and peace returned, the issue surfaced once again. Before long, the cause of the problem was pinned down to the photochemical reaction of carbon monoxide (CO), hydrocarbon (HC) and nitrogen oxide (NOx). These substances were included in the exhaust of factories and automobiles.

An upswell of activity in the U.S. on the part of a grass-roots movement led by Ralph Nader led to the enactment of the Clean Air Act in 1963. An amendment proposed by Democratic Senator Edmund Muskie focusing solely on auto emissions (commonly referred to as the Muskie Bill) passed through U.S. Congress in December 1970.

Senator Muskie wanted to roll back air pollution by requiring automakers to drastically reduce auto emissions. More specifically, the amendment called on automakers to cut CO, HC and NOx emission levels down to one-tenth that emitted in 1970—within five years.

U.S. auto industry was in an uproar over the numerical targets set out in the bill. It was common knowledge that, given the then-current level of technology, it would be impossible for automakers to scale back toxic exhaust by 90 percent in only a few years. This was when Jurassic full-sized vehicles were in vogue. The Big Three of GM, Ford and Chrysler signaled their adamant opposition.

Yet, despite the political clout of the Big Three, they could not buck the tide. It became clear that opposing the measure would brand them as public enemies. If a group of automakers managed to develop the technology to satisfy the standards, the remaining makers would be instantly ostracized.

The Muskie Bill movement had a significant impact on the

Japanese auto industry. Photochemical smog was discovered in Tokyo in the summer of 1970, the year before the Nixon Shock, turning auto emissions into a major social issue. In July 1971 the newly-formed Environmental Agency, seeing emissions as a serious threat, passed its own version of the Muskie Bill in line with regulatoy values in the U.S. as early as the next year. Japan's auto emissions regulations were considered to be the strictest in the world; the law stipulated that cars that did not meet the required standards by the deadline would not be allowed on the market.

The greatest challenge for automakers was coming up with measures to combat NOx. They would ultimately have to reduce emissions of the toxic substance down to 0.25 grams per kilometer traveled. Even if they did meet regulations, their efforts would all be for naught if vehicle performance suffered as a result.

The only car guy who derived any measure of pleasure from the emissions standards was Honda's founder Soichiro Honda. "This is Honda's chance to vault into the global market for four-wheel vehicles. Automakers around the world are all lined up on the same starting line. Technology isn't a matter of money. The world's automakers, lined up side-by-side, start running when the gun goes off. This kind of opportunity comes around once in a blue moon. Honda gets to go head-to-head with the world's major players based on ideas and effort alone. If it's a contest of technology, there's no way Honda can lose. Without fail, we'll design an engine that clears the Muskie Bill."

Soichiro, by building a low-emission engine before all other automakers, tried to rectify the blemishes to Honda's good name suffered during the previous year or two from withdrawing from F1 racing, the tumult surrounding the defective "N360" k-car, and slumping sales of the "H1300" car mounted with an air-cooled engine. Resolving to deliver a surprise blow to the older automakers, Honda's innate fighting spirit reared its head and he led the way in developing a low-emission engine.

In a meeting with the president of French Renault just after the Muskie Bill was passed, Eiji was asked his thoughts on the U.S. emissions regulations. "It's terrible," he replied. "It's a matter of life or death for automakers."

Renault's president seemed genuinely happy to hear this. "I can't do business with such a ridiculous country," he said, pouring it on nice and thick. "French Renault is going to halt exports to the U.S." And that is exactly what they did.

Although European countries still did see the need to institute regulations on auto emissions, Japan had already made it known publicly that it would pass a Japanese Muskie bill with the same numerical targets as the American version. Toyota would also have to adopt a serious stance toward auto emissions as it was beginning to become an issue of national health, but Eiji questioned whether Japan really needed regulations that copied the Muskie Bill ad verbatim. He hung it on the Environmental Agency to demonstrate that such restrictions were really necessary.

The agency responded only with a message stating that "it's better for the air to be clean than dirty." Eiji rearticulated his question. "Implementing measures to combat auto emissions will drive up the price of passenger cars. Is this desirable?"

"Money is no issue when it comes to people's health," the Environmental Agency responded, giving full rein to sentiment. "Money is no substitute for health."

Eiji agonized over the issue, eventually answering his own question. "Nothing will come of meeting the standards if vehicle performance falls off. A car won't create exhaust if it doesn't run, but if a car doesn't run it's no longer worthy of the name. They're cars, so we need to meet past performance standards as well as the regulatory values."

Eiji was also summoned by the Diet for his role as chairman of the Japan Automobile Manufacturers Association (JAMA). The more he explained how truly difficult it would be to meet regulations, the more Toyota was criticized as "dragging its feet on auto emissions regulations" and bashed by the media—"just shut up and clean up." The witch-hunt was on.

Developing all technology "inside"

Nevertheless, Toyota was not just sitting back and doing nothing about exhaust emissions measures. At Eiji's direction, Kiyoshi Matsumoto (later executive vice-president) and his team were on a quest for technology that could satisfy both regulatory values and performance quality. What especially got Matsumoto's attention was a catalytic converter. Eiji, too, had previously been interested in a catalytic converter that could maintain performance levels without requiring an overhaul of existing engines. The problem was how Toyota engineers, who knew only about machinery, might master catalytic technology.

In addition to catalytic converters, they were also looking into a lean-burning system that could stably burn homogeneous lean air-fuel mixtures by controlling combustion. But the system would not only not lead to improved mileage but also bring with it a number of issues that would complicate development and commercial viability, such as poor ignition and unstable combustion due to the leanness of the air-fuel mixture.

One of Eiji's trademark phrases was "do it 'inside.'" That meant "in-house." Matsumoto called in a university chemistry professor to explore the potential for catalysts and brought to light all available foreign literature on the topic. Although Toyota was leaning towards a catalytic converter as the technological answer to combating emissions, the company regrettably still did not have any engineers proficient in chemistry.

Matsumoto therefore went ahead and proposed to Eiji, "Catalysts are chemists' domain. Unfortunately, Toyota doesn't have any chemistry experts, so I was thinking about having a company that specializes in catalysts help us out. If that's not going to work, then I want to purchase catalytic technology."

"You said we could make catalysts work," Eiji objected. "No matter what it takes, we'll do it 'inside.' If we entrust critical technology to some party outside the company, we'll be in a fix when something goes wrong. In that regard, if we do it 'inside,' we'll at least have some way to deal with it. When we're not sure of an outcome, we can't entrust risks to outside parties."

Eiji thus flapped the presidential banner in favor of the catalytic method as a measure to control emissions. Matsumoto was in fact overjoyed that Eiji understood and embraced the method he had proposed. He went out on a limb and promised, "I'll stake my pride as an engineer on this."

Eiji held firmly to the idea of doing things "inside." Auto emissions regulations were not only about clearing regulatory values. Toyota would also have to weigh fuel economy, driving performance, serviceability, cost, and so on and so forth. Catalytic agents were highly sensitive to external conditions and, unlike in the apparatuses used in chemical engineering, their use conditions fluctuated widely when applied to automobiles.

Although joint development was also an option, a company specializing in catalysts might know all about catalysts but not be familiar with automotive technology. Toyota would then have to school the catalyst manufacturer in the ABCs of autos. As the compliance schedule for emission controls was already set, Toyota could not exactly take its time getting around to a solution. In the end, it might be quicker if Toyota's engineers studied up on catalysts from scratch. In the long run, the resulting technology would be an asset for Toyota. It was in December 1971 that Toyota decided to develop its own catalytic converter as a measure for reducing auto emissions. At that point, only two companies, Toyota and GM, were focusing their attention on catalysts.

Toyota charged into development full steam ahead but, plagued by many different lines of cars, the prospects for meeting emissions standards with every one of their models was not looking good. Even if something worked in the labs, immediate commoditization wasn't guaranteed. Moreover, even if, say, the Corolla could be made to meet regulatory values without losing performance, the same technology might not be applicable wholesale to the Crown.

The Environmental Agency held a hearing in May 1973. Honda, which had developed a CVCC (Compound Vortex Controlled Combustion) engine the previous year, and Toyo Kogyo (now Mazda), which had concentrated its efforts on the rotary engine, indicated that they would be able to meet the final NOx regulations. Toyota was close to compliance on a number of its models but wasn't ready to certify that every one of its models would be in compliance. Eiji's thinking was that "it was a matter of responsibility for a company to distinguish clearly between success at the lab level and at the commoditization level."

Public criticism centered on Toyota. "How come Honda and Mazda say they can but not leading maker Toyota?"

What really put Toyota in a bind was that Eiji was concurrently serving as JAMA chairman. As the chairing company of the association, Toyota would have to keep pace with the industry. Matsumoto's daily progress reports began to inspire Eiji's confidence in catalysts, but, alas, time was running short.

As far as Toyota itself was concerned, any vehicle models that weren't meeting the standards could just be temporarily discontinued so the company could announce compliance. However, such a move would put the industry's stragglers in a highly precarious position. The chairing company could not afford to make careless remarks.

While Honda and Mazda announced their projected compliance, chairing company Toyota had, really, one option only: being the bad guy.

Chapter 19
Virtue out of Vice

EMISSIONS REGULATIONS INCLUDED IN THE Japanese Muskie Bill called for a two-phase reduction of both CO (carbon monoxide) and HC (hydrocarbon) by fiscal 1975 and NOx (nitrogen oxide) by fiscal 1976 down to one-tenth the levels emitted in 1970. The seconds were ticking as the enforcement period drew near.

Doubling as Toyota president and chairman of JAMA, Eiji requested an extension of the deadline at hearings held both at the Diet and the Environmental Agency, but the more he tried to justify it, the more Toyota was seen as "dragging its feet on emissions regulations."

"The catalytic converter will definitely be our answer to emissions," Eiji thought, "but unfortunately it'll take a considerable amount of time before it becomes commercially viable. If we get hung up on the catalytic converter as our only option, however, Toyota will be forced out of the market." A panic-stricken Eiji had Toyota engineers explore the feasibility of a lean combustion system or developing something other than reciprocal engines, such as a gas turbine engine, rotary engine or an electric vehicle in addition to their current work with catalysts. In the meantime, Eiji temporarily put a lid on his policy to "do everything 'inside,'" saving face be damned, and paid a visit to Soichiro Honda at Honda's Yaesu headquarters just before Soichiro's self-decreed retirement to propose that Honda license its CVCC engine technology to Toyota.

Catalysts improve gas economy

In the end, Toyota somehow sailed safely through to comply with 1975 regulations with an "oxidation catalytic converter," which uses an air pump to feed oxygen into the engine. The problem now would be 1976 regulations.

The Environment Agency held another hearing in June 1974 to get an idea of how automakers were coming along. The main purpose was to see what kind of numerical targets companies would be able to meet.

"At the present stage, we're still nowhere near achieving the regulatory values for all our vehicles," one of Toyota's technical directors stated cautiously, based on Eiji's capacity as chairman of the Automobile Manufacturers Association. "To productize our emissions systems, we will need a preparatory period of several years once things start looking more promising at the experimental stage." He also requested, rather too hopefully: "We would like to ask that you continue the 1975-level regulations for a few more years and then take an across-the-board look at improvements in air pollution, technological advances, and changes in the social landscape to determine new targets." The request was made not so much for Toyota's sake as out of responsibility as JAMA chairman to do what could be done to avoid leaving some automakers behind.

Based on findings from the Central Council for Environment Pollution Control, the Environmental Agency reached a difficult decision in February 1975. They would extend for another two years the deadline to meet 1976 regulations. As a stopgap measure for the interim period, they also announced new 1976 regulations that would require NOx emissions levels to be cut to 0.6 grams per kilometer traveled.

Although the 0.6g target was still strict, in addition to the catalytic converter and CVCC engine, Toyota was already close to meeting standards with its lean combustion engine. Despite an extention of two years, however, keeping NOx emissions under 0.25 grams would be virtually impossible. Toyota had known early on that the oxidization catalytic converter would not cut it. On the other hand, it would be an unreasonable stretch to install a CVCC engine in all of Toyota's vehicles.

After a battle against unforgiving odds, Matsumoto's solution was a three-way catalytic converter that reduces or oxidizes the three toxic substances by using precious metals such as platinum and rhodium. As this method creates less of a strain on the engine, it would not only maintain driving performance but also improve fuel consumption if done well. The main drawbacks were the high prices of precious metals and whether Toyota would be able to maintain a stable supply. Eiji, believing that catalysts were a sure-fire way to curtail emissions, jumped at the idea, saying, "We'll find a way to get a hold of the precious metals. Since we're going to use such valuable metals, find a way to boost fuel economy and driving performance even if only by a little bit."

Toyota, staking the company's very existence on three-way catalysts, jumped right into development. The technology evolved at a very rapid clip. The efforts of its engineers paid off as Toyota, with the release of the Crown, Mark II and Chaser in June 1977, became the first in its field to bring all of its vehicles in conformance with 1978 regulations by the deadline. And just as the "Toyota's dragging its feet on auto emissions" line began to wear off, Toyota was criticized for having said they could not do it when they really could.

Although vehicles conforming to 1975 and 1976 regulations suffered a decline in driving performance and fuel economy, those in line with 1978 regulations had improved fuel economy and performance just as Matsumoto had anticipated. Toyota had made virtue (better mileage and performance) out of vice (auto emissions regulations mandated by pollution).

Emissions regulations had thus brought Toyota better fortune than they would have had otherwise. As the first oil crisis occurred just after the 1975 regulations took effect, sending crude oil prices soaring, Japanese cars flew out of dealership lots all around the world. Inexpensive and fuel-efficient Japanese cars such as those of Toyota were lionized as efficient economy cars particularly in the U.S., facilitating a quick recovery in price competitiveness after a setback in the wake of the Nixon Shock and spurring on further growth in exports of Japanese cars to the American market.

In 1970, the year that Toyota began full-fledged efforts to counteract auto emissions, it employed 519 researchers and spent ¥2.8 billion on research. These numbers had swelled to 1,567 and ¥12.2 billion by 1973, then to 2,250 and ¥27.3 billion by 1976. One of the reasons Toyota was able to meet emissions standards was that it spared no expense in channeling people and money into the project.

Eiji's investment did not go to waste. He continued to pour generous amounts of money and manpower into research thereafter, developing a new engine equipped with an ultra-lean combustion control system utilizing electronic technology. Toyota's efforts to prevent the release of exhaust as much as possible at the engine stage brought them within reach of meeting regulations with oxidizing catalysts alone.

What was so ground-breaking about this engine was that it greatly improved fuel economy by ensuring stable combustion even with lean air-fuel mixtures. Moreover, Toyota would be able to keep prices down by not using precious metals. Toyota adopted this system in May 1984 for use in the new FF (front engine, front-wheel drive) layout of the Carina.

Honda's CVCC engine, the first in the world to meet emissions standards, never established a global trend because its combustion configuration was so complex that the surface area of the combustion chamber underwent significant heat loss, thus causing a decline in horsepower. Before long, the development-based automaker Honda stopped using this system entirely, changing over to the catalytic method. Just as Eiji had prognosticated, the catalytic method became the predominant strategy for counteracting auto emissions.

After meeting standards, Toyota got down to work on improving fuel consumption. In 1997, a quarter-century after the passage of the Muskie Bill, Toyota would release the Prius, the world's first hybrid vehicle, to combine electricity with a gasoline engine.

Toyota cuts output, while Mazda ramps up production significantly

The first oil crisis struck in October 1973, just as the battle over emissions regulations came to a head and Eiji was summoned to the Diet.

Looking back on it now, this was an anomalous year from the very start. With the Japanese economy at the time threatening to overheat, automobiles were selling left and right as fast as they could be produced. At the same time, however, a series of explosions at chemical plants halted production of chemical products. Due to a shortage of tire materials, for a time many cars were driving around without a spare tire. Cars continued to sell regardless.

The "if you make it, it will sell" economy persisted well into the summer, prompting a shortfall of labor at the production site, which Toyota compensated for by having dealers send extra hands to help sustain production. Meanwhile, materials began to dry up as the months wore on and, by early autumn, they stopped coming in altogether.

Then, in the middle of all this, the Yom Kippur War broke out on October 6. Although the skirmish came to an end in a relatively short period of time, OPEC member nations seized the occasion to go on the offensive and drive up the price of oil, sending crude prices soaring and setting off the first oil crisis.

Not only did gas prices rocket to stratospheric levels, but neon signs in Japan's downtown districts went out and people were asked to voluntarily refrain from using their cars. A supermarket scramble for toilet paper also ensued; detergents disappeared from store shelves, and for those waiting to get a hold of some, what had previously sold for ¥100 was now upwards of ¥200 to ¥300. Prices rose almost overnight not only for petroleum-based products but also for everything else, breeding a maelstrom of chaos in ordinary people's lives.

Exhausting all possible means to scare up materials, Toyota somehow managed to get back operating at full capacity within the year but, unable to bear the astronomical price of materials, the company twice hiked the prices of its existing lines, once in December 1973 and then again in January 1974, rather than change models. This was the only time before or after that Toyota raised prices instead of changing models.

Sales fell off sharply as payback for the markups. Hit with the double whammy of a rise in both the price of gas and the price of new cars, consumers held off buying cars, sending the automotive market into a tailspin. Dealer inventory had been piling up since just before the second round of price hikes, inducing Toyota to shift its stance and significantly cut production. Extending through February and March, scaled-back production lasted just under three months.

In contrast to Toyota's move to slash output, one automaker dramatically increased output. This automaker was Toyo Kogyo (now Mazda). "The shortage of materials due to the oil crisis is a temporary phenomenon," Mazda president Kohei Matsuda said luridly at a press conference in the beginning of the year. "It'll work itself out by early spring. Mazda's been stockpiling materials in preparation for ramping up production after the turn of the new year. While increasing production, we will sequentially replace the engines of all our passenger cars with rotary engines (RE) to meet emissions regulations."

German companies NSU (now Audi) and Wankel held the basic patent for the rotary engine. The engine, which used a rotor instead of pistons, stood out for the high speed at which it operated as compared to a reciprocal engine. GM and Mazda were the first ones to latch on to this engine. Although Eiji never thought that the RE would edge out the reciprocal engine, if GM had already bought the license and begun investigating its uses, the engine had to count for something. So as an insurance policy, Toyota purchased the rights to use the engine from the two German companies and moved forward with research. This, of course, was prior to the emergence of emissions standards.

Once research was actually underway, however, Toyota found out that Mazda held all application rights to the engine. As long as Toyota did not have access to these rights, it could not productize the RE in its vehicles. Just as this was going on, Toyota came across information that GM had decided to pay Mazda $50 million in royalties to obtain application rights for the purpose of installing the RE in its Vega sports cars. GM had also built a plant specifically for the RE and ordered the necessary production machinery. This was an era when the global automotive industry revolved around GM. It was a very real possibility that the RE would come to dominate the industry if GM followed up the Vega with a whole line of other RE vehicles.

Given this, Toyota rushed into negotiations with Mazda. Talks expanded from the initial plan simply to buy application rights to the RE to purchasing the stand-alone engine. Negotiations began to traverse a difficult path once Mazda asked Toyota to supply the Crown's body in return.

Then came the oil crisis. Toyota scrapped the productization of the RE based on its poor fuel economy, essentially ending talks with Mazda. Almost coincidentally, GM also abandoned the rotary engine and President Cole resigned to take responsibility. In a terrible stroke of misfortune, Cole later died in a plane crash.

What had thrown off Kohei Matsuda's judgment was the oil crisis. Although the main selling point of the rotary engine—

developed at great risk to the company—was the high velocity at which it operates, the engine's poor combustion efficiency due to the sharp angles of its crescent-shaped combustion chamber prevented it from emitting NOx. Had it come at a time when gas was cheap, the engine would have given Mazda an insurmountable advantage with its high performance and potential effectiveness as a measure to reduce emissions. Kohei had ramped up production based on the belief that, "once the oil crisis abated and gasoline prices returned to their former levels, people would take another look at the rotary engine as the odds-on solution for reducing emissions and give rise to a rotary boom."

Just after Kohei initiated a massive increase in RE vehicle production, the U.S. Environmental Protection Agency (EPA) declared RE vehicles to be "gas guzzlers." As the oil crisis had quadrupled crude oil prices in a very short period of time and consumers were sensitive to gas prices, sales first fell off sharply in the U.S. market, a situation which then spilled over into Japan, plunging Mazda into a full-blown financial crisis in no time at all.

While Mazda sales slowed down, Toyota completed its inventory adjustments, turned around and boosted production significantly in April. The Corolla was the principal component of this increased output. After peaking at 1,564,700 vehicles in 1973, Toyota's domestic sales went downhill in 1974. It wasn't until 1979—six years later—that Toyota surpassed the level of performance it had achieved in 1973. During this period, the Corolla alone kept on selling like hot cakes.

In the meantime, however, Toyota began throwing its strength into exports due to stagnant domestic sales in the wake of the oil crisis. Exports shot past the one-million mark in 1976, going from 720,000 vehicles in 1973 to 1.18 million in 1976. In addition, Toyota's export ratio rose to 47.6 percent. This went on to exceed 50 percent in 1980. By 1984, Toyota had exported a total of over 1.8 million vehicles.

The Toyota Production System is born

All the dry, innocuous stats came with an intriguing subplot. Through the process of weathering emissions standards and the first oil crisis, Toyota had built the foundation for taking a big leap forward into the rest of the world.

It was in order to survive even with a limited quantity of manufactured vehicles that Taichi Ohno originally worked out a rationalization technique using *kanban* to completely eliminate waste. Ohno first introduced the system at the main machinery plant at which he served as plant manager. Eliminating overproduction at each process and averaging out production for all processes through the use of *kanban* enabled highly efficient operations using limited equipment and personnel.

He used the same *kanban* at the machinery plant even with the delivery of parts from parts suppliers. But suppliers were slow on the uptake of Ohno's intentions for using the system, with some leveling the criticism that "the *kanban* system allows Toyota to produce with little inventory, while all the excess inventory puts a strain on parts suppliers."

This type of misunderstanding is sure to emerge from companies who adopt the *kanban* system in form only rather than improve their own method of production. Ohno therefore took it upon himself to explain to these companies with dogged persistence that they could improve their production methods if they were to take the same approach as Toyota; he would help guide the companies through the process to boot. The misperceptions and criticism faded as *kaizen*, or modification and improvemement, gradually began to produce results for both Toyota and its parts suppliers. It was only in the 1970s that the series of rationalization measures based on the *kanban* system came together into a system that integrated all the companies. This fundamental approach and body of streamlining techniques were duly systematized and named the Toyota Production System (TPS).

At the same time, Toyota created the Operations Management Consulting Division within the Production Management Department as a framework for implementing TPS expertise not only within the company but with respect to parts suppliers as well. Current chairman Fujio Cho volunteered to join the Operations Management Consulting Division under Ohno's tutelage. When Toyota built a factory in Kentucky on its own initiative following the joint venture with GM, Cho was chosen to head up the new plant because he aimed to firmly entrench TPS in the United States.

The *kanban* system, initiated as a method for improving performance by eliminating even minimal amounts of waste, was also extremely effective for expanded mass production. While increasing output day in and day out throughout the late 1960s, Toyota established the Kamigo, Takaoka, Miyoshi, Tsutsumi and Myochi plants in rapid succession, implementing TPS as each one got up and running.

Toyota reached a turning point when it geared down production in the immediate aftermath of the oil crisis. At Ohno's direction, Toyota undertook a comprehensive review of all of its plants and equipment from the standpoint of "whether costs could go down when production stalls." The company first put a freeze on all capacity-building investments that were currently in the works. Switching over from a large-scale production model to a type of management geared towards low growth, Toyota kept capital investment at a minimum to facilitate the change in models. More specifically, Toyota thoroughly abandoned the "it would be good to have" approach in favor of limiting capital investments to that which "production would be impossible without." Although in the past Toyota would quickly bolster plants and equipment whenever capacity was insufficient even on production lines at facilities that were already up and running, from this point on they tried to outride the capacity shortfall by increasing the *kadoritsu*, or operational availability, of existing facilities.

Kadoritsu is a term specific to Toyota that means making equipment available whenever it is needed. The Toyota Production System does not attach as much importance to the more general term *operating rate* than it does operational availability. The reason for this is that it makes more sense to leave equipment idle than to increase the operating rate and create waste. This was no less than a Copernican shift in thinking.

The head banto enters the foray

Ohno's was a thankless job, as it were, with very few opportunities to stand at the center stage of management when it came to announcing new releases and giving press conferences. Meanwhile, Masaya Hanai lived up to his name demonstrating exceptional ability as Eiji's number two man.

The distinguishing feature of Toyota management is how it follows the uniquely Japanese *banto* system.[37] A *banto*'s job is not

---

37. *Bantosei* is a system in which head butlers/clerks are responsible for a family's

simply money man or the president's assistant. This person must keep a sharp eye on all aspects of management and step in for top leadership and take over management if the situation calls for it. Tojiro Okamoto filled this role before the war, while Hisayoshi Akai, scouted by Okamoto from Mitsui & Co, did it during and after the war.

It was most regrettable for Toyota to lose Akai in a car accident in the winter of the final year of the war. Toyota settled on one of Kiichiro's friends from the University of Tokyo as his replacement but, when he proved unable to perform the duties inherent to a *banto*, the position was ultimately left vacant, leading the company to the brink of collapse and forcing Kiichiro's resignation.

Chosen to succeed Kiichiro as president was Taizo Ishida, a true *banto* of the Toyoda family, similar to Okamoto. Although former banker Fukio Nakagawa was the guardian of the Toyota vault during Ishida's tenure as president, Nakagawa was merely a money man— not a *banto*. Ishida had acceded to the president's seat on a temporary basis until Kiichiro was to return, but because of Kiichiro's untimely death just before his reinstatement Ishida continued to stay on as president under the understanding that he do so until the next capable individual from the Toyoda family could step up.

The cushion to the money man's seat was then passed to Hanai, managing director in charge of accounting, when Eiji became president consequent upon Nakagawa's sudden passing. A money man holds vast powers over a company's financial expenditures, including capital investment. Since adopting advanced technology involves a great deal of capital investments in plant and equipment, which technologies to adopt is an issue that requires input from outside the engineering department as well. The lot of Toyota's financial watchdog is to know exactly what is going on in the finance department and to constantly work to increase retained earnings. Hanai was the perfect man for the job.

The only two people in Toyota's seventy-year history who have risen from executive vice-president to chairman are Shoichi Saito and Hanai. Saito was Eiji's so-called "comrade-in-arms" who shared in Toyota's multitudinous hardships since the days of its inception. Eiji

business affairs. Without titles such as general manager or managing director, all top managers, with the sole exclusion of the president, are eligible to become *banto* (Nagashima, Soichiro; Niche Marketing: 60 Success Stories, APO, 2007).

gave him the title of chairman to reward him for his service.

Prior to the oil crisis, Hanai lived in Tokyo wrapped in a veil of relative obscurity, hidden from view in the shadow of executive vice-president Masao Yamamoto, but he quickly cut a fine figure for himself after Yamamoto moved out to become chairman of Daihatsu. The springboard for Hanai's "promotion" from money man to *banto* came at the end of 1972 when Saito, taking over the chairmanship left vacant upon Ishida's retirement, essentially stepped down from day-to-day management.

Squeezed by the emissions issue, Toyota was also at wit's end with the runaway price of materials due to the first oil crisis. With his concurrent duties as chairman of the Automobile Manufacturers Association, Eiji was under pressure to deal with the issue without delay. As such, he had at most three hours a day to spend attending to company business. During this time, Hanai stepped in to manage as Eiji's right-hand man.

Hanai single-handedly took over for Eiji in terms of responding to media requests with respect to the emissions issue. What set Hanai apart from other directors was how he came to Eiji's rescue by saying the things that Eiji wanted to say but was not at the liberty of saying in his position.

Perhaps because he was an old engineering hand, Eiji had a limited command of vocabulary and often lacked expressiveness. In this sense, Hanai was as eloquent as he was competent, giving him all the right qualifications as Eiji's spokesman. Hanai's words was backed by Eiji's approval.

Although he was perfectly suited to be Toyota's spokesperson, Hanai's primary task was to drive home the streamlining policy of "squeezing water from a dry towel" from the perspective of accounting and purchasing. During the period when materials were appreciating rampantly following the oil crisis, Hanai had accounting staff who worked under him go over every square centimer of the plant premises with a fine-tooth comb to conduct thoroughgoing cost-accounting.

What cemented Hanai's reputation was a series of negotiations over price increases on steel products that took place after the oil crisis. In response to how blast furnace steel manufacturers such as Nippon Steel Corporation pushed the "Inayama Theory," a theory long argued by Nippon Steel Chairman Yoshihiro Inayama that "price = costs + the appropriate profit," the auto industry developed the Hanai Theory that "price minus costs = profit." This was to say that companies should cut costs rather than raise prices.

In negotiations that took place in 1975, Hanai broke steel makers away from their law of uniform pricing whereby the per-tonne price was the same for both low-volume and bulk purchases. This, the steel industry had held to obstinately in the past. In 1977, Hanai also bargained big steel down from their marked-up prices to official market prices. Watching how Hanai worked, Nippon Steel's Inayama regretted not having someone like Hanai at his own company.

While Eiji and Hanai were teased by media as being "identical twins," Eiji rewarded Hanai for his achievements by promoting him from executive vice-president to chairman in 1978. Hanai was always in the habit of saying "Toyota's chairman is the president's minus." In other words, Hanai's role was to tell Eiji outright whenever Toyota went too far and to bluntly say the kinds of things to him that anyone else would have hesitated to say. He became what one might call Eiji's best critic.

Chapter 20
The Global Compact Car Wars

T HERE ARE TIMES WHEN COMPANIES have to go into hibernation to prepare for their next big expansion. The equivalent for Toyota was the period starting in the late 1970s, when the company took aim at meeting emissions standards, until the 1980s. But rather than holing up in a den like a bear, this was a time when Toyota was getting ready for the global car war that had engulfed automakers in the U.S. and Europe.

Toyota's hibernation policy was based on a two-pronged strategy to formulate a system whereby the company could generate profits while operating at 80 percent capacity, as well as diversifying its financial policy.

The rationale for operating at 80 percent was to build an operational structure that could be quickly mobilized to increase or decrease production in the event of an unforeseen contingency such as an oil crisis. Toyota takes an annual one-week summer holiday in August; with fewer operating days, the operating rate drops to 80 percent. As a matter of course, the month always showed a deficit. Yet, in August 1977, Toyota recorded its first surplus, albeit a slight one. Seeing this, Masaya Hanai issued a rallying cry: "If we're operating in the black at 80 percent capacity in August, then let's do it at 70 percent capacity in other months."

In financial terms, Toyota finished redeeming its bonds in June 1978, becoming the first debt-free company among major Japanese corporations. Then, after raising capital by issuing new shares at market price, Toyota's capital adequacy ratio rose to 61.4 percent by the end of June 1982, while excess cash that Toyota could use at its own discretion reached ¥578.9 billion. To put these excess funds to effective use, the company began to invest the money carefully and meticulously in a way that underscored safety and profitability, inaugurating the so-called investment-based "Toyota Bank." The first "president" of the newly founded "bank" was of course Hanai, who had become Toyota's chief *banto*. His philosophy was that "Toyota's excess cash is a contingency fund, so we will invest it only on a short-term basis so as to have liquidity at any point. Toyota's foundation will be rock-solid once excess cash reaches two trillion yen."

Then, in September 1979, just as the global car war was finally getting underway, "Toyota's savior," Taizo Ishida, passed away at the age of 90. The next year, Toyota Motor Sales's Shotaro Kamiya, praised as the "god of sales," died in December 1980 at the age of 82, while Shoichi Saito, Eiji's confidante, passed away in October 1981 at 73. The flurry of deaths among Toyota elders poignantly reminded everyone affiliated with the company that times were changing—and they were changing fast.

The Big Three's world car strategy

The two oil crises were what triggered the global car war. Before the scars from the first oil crisis could heal, in December 1975 President Gerald Ford signed the Corporate Average Fuel Economy regulations. Effective from 1978, the main provision of this bill was to implement fuel economy regulations requiring automakers to increase the average mileage per gallon of gasoline to 22.5 miles—standard for Japanese cars—by 1985, the final year of the bill. Automakers who failed to meet this standard would be levied a surcharge. The Big Three, who produced a large percentage of full-sized vehicles, would need to shift to compact cars to meet the regulatory values. In other words, downsizing.

At this point, there would be no avoiding a car war from flaring up between Japanese and American automakers with the U.S. market as the battlefield. With its broad base of component and parts manufacturers, the automotive industry is tied in with issues of national security for the United States. If it became clear that the Big Three were lagging behind, there was an undeniable possibility that the U.S. government would move to restrict Japanese car imports.

The Big Three would invest a tremendous sum: $80 billion,

three times that poured into the Apollo Program to send people to the moon. Ford president Caldwell called this the "largest and deepest industrial revolution in a time of peace."

Top automaker GM started things off with a bang, announcing an initiative to transition over to compact cars. Investing $50 million, GM would develop a series of cars, starting with the 3000cc-class "X Car," followed by the 1500cc "T Car" and finally the 1000cc "S Car," with plans for annual production of one million vehicles each.

Although GM's world car strategy was a measured response to U.S. fuel economy regulations, at the same time GM was predisposed to waylaying imported cars such as those from Japan. GM's basic strategy hinted at a world car concept that the company would produce and mass-market not only in the U.S. but also at its subsidiaries scattered around the world.

Japanese automakers were quaking with trepidation at GM's world car concept. Toyota may have been Japan's leading company, but it paled in comparison to GM on all fronts. After all, its sales were still only one-fifth that of GM's and brought in only one-sixth of its profits.

Prior to the announcement of fuel economy regulations, the U.S. market clearly pigeonholed the Big Three into the category of full-sized cars and Japanese and European cars into the category of compact cars, a symbiotic relationship of co-prosperity. If GM were to storm the compact car market monopolized by Japanese and European carmakers on the back of its vast material resources, intense competition between Japanese, American and European automakers would be inevitable. The Big Three may not have had any experience in compact cars, but their latent potential was a force to be reckoned with.

The media spoke a "global compact car war" and the "Japan-U.S. compact car war." Masaya Hanai, having been promoted to Toyota chairman, agreed with the media and treated it as a war. Hanai spoke in February 1980 of the nature of war at a gathering of one thousand frontline managers in the large hall of the Toyota Kaikan Exhibition Hall:

"At first I thought the global compact car war was merely a sort of compact-car competition," he said to the gathered crowd. "Recently, however, I've had a change of thinking. It's a war. Losing in a competition, you can get by with a shuffle in the rankings. But a war's a life-or-death struggle. A disastrous outcome lies in wait for the vanquished; either become a vassal (subsidiary) or be killed (bankruptcy)."

Hanai, however, was not exactly pessimistic about the upshot of the war that was beginning to rumble. "I'm treating the global car war as a chance for Toyota to take a big leap forward," he said. "Rather than just accept that the compact car market—Toyota's forte—is going to be devoured by the Big Three's world cars, we'll expand the compact car market even more with a bit of hard work. This sets an even greater stage for Toyota's advance."

Toyota meted out a number of additional hibernation initiatives to come out on top of the war. At the core of all of them was further cost-cutting. Hanai with his pet phrase—"Toyota's chairman is the president's minus"—spearheaded cost-cutting. Hanai's stance, however, was in sync with Eiji's: rationalization in the vein of "squeezing water from a dry towel."

A combination of the two oil crises prompted all Japanese companies to work towards cutting costs. While many were definitely seeing good results, others cried out that they were squeezing the towel for all it was worth but weren't gaining a single drop more.

"Japan has a high humidity," Hanai would counter coolly. "Even a parched towel will become sopping wet over time."

What Hanai was trying to say was that there are many ways to streamline with a slight change of perspective; for example, switching from a cost-cutting campaign pursued through a vertical office organization to a more cross-sectional approach. Technology will continue to advance during the intervening period, enabling cost-cutting that had been impossible in the past. As time passes, this allows for some breathing space. Even a dry towel will naturally get wet over time.

One of the remarkable things about Toyota is that it makes good on its promises. A typical example of this was the 1978 "Corolla ¥10,000 cost-cutting campaign." To realize its objective, Toyota attempted to cut costs not up and down the ladder but cross-sectionally instead. The company's design garrison thought out ways to cut costs within their own territory of expertise. The plant devised ways to implement a more efficient workflow.

Setting the initial goal of cutting a total of ¥10,000 per car, the production, engineering and purchasing departments were assigned several thousand yen each. In the end, they exceeded their goal, successfully cutting costs by ¥12,000. As Toyota was producing around 800,000 vehicles annually just in Japan at the time, this campaign alone led to a streamlining of nearly ¥10 billion.

The Toyota chief executive tends to know the difference between rationalization and decrement management inside out. Decrement management leads to a contractionary equilibrium, which at some point will enter a blind alley. On the other hand, since rationalization is a way to eliminate waste, assuming unlimited will and knowledge, it can continue ad infinitum.

The rationalization methods that Hanai took the initiative to implement were based on the creative ideas suggestion system that Eiji picked up from Ford and subsequently introduced at Toyota. There were a total of 530,000 employee suggestions—twelve per person—in 1978, the year that Hanai became chairman. Employees made one suggestion per month. Although it would seem that fielding so many suggestions the first year would lead to a decrease the next, the number actually increased to 580,000 the next year in 1979.

The company screens suggestions one by one, adopting them without hesitation if deemed that they would lead to costs being cut. Employees whose suggestions are taken up receive a bonus. The suggestion system is a company-wide system and not confined solely to plants, enabling savings despite the fixed expense. Hanai boasted that it is possible to minimize payroll costs without cutting back personnel, for example by "coming up with ingenious ways to shorten overtime."

Rather than a one-way street of instructions from management to workers, Toyota's cost-cutting only works when stirred up by employees at the working level. The entire staff takes up the challenge of cutting costs. When one's own rationalization proposal is successfully adopted, it automatically breeds a sense of participation in the company's operations. The texture of the system was established with the labor-management joint proclamation of 1962 and then fortified with time.

Deterioration into U.S.-Japan auto friction

The endgame to the global compact car war over which the media raised such a fuss fizzled out all too quickly with a sweeping victory of the Japanese side before the 1970s were out. What foiled the Big Three was their inability to develop a compact vehicle to rival Japanese cars no matter how massive a capital investment they made. To make a boxing analogy, it was as if the American contender pulled out of the fight before getting into the ring.

The Big Three even tried enlisting the cooperation of its capital partnerships in Japan. GM-affiliated Isuzu's main line of business was less in compact passenger cars than large trucks. Consequently, GM, leaning on its vast financial resources, formulated a plan to affiliate with Honda, but eventually switched over to Suzuki Motor Company through the generous offices of Isuzu president Toshio Okamoto. Suzuki's core business at the time was in light-duty k-cars, which do not fly in the U.S. market, thus providing very little in the way of adaptable fire power. The tie-up with Suzuki did no more than sate GM's hegemonic bent.

It had only been a short time since Ford had allied with Mazda. A "what's Ford up to now" mood still loomed heavily within Mazda, and more time would be needed to build an amicable relationship.

The relationship between Chrysler and Mitsubishi Motors was complicated as well. Mitsubishi was prevented under agreement from marketing its own brands of vehicles in the U.S. market. Mitsubishi's past presidents had wrestled with the pros and cons of unequal treaties. With Chrysler's operations already sliding, the cars supplied by Mitsubishi were a lifeline. Nevertheless, Chrysler's debt swelled from $200 million in 1978 to $1.1 billion in 1979, and then to $1.7 billion in 1980.

Chrysler took on Lee Iacocca, fired by Ford, as its CEO for a reorganization, but the company's financial crisis worsened markedly at the beginning of 1981. Iacocca thereupon brought his political clout to bear in getting a $700 million loan from the U.S. government, and the company somehow managed to stay afloat. Although he put in for another $400 million in additional loans at the end of the year, the industry consensus was that Chrysler's collapse was almost hopelessly imminent.

In its 1980 accounts, Ford, too, wrote down a loss of $1.54 billion, the largest in its history. Furthermore, leading automaker GM had rolled into the hole as well. Deficits among the Big Three reached $4 billion that year.

Japanese cars had initially been valued as inexpensive economy cars, but the perception transitioned to "fuel-efficient" economy cars with the oil crisis. In due time, they came to be praised as high-performance cars and reliable cars. It would be strange for inexpensive, fuel-efficient, high-performance, and reliable cars not to sell.

With the U.S. economy stagnating during the latter half of the 1970s, every Japanese car that sold was one less American car sold. The strain from this resulted in layoffs at the United Auto Workers (UAW) union. The UAW, irate about such substantial layoffs, put on displays, such as jumping atop and smashing Japanese cars, which was highly publicized by the media.

Although it is standard practice in war for the winner to subjugate the loser, business battles do not work that way. If anything, the defeated country is more likely to turn to protectionism, especially since automobiles are a strategic industry for both industrialized and industrializing countries. So, to nobody's surprise, before long Japan's triumph in the global compact car war deteriorated into U.S.-Japan auto friction.

As a way to alleviate the friction, the U.S. proposed the idea that Japanese automakers set up local production in the U.S. UAW president Douglas Fraser came to Japan in February 1980 to urge Japanese carmakers to build passenger car plants to help allay tensions. From the UAW's perspective, getting Japanese automakers to establish U.S.-based production meant more jobs for UAW union members.

Honda, the first to pick up on this, announced in early 1980 that it would build a car plant adjacent to its two-wheeler plant in Ohio to produce the Accord line of compact cars. Nissan followed with an announcement in April that it would begin U.S. production of pickup trucks.

This left Toyota. But the only action Toyota took was to commission three think tanks in the Japan and the U.S.—the Nomura Research Institute, Arthur D. Little and the Stanford Research Institute—to conduct field studies. The public took this report to mean that Toyota has no intention of setting up U.S.-based production.

As the days went by, of course, criticism of Toyota mounted. "Those Mikawa yokels have no international sensibilities," critics claimed. "Our entire auto industry is going to go down the tubes while that company dillydallies around."

It was obvious to anyone that the friction between the U.S. and Japan over automobiles would remain unresolved until Toyota made the decision to shift production to the U.S. In time, the matter inevitably escalated into a political issue. The impending step was import restrictions on Japanese cars. If it failed to act, Toyota would be made out to be the principal cause of the friction.

Nissan, investing in longer-term projects

One of the cardinal rules of investing in highly competitive industries is to choose projects that are sure to generate profits in the short term. Investing in longer-term projects, even if there is a high probability of success, runs the risk of squandering one's investment before reaping the rewards.

As the global car wars deteriorated into U.S.-Japan auto friction, the situation, coupled with yen appreciation, forced Japan's automakers to commit to internationalizing operations whether they wanted to or not. Honda and Nissan, who launched U.S.-based production before Toyota, had their reasons for doing so. While Honda invested in a project that would bring in profits in the near term, Nissan, however, was investing in a longer-term project while trying to maintain their current level of profitability.

First, Honda. Although their first compact car, the Civic, sold much better than expected, it did not manage to break into Toyota and Nissan's stranglehold over the Japanese market. Honda had no other option than to fortify its base in the American market in which it was doing so remarkably well if it were to survive as an independent automaker.

With the popularity of the Civic in the U.S. market climbing year by year after the first oil crisis, sales promised to increase geometrically if Honda supplied its vehicles to the market in a timely fashion. If this trend were to continue, it was entirely conceivable that Honda could surpass Toyota and Nissan in five years.

Honda would be done for if something happened to prevent them from exporting finished cars to the U.S. just as they were gaining momentum. If there were any way to slip through the net, it would be to begin producing its vehicles in the U.S. But it would need to move fast to preempt the politicization of tensions between the two countries. What made such a move more feasible for Honda than for Toyota or Nissan was that Honda had been producing motorbikes in the U.S. Learning from its existing operations while examining economic trends in the American market allowed for a smooth transition into four-wheel vehicles.

Since Honda initially had no experience manufacturing in the U.S., it commissioned a feasibility study on U.S. production from an American consulting firm in 1976. In June 1977, Honda decided to first build a motorbike plant in Marysville, in the outskirts of Columbus, Ohio.

An agreement signed with the state government provided for the acquisition of additional land under the assumption that Honda would transition into producing cars in the future. Then on October 11 of that year, executive vice-president Kihachiro Kawashima made a resounding proclamation at a press conference held to announce the establishment of the motorbike plant. "Depending on trends in car demand, as well as trends in exchange rates and import restrictions," he said, "we would like to come to a decision on whether to build a passenger car plant as early as two years from now and within four years at the latest."

Around the time Honda began a feasibility study, Nissan was also quietly looking into shifting production to the U.S. At the suggestion of Ichiro Shioji, president of the Confederation of Japan Automobile Workers' Unions, which was on amicable terms with the UAW, President Tadahiro Iwakoshi sent an investigation team to the U.S. to get a sense of whether U.S. production "would fly." In the spring of 1977, he flew to the United States to personally inspect the site for the plant. Iwakoshi considered U.S.-based production to be a little something extra while maintaining exports of finished cars.

Iwakoshi left the task of announcing Nissan's shift into the U.S. to his successor, Takashi Ishihara. Ishihara, however, objecting to shifting operations based on a suggestion from a union leader, put a freeze on the project claiming that wages were high in the U.S. and the quality of labor poor.

But there was a reason that Nissan opted to produce pickup trucks at a time when U.S.-Japan friction was scorching. Rather than alleviate friction, Ishihara's intention was to deal with the issue of import duties on light trucks (the "chicken war")

In the early 1970s, West Germany significantly raised import duties in response to a sharp rise in imports of U.S. poultry products. The U.S. retaliated by raising import duties on light trucks to 25 percent, essentially barring VW's light trucks from the U.S. market.

Caught in the crossfire, Japanese automakers obtained the consent of customs authorities to remove the truck beds and install them in the U.S. As an unfinished product, called a cab chassis (the body without the bed), the product was treated as an auto part and got by with only a 4 percent import duty.

Japanese-developed light pickup trucks, which were also the beginning of Japanese RVs (recreational vehicles), were convenient in that they could be used not only for leisure but for commuting to work as well. As such, the market grew quickly. Within five years, light truck exports to the U.S. surged, from 250,000 in 1975 to 580,000 in 1980.

Nonetheless, in May 1980 the U.S. Treasury changed the cab chassis duty classification from parts to unfinished trucks, slapping on a 25 percent tariff. With this, Japanese-produced light trucks lost their price competitiveness while the Big Three, lying in wait to enter the market, widened their share of the market.

Judging by the sequence of events that led up to this point, it would be difficult to say outright that Ishihara's decision was wrong. The problem was what happened afterwards. Although Honda had led off with motorbikes and then transitioned into cars, Nissan, rather than produce passenger cars, moved ahead with a longer-term project with uncertain prospects.

Starting off with capital participation in Motor Ibérica in November 1979 (it later became a wholly owned subsidiary), Nissan launched a series of bold overseas projects in less than a year, including joint production of passenger cars with Alfa Romeo in Italy, licensed production of VW's compact car, the Santana, and local production of passenger cars in Britain.

Ishihara thought of nothing but chasing down Toyota. Even though he sent out signals just after his accession to president in June 1977 that Nissan would "recapture a 30 percent market share" of domestic sales, the truth was that they were still many years away from achieving this; they had to abandon their pursuit of Toyota in the domestic market. "We're now in an age of consolidated accounting," reasoned Ishihara. "Nissan will take out Toyota in a consolidated way by internationalizing operations. That's the chink in Toyota's armor."

The media wrote this off as "Nissan's wild international projects," and collapse was quick in the coming particularly for such grab-bag international strategies. The labor union had opposed Ishihara's tactics all the way, a confrontation that came to a head with Nissan's announcement in January 1981 that it would begin production in Britain.

The operational foray into Britain developed into a family feud, with chairman Katsuji Kawamata taking the union's side. The original plan to produce 200,000 vehicles annually was downgraded to a pilot plant that would initially produce 50,000 cars. The Alfa Romeo and VW projects had already begun but were eventually shut down after facing mounting deficits.

If Nissan had foregone its European projects and instead concentrated its financial resources on the U.S., it would have surpassed Toyota. Furthermore, Nissan probably would not have been outpaced by Honda, much less come under the control of Renault. It was in 1985 that Nissan realized the importance of the American market and forced the conversion of the production line at its truck plant to produce passenger cars instead.

In the past, present and future, the U.S. is the ultimate reliably profitable market. Carlos Ghosn, sent in to Nissan by Renault, knew this when he put the company back on the road to recovery by closing a plant in Japan and building a new one in Mississippi.

Chapter 21

The Decisive Tie-Up Negotiations with Ford and GM

B USINESS IS LIKE HORSERACING. IN the paddock, the Honda and Nissan entries looked ready to run. The starting gate flies open and Honda jumps out to an early lead, tearing through the first and second turns. Nissan is right there alongside Honda at the start but, unable to corner the second turn, strays off course. The odds-on favorite Toyota refuses to budge at the starting gate. The difference between horseracing and business is that, while the finish line at the horse track lies just around the fourth turn, business is a competition without a finish line.

Eiji felt a tinge of loneliness as the global compact car war fizzled into auto friction. Ishida, who Eiji looked upon as his managerial guru, had passed on to the next world, while Saito, Eiji's close friend with whom he had gone through thick and thin since Toyota's early days, was bedridden.

"The auto tensions stem from the management failures of the Big Three. There's no logical reason whatsoever to criticize Japan. So we'll just hang tight until Toyota finds a compelling reason to shift production into the U.S.," intoned the trustworthy chairman Masaya Hanai, a principle to which he frequently returned.

Eiji expected that setting up production in the U.S. would be unavoidable in the long run. Still, what kept him from making up his mind was that, even if Toyota did shift production to meet the request of the American side, he was not at all convinced that U.S.-based operations would be capable of manufacturing cars with the same level of performance as those produced in Japan. There was a genuine risk that a difference in performance between American-produced and imported cars—even if the cars looked the same on the outside—

would damage the Toyota brand and cause serious inconveniences for American consumers.

Tie-up negotiations with Ford fall short once again

Toyota is able to make high-performance cars at low cost because they are made with meticulous attention to detail by lifetime-employed skilled mechanics according to the Toyota Production System. Eiji thought that it would be difficult to implement in the U.S. an ever-evolving Toyota Production System that had taken years to develop. At the same time, however, he was spinning his wheels for the best way to go about doing just that.

As a president who'd risen up as an engineer, Eiji took pride in not capitulating to anyone when it comes to automaking. The Crown, a concept which Eiji had come up with himself, had brought Toyota into the ranks of the automaking elite, while the Corolla had solidified the foundation for Toyota to expand into the rest of the world.

Exportation and foreign sales might have been the realm of Toyota Sales, but it was Toyota Motor that developed the cars. Toyota Sales was sending an incessant barrage of requests to "find a way to make it happen" but no specific suggestions. Inside Toyota Motor it was the same. It was then that Eiji first got a taste of the loneliness that visits those at the top. Unless the company came up with some sort of measures for shifting production—and quickly—they would stall themselves out of options.

The study that Toyota had commissioned to various think tanks in Japan and the U.S. did not turn out very well. Nonetheless, they could not just stand around waiting for things to happen. In the beginning of summer, Eiji braced himself to make a decision to pursue U.S.-based production.

Two things prompted the decision. The first was a letter that came in from Donald Petersen, who had taken over as Ford's new president in the beginning of spring, saying that he would like to pay a courtesy visit to Toyota to offer his greetings as the newly-inaugurated president. Soon thereafter, President Carter proposed joint production between Japanese and American automakers as a solution to U.S.-Japan auto friction at a U.S.-Japan summit meeting held at the White House on May 1 between Carter and Prime Minister Masayoshi

Ohira. "This is it!" cried Eiji, seizing on Carter's idea. Eiji had always devoted much of his energy to gathering such information.

After making a solo effort to work out a framework for joint production, Eiji handed a memo to Mamoru Tanabe, senior managing director of Nippon Denso (now Denso) who, originally being from Mitsui & Company, had a lot of friends among Big Three leadership from his time selling auto parts. Eiji sent Tanabe to Ford headquarters to deliver it personally. Contained in the memo was a message to the effect that Toyota was ready to propose establishing joint production when Petersen visited Toyota to bring tidings as Ford's new president.

"You want to set up joint production with Ford, not GM, right?" Tanabe confirmed when Eiji called him in to run him through the itemized provisions of his proposal.

"GM's too big a business partner," Eiji said in response, nodding his head as if to convince himself. "Plus, U.S. antitrust laws make it totally impossible for us to tie-up."

One of the reasons Eiji chose Ford as a business partner was partially out of gratitude for their taking care of him during his study abroad. Ford had been a mentor to Toyota and the two companies had entered talks to form a partnership four times in the past, but nothing had ever come of it. Although Eiji had never had a direct part in any of the negotiations, he had been observing them very closely and was eager to try his hand, thinking, "I'll see to it myself this time around."

They would produce the Camry, a 2000cc compact sedan with an FF (forward engine, front-wheel drive) layout, which Toyota had developed for the U.S. market.

The wheels of fortune kept turning. Tatsuo Hasegawa, senior managing director of development, had nixed the FF layout suggested by Eiji for the Publica and instead adopted the FR layout. Over twenty years later, Hasegawa took the lead in developing the Camry, Toyota's first vehicle with an FF layout. Now in the final stages of development, Eiji was sure the car would be a hot-seller in the U.S. market.

Toyota would soon present the eye of its automotive apple to Ford. Ford could study TPS if the two companies would be working together for joint production. Rather than simply use it as a tool for Ford's workers, Toyota could put TPS to the test to see if it could take root in the United States.

Eiji also looked forward to the positive political impact from Toyota taking the initiative on joint production—as proposed by President Carter at the U.S.-Japan summit meeting—and turning it into reality. The world's second and third largest automakers joining hands would of course exert pressure on the industry-leading GM. The agreement would not only bring the short-term benefits of alleviating trade friction and giving Toyota the opportunity to set up U.S.-based production, but also offer an opportunity to build an amicable relationship with one of the Big Three companies.

Petersen visited Toyota headquarters on June 24 accompanied by two vice-presidents. The meeting, including Petersen's presidential greeting, was held in the VIP room of the Toyota Kaikan Exhibition Hall from 10:30 a.m. and lasted a modest three hours, including a break for lunch. Judging by the members of Ford's team and by Petersen's enthusiasm, Eiji felt all the more confident, convinced beyond doubt, in fact, that the negotiations would produce an agreement in a short period of time.

Joining Eiji and Hanai on the Toyota side were the head of Toyota Sales and the vice-president for overseas sales. Most of those in attendance were finding out the details of the negotiations for the first time. Masaya Hanai was one of them, and he described Eiji's keenness thus: "the slow-to-act monarch took off on horseback like a bat out of hell."

Full-fledged negotiations began at the end of July, but contrary to expectations, Eiji began to view Ford's behavior with skepticism. The seeds of distrust were planted when on August 4, just after negotiations had gotten underway, Ford followed suit with the UAW and abruptly filed a dumping complaint against Japanese cars with the U.S. International Trade Commission (ITC). Shaking hands (negotiating a tie-up) with the right hand, while exchanging blows with the left (appealing to the ITC). Eiji was shocked by such a dry approach to business.

Eiji directed the Overseas Operations Division, the contact for negotiations, to lodge a complaint. "Kicking you under the negotiation table is a technique used by foreign companies, not just Ford," he was advised to the contrary. "You should just ignore it." Eiji passed on lodging a complaint.

The all-important negotiations hit a snag when it came to choosing which model to lead with. Ford appeared reluctant to proceed

because the Taurus, which it had developed to buttress the company's
future, and the Camry competed for the same segment of the market.
Toyota would have to drastically overhaul the design of the Camry to
avoid this.

Although Ford stridently insisted on changing the Camry's
design, Hasegawa refused to budge from his stance that Toyota had
developed the Camry "for the American market, not for Ford." Readily
acquiescing could potentially derail not only Toyota's development of
new models, but also its entire approach to development. The Camry
idea flickered out in early fall without the parties having reached an
agreement.

Talks had run aground because of Ford. Ford had two separate
teams for development and negotiations with Toyota. Consisting of
production and marketing people, members of the negotiation team
knew hardly anything about the details of the cars their company
was producing. No matter how hard and how long Ford's Toyota team
negotiated, any agreement would be shot out of the sky by Ford's own
development team in Detroit—even if the two negotiation teams
managed to find a middle ground. Since it was Toyota that had
approached Ford about partnering up, Ford was in the easier position
of making Toyota present as many different models as possible so Ford
could choose the car that best fit its own line-up.

Eiji awoke to the fact that he had swung and missed with
his executive initiative to collaborate with Ford as soon as the two
companies failed to agree on what model to launch first. Further
pursuing the issue would only disrupt Toyota's operations.

Continuing to limp along into 1981, talks were moving away from
the realm of business. In May, the U.S. government muscled Japan
into accepting voluntary export restraints (VER) to reduce exports of
Japanese passenger cars to the U.S. from 1.82 million vehicles in the
previous year to 1.68 million to resolve the highly politicized issue of
autos. Japan was to voluntarily restrict exports for three years with the
understanding that it would be indirectly assisting the reconstruction
of the Big Three.

At this stage there was no longer any reason for Toyota to draw
out negotiations. Eiji nonchalantly expressed Toyota's intent to drop
talks with Ford at the new-car release announcement in July. Toyota
Motor Sales Chairman Seishi Kato said it well when he described
negotiations to form a major alliance that would have rocked the

entire global auto industry: "the mountain labored but didn't bring forth a mouse—not even a mouse turd."

Whether to give China priority over the U.S.

Driven into a corner, Toyota had two options. One was to set up U.S.-based production on its own. The other was to temporarily put U.S. production on ice and focus instead on moving into China.

Japan and China signed the Japan-China Joint Communiqué to establish diplomatic relations when Prime Minister Kakuei Tanaka visited China in September 1972. Six years later, Takeo Fukuda, the father of the recent prime minister Yasuo Fukuda, signed the Treaty of Peace and Friendship between Japan and the People's Republic of China in August 1978. Deng Xiaoping, supreme leader of China, visited Japan in October as a gesture to reciprocate good feelings.

Deng, who was in the process of modernizing Chinese industry, energetically toured Japan's state-of-the-art factories. Among the factories he visited, he took a particularly keen interest in Toyota's and Panasonic's plants. At Deng's request, Panasonic owner Konosuke Matsushita was quick to announce that Panasonic would be building a plant in Beijing to produce cathode ray tubes for color televisions.

Toyota, for its part, felt a kinship with China. The founder of the Toyota Group, Sakichi Toyoda, had run Toyoda Spinning and Weaving Works' Shanghai plant and produced piston rings in Tianjin before the war. Toyota itself had also made trucks in Tianjin through knockdown production. With a population of 1.3 billion people, the Chinese market would undoubtedly grow to become one of the largest markets in the world. Although Toyota had previously classified China as a market that would develop in the longer term, the company thought that the market may be worth serious consideration partially because the automaker's U.S. strategy was nowhere near resolution.

One company was a highly successful paragon of a firm that had given up on the U.S. and turned its priorities to China: Volkswagen. As a pioneer that had firmly established its cars in the U.S. market, VW launched U.S.-based production of the Golf, a new line of vehicles to succeed the Beetle, in Westmoreland, Pennsylvania in the mid 1970s. Unable to get the plant off the ground, they soon began looking into downsizing its operations (discontinuing production in 1987).

VW, figuring that investment in China would be sure to profit in the longer term, decided to devote the three managerial resources of people, goods and money to China. Seeing VW's shift in strategy, Eiji agonized whether to follow suit. "I wonder if Toyota could succeed with U.S.-based production where VW failed," he wondered. "China's a massive market but—putting aside its future potential—for the time being it's still a market with longer-term prospects."

Saving the best for last

GM kept an intent eye on Toyota's woes throughout. GM was finally starting to realize that the reason its world car strategy came unraveled was that the company did not have sufficient expertise in compact cars. Chairman Roger Smith momentarily thought GM was done in when Toyota and Ford announced plans for joint production. Not even GM could let down its guard if the world's second and third biggest automakers were to come together.

Although GM had initially taken a wait-and-see approach, they began to take an interest in Toyota's activities as negotiations with Ford went sour. Still, the pride that went with being the world's biggest automaker prevented GM from acting precipitously while the negotiations were still underway. Enter J.W. Chai, vice-president of Itochu International and businessman extraordinaire who played an active role in GM's tie-up with Isuzu.

Chai, who also served as an outside director for Isuzu, was remarkably familiar with the Japanese automotive industry. His view of why Toyota-Ford talks had gone south was that Toyota went straight into proposing joint production without negotiating in advance. In bringing this type of partnership to a successful conclusion, the negotiating parties had to firm up the details of the agreement only after first ascertaining what both companies' heads intended to get from the deal.

When Chai visited Japan to see the Tokyo Motor Show in November 1981, he met with Hideo Kamio, managing director of Toyota Motor Sales. Kamio had a close personal relationship with not only Eiji but Hanai as well. These relationships would be a boon to Toyota.

Upon hearing from Kamio all the difficulties Toyota had been having trying to penetrate the U.S. market, Chai also learned that Toyota would be open to negotiating a deal if GM were to approach them about it. While GM was at pains trying to produce passenger cars, Toyota was going nowhere fast with its U.S. strategy. If it could be reliably determined that both parties were open to potentially forming a partnership, the fantasy alliance between the top Japanese and American automakers could become reality.

When Chai mentioned a possible pairing between the two automakers, Roger Smith leaned forward and asked Chai to do something for him. "GM's not on familiar terms with Toyota management, much less with Toyota's internal affairs," he said. "I'd like to give you full plenary powers to set up a meeting between me and Toyota's president."

Chai drew up a scenario for a partnership between Toyota and GM. Then, according to plan, Toyota Motor Sales Chairman Seishi Kato first flew to GM headquarters in Detroit on Christmas Day in December of that year to meet with Smith and formally express Toyota's willingness to negotiate a joint venture with GM. Kato identified strongly with GM from his experience working at GM Japan in the past.

Striking while the iron was hot, Chai made an undisclosed trip to Japan in early January 1982 to deliver Smith's personal message to Toyota's Tokyo office in Hibiya while the media was distracted by the mania surrounding the merger between Toyota Motor and Toyota Sales. Although the message was simple—"I would like for the heads of both companies to personally get together to exchange opinions on a joint venture"—Chai explained the finer point of GM's actual proposal: using idle plants on the west coast to jointly produce Corolla-class compact cars on a scale of 500,000 vehicles annually. Toyota and GM would then split the finished cars down the middle and each sell them under their own corporate name.

Eiji, who had been receiving detailed reports from Kamio on advance backroom negotiations, found GM's offer attractive. But at the same time, he also harbored suspicions as to whether "a company as bureaucratic as GM would confer full plenary rights to a third party."

Hanai also sat in on the talks and was aware of Eiji's suspicions. "Heaven itself calls for a partnership between Toyota and GM," he muttered to himself, making sure that Eiji could hear.

With this input from Hanai, Eiji resolved to attend high-level talks with GM. With every one of Eji's moves being watched by the media, however, a trip to Detroit would let the cat out of the bag. Consequently, Toyota decided on short notice to hold a dealer convention in Canada, during which Eiji would drop by New York and attend the meeting there.

Advance negotiations were going so well—actually working in Toyota's favor, no less—that it occurred to Eiji as the meeting approached that he must be getting duped by someone. "I know Roger Smith's face," he assured himself to dispel such a gloomy state of mind. "We've never talked face-to-face before, but I haven't forgotten his distinctive reddish-copper face. If some impostor comes instead, I'll be on to him right away."

As for impostors, a financial fraud called the M-Fund was going around at the time. The M-Fund referred to treasure plundered by the former Japanese military during the war and subsequent occupation that was brought back to Japan, confiscated by William Marquat, chief of GHQ's (General Headquarters of the Allied Forces) Economic and Scientific Section, and then held in joint custody by Japan and the U.S. as a postwar recovery fund for Japan. The M stood for Marquat.

Stories like this often morph to reflect the times, including rumors that the fund is being used as oil dollars, as a secret source of funds for the Imperial family or as an operational fund for the Ministry of Finance. All these anecdotes were entirely fictional; such a vast store of money does not exist. It really is just a financial fraud.

The would-be perpetrators bring in letters of introduction and other correspondence from powerful politicians, tycoons, and high-ranking bureaucrats, letters that are difficult to pin down as fraudulent, and present financial schemes to corporate executives that seem to be in need of money. Forging letters of introduction and other correspondence is a piece of cake for the criminal elements of society.

Some businessmen end up falling for these kinds of things even if they know such financial schemes tend to be frauds. One such incident blew up into a major controversy in the auto industry. Before Nissan tied up with Renault, Nissan's executive vice-president of sales drafted a letter of undertaking believing a fictitious loan for ¥1 trillion to be genuine. It is rumored that Nissan ultimately bought back the letter of undertaking for several hundred million yen.

A basic agreement reached at the first top-level meeting

The Links Club, right in the heart of Manhattan, served as the venue for the meeting between the heads of Toyota and GM. Bustling as a meeting place for movers and shakers of the U.S. economy to share information during the day, only a smattering of people show up at night.

"This guy looks exactly like the person I met at the tenth anniversary party for the Isuzu-GM alliance," Eiji thought as he walked in. All Eiji's doubts cleared up the moment he firmly shook hands with Smith at the Links Club.

It was here that Eiji made a bold step towards a "World Toyota." Already certain that both parties were going into the talks with the same unflagging resolve, the two reached a general agreement at the very first meeting. This being a negotiation between two of the top companies in Japan and the U.S.—both too proud *not* to be persnickety about cost-benefit calculations—difficulties naturally arose every so often during subsequent negotiations.

The two companies very nearly cashed in their chips and started anew over the valuation of the Fremont Plant, which emerged as a candidate for the facility to be used for joint production. The assessed values that each company came up with were miles apart and, moreover, neither was about to budge. Worn down by early autumn, Masatoshi Morita, head of Toyota's negotiating team, proposed to Eiji—now chairman—that Toyota start over.

"If the talks flounder," Eiji responded unsympathetically, "then of course we'd have to call it quits. But we can't skirt around entering the U.S market. Failing to form a partnership with Ford and *then* GM would leave us no option but to go it alone. Are you guys all confident that we can go it alone? Negotiations take persistence. Hang in there and you'll end up finding a solution. Whether Toyota can metamorphose into an international corporation depends on this tie-up with GM. I want you to give it some thought and go back out there."

Eiji's words once again reminded Morita of the enthusiasm that Eiji invested in a partnership with GM. While advising the negotiation team as to what to do, Eiji himself then moved into action. Sending executive vice-president Shigenobu Yamamoto as emissary, Eiji wrote a letter to Smith. Smith responded to the letter by offering a package of concessions, leading the two companies to reach a basic agreement in the beginning of 1983. On February 14, each company's board of directors accepted the joint venture.

The tie-up rumors between Toyota and Ford that had shaken the global auto industry came apart within the year, but talks between Toyota and GM, gawked at in utter disbelief by the industry as a whole, gelled in just under a year after the first meeting between the companies' leaders took place.

Eiji's final task in a presidency that lasted fifteen years was to form a partnership with GM to forge a path towards internationalizing operations and building a solid framework for Toyota as a worldwide enterprise with the long-awaited merger between Toyota Motor and Sales. On the day of the merger, Eiji delivered a message to all his employees:

"Toyota Motor's 'postwar' ended on June 30, 1982," he said. "As of July 1, we are taking a new step forward."

Chapter 22
The Vicissitudes of an International Corporation

JAPAN CAME OUT ON TOP of the global compact car war of the 1980s. Although this spawned auto friction as a side effect, the situation was headed towards resolving itself through the Toyota-GM merger. Voluntary export restraints on Japanese-made passenger cars, which began in fiscal 1980 for the purpose of indirectly assisting the reorganization of the Big Three, ended up lasting twelve long years. If VERs had expired after three years according to the original plan, Toyota's international strategy likely would have been dramatically different. It is ironic to note that Toyota was able to grapple with internationalization so successfully precisely because VERs were so protracted.

The eagerly-awaited first quality-assured car (Chevrolet Nova) produced at the Fremont Plant of the New United Motor Manufacturing (NUMMI), the joint venture formed by GM and Toyota, rolled off the line on December 12, 1984.

The plant's dedication ceremony was held in grand style at the same plant on April 4. Although President Reagan initially had been slated to return to his home turf during Easter break to attend the ceremony, he would be unable to leave Washington due to a busy schedule tending to state affairs. Instead, Eij Toyoda went to the White House the previous day to pay a courtesy visit to the president, telling him of the joint venture's dedication ceremony.

Eiji was the first to say a few words at the ceremony, speaking to a crowd of over 500 people from government and financial circles, joined by 1,500 employees. "I hope to contribute to the vitalization of the U.S. automotive industry by bringing together all the best qualities of American and Japanese automakers to build an outstanding, internationally-recognized production system."

"This venture represents a deal between Toyota, GM and the UAW to face new challenges, bringing together the collective wisdom of the East and the West," GM Chairman Roger Smith added. This marked the beginning of the honeymoon between Toyota and GM.

Fear of falling to number three

Although the joint venture had gotten off on the right foot, Toyota had cause for concern. The top spot in passenger cars sales in the American market was coming under threat from Honda. When trade tensions peaked in 1980, Honda had sold no more than 387,000 vehicles in the U.S market in contrast to Toyota's 568,000. By the time the construction of the 150,000-annual-capacity Ohio plant was completed at the end of 1983, Honda was rapidly gaining ground on Toyota, firing away with its U.S.-based production weaponry. It then drove right past Toyota in 1984.

Showing no signs of slowing down, Honda's expansionary policy was to first verify that the company could successfully operate its plant at full capacity without any problems. After doing so, Honda began construction to double its plant's capacity with a view to being up and running by 1988. The company simultaneously announced that it was to set up a plant in Canada with an annual output of 40,000 cars. Honda not only caught up to Toyota, but also, between its finished car exports and local production, it built a network to supply some 800,000 vehicles per year to the U.S. market.

Nissan, too, was building a passenger car line with a 10,000-vehicle capacity in its light truck plant in Tennessee, which it planned to have up and running by the spring of 1985.

Toyota compared favorably with Honda and Nissan in terms of U.S.-based production, but with all the cars produced by NUMMI going to GM and the agreement calling for the provision of a maximum of 250,000 vehicles per annum, Toyota could not channel production to its own sales network even if the plant was operating at full capacity. It was consequently only a matter of time before Toyota fell to number three among Japanese automakers in terms of U.S. car sales. Having taken the lead in opening up a new market in the U.S,

Toyota was too proud to let this happen.

The question then was what Toyota should do to regain the top spot while mitigating as much of the risk as it could. The first attempt at a concrete plan to emerge from a continuum of heated debate was shifting into Canada. Following the U.S. lead, Canada had also implemented import restrictions on Japanese cars. But with a limited track record in Canada, Toyota resigned itself to the number two spot behind Honda.

Toyota had its reasons for considering a move into Canada. The Canadian and American governments signed a zero tariff agreement between the two countries. Japanese automakers would be able to reap the benefits of the agreement if they were to become a member of both countries' Automotive Industries Association. Canada is a big place, but being in the proximity of Ontario—near the Great Lakes and within the extended territory of Detroit—would be indispensable for sourcing parts. Meanwhile, the labor unions there were not all that strong.

What made the idea even more appealing was that the Canadian dollar was cheaper than the U.S. dollar. Building a plant in Canada would have the effect of killing two birds with one stone. Toyota began a field study with an eye on establishing production in Canada in the fall of 1984, but the company scrapped the plan well before the end of the year. Exporting cars to the U.S. from Canada may have been a legitimate option, but Toyota feared that the move would invite hostility from the United States.

Softening its tone towards Toyota with the GM merger, American media instead anticipated that Toyota would construct its own plant in the U.S. sooner or later. Forcing its way into Canada at such a time would ruin the good reputation within the U.S. that Toyota had built with the GM alliance.

Thus, U.S.-based production would be unavoidable. The first idea that came up was to utilize NUMMI. GM's former Fremont Plant was situated on a 890,000m² lot, of which NUMMI used only a third. Toyota could make efficient use of related facilities such as supply water and drainage by borrowing unused land from NUMMI to construct its own factory next to the joint-use plant, thus enabling Toyota to save that much more in investment overhead. Even in terms of production, Toyota could draw on subcontracted plants fostered by the joint venture and train employees through NUMMI.

It would not at all be impossible to take back the lead in sales among Japanese automakers now claimed by Honda if Toyota were to install an assembly line with a 10,000-vehicle monthly output. Capital investment could be kept to $100 million. Although it looked like a deceptively risk-free move, there was always the concern that Toyota was turning a blind eye to possible future ramifications of such an endeavor.

The first problem was the relationship with GM. The joint venture had been authorized by the U.S. Federal Trade Commission (FTC) to operate for a maximum of twelve years. The venture would automatically be terminated once this period was up, at which point either GM or Toyota would buy out the other for rights to the plant and equipment. It was difficult to say how it would pan out if Toyota constructed its own factory on the same premises as the current plant. Toyota did not yet know about buying out GM for rights to the plant, but if GM were to buy it back, then this would certainly complicate management of Toyota's own facilities.

Some issues would still remain unresolved even if Toyota were to buy out GM. Including planned future production, the number of Japanese cars manufactured in the U.S. would have already exceeded one million vehicles annually. As Chrysler—one of the Big Three— was producing around 1.2 million cars per year, Japanese automakers' U.S. production would be the equivalent of the emergence of a fourth major automaker in the United States.

Be that as it may, the fourth major automaker's production entailed assembly only, as Japanese automakers imported engines, transmissions and other principal components from Japan. It may be considered local production, but it was really the same kind of knockdown production as that pursued in developing countries. If this formula became firmly rooted, it would incite parts suppliers and other sectors of the U.S. automotive industry to whip up another round of U.S.-Japan auto friction. At that point, it would be a foregone conclusion that Congress would move to enact local content legislation (parts supply from within the U.S.).

A west coast plant far from Detroit would be extremely disadvantageous considering prospective local parts procurement. A stream of Japanese parts manufacturers had followed Japanese automakers into the U.S, but with their sights set on supplying parts to the Big Three they were all concentrated near Detroit either in the northeastern snowbelt or in the Midwest.

A plant on the west coast would serve the greatest advantage if Toyota were to set up operations with the intention of bringing parts over liberally from Japan. By centering its plants on the west coast Toyota would have to run the risk of some level of deterioration in cost competitiveness.

Many within the company had come to espouse the view that Toyota should build a full-scale plant in the U.S. on its own initiative. Even so, the lingering prospect that local production would become excess baggage if voluntary export restraints were repealed prevented Toyota from making a decision. Hesitating, however, would set dealers a-grumbling.

Toyota's initial aim was to take back the industry lead. But both shifting operations to Canada and using the Fremont Plant were only superficial, small-time attempts to set up local production through a notional accounting and purchasing mindset. Even if it were to wrest back the top spot, Toyota would never come to be recognized as "World Toyota" by employing such tactics.

Independently shifting operations into Kentucky

No matter how saturated the American market, demand for Japanese cars remained strong. As long as there were no major changes in the demand structure, competitive automakers could survive even if hit by temporary financial challenges. In fact, unless Toyota could find a way to thrive amidst such intense competition, Eiji Toyoda's goal to achieve "Global Ten" status by nabbing a 10 percent share of sales in the global market would end before it had scarcely begun.

The one who had first strongly suggested independently building a full-scale plant was Hiroshi Okuda, head of both the Fremont Operations and Overseas Planning Department. After exhaustive study, Toyota decided to locate its new plant in Georgetown, Kentucky, a center of activity for Big Three plants. Although the initial scale of production would be 250,000 cars per year, Toyota purchased a sizable plot of land with future expansion in mind.

The first line of cars that Toyota would produce at the new plant would be the Camry, developed for the U.S. and which Toyota had offered when it approached Ford to engage in joint production in the summer of 1980. Built with Americanized styling and streamlined features, the Camry was designed to be conducive for local production.

Including the cost of land, Toyota scraped by with a capital outlay of $500 million, as operations at start-up would utilize a knockdown production system where all major parts from engines to transmissions would be brought in from Japan. While setting up production in the U.S. would be a huge hit-or-miss undertaking for a corporation of weak financial standing, Toyota could comfortably meet the challenge with its nearly ¥1 trillion of excess cash.

The only foreseeable problem was that it would take a minimum of three years until completion and four years to be running at full capacity if Toyota decided to move forward with converting the expanse of corn fields into industrial land to build a plant with an annual capacity of 250,000 cars. In the interim, Toyota would have to brace itself to surrender the top spot in passenger vehicle sales to Honda. Not to mention the issue of Toyota's pride, the problem would be how to assuage dealers' disquiet towards the shortfall in supply. Dealers could very well seek recourse in court for a breach of contract if Toyota simply ignored the issue.

While Toyota's presidency changed hands from Eiji to Shoichiro in July 1982, Eiji continued to deal the cards of Toyota's U.S. strategy in his new capacity as chairman. In a top-level meeting held during his visit to the U.S. to attend the dedication ceremony of the Fremont Plant in April 1985, Eiji proposed to GM Chairman Roger Smith boosting production at the Fremont Plant by 50,000 cars and requested that Toyota be permitted to distribute the cars manufactured through increased production to Toyota's own sales network. Getting a hold of 50,000 more cars starting with the 1987 model would not be enough to recapture the lead, but would mollify dealers.

Smith accepted Eiji's proposal. Increased production at NUMMI would allow for a simple transition over to consigned production even if the joint venture terminated after the scheduled twelve years and GM took back the plant. On the other hand, if Toyota took over the plant, it would also be possible to convert the plant for small-lot production of many different models to take advantage of the benefits of being on the west coast. Furthermore, the company would also be able to turn it into a light truck plant in collaboration with the truck bed plant in Long Beach. There was any number of ways to put NUMMI to practical use. Luckily, in 1992 the FTC granted permission for the joint venture to continue operations after the initial twelve years were up.

Toyota wasted no time in establishing Toyota Motor Manufacturing Kentucky (TMKK) in January 1984, immediately breaking ground on construction of the new plant. The first car rolled off the line in May 1988.

Toyota charged its way up the ranks to third in production volume behind GM and Ford, but it was still a long country mile away from casting off its image as "Toyota Japan" and levitating to "World Toyota" in terms of standing. The firm would have to kick its U.S-based production into high gear to go head-to-head with the Big Three and live up to the name of "World Toyota."

Between the two banners of Toyota's U.S. strategy, the Fremont Plant, accessed through the merger with GM, was a good testing site for U.S. local production, while the independently-built Kentucky Plant served as a showroom. Prior to Toyota's arrival, Georgetown, an agricultural zone underdeveloped even by Kentucky standards, brought in no more than $18.6 million a year in tourist revenue. After the plant was up and running, however, this shot up to $50 million. Although the state government had passed the first $140 million incentives package in state history to entice Toyota, tourist revenue more than made up for it.

The challenge for the Kentucky Plant was implementing TPS. At the Fremont Plant, Toyota had given priority to former GM employees in hiring, and trained them in TPS. Outcome aside, they were quick to pick-up on TPS, having had previous experience working at automotive plants. But the complete amateurs at the Kentucky Plant would have to be trained from scratch in the art of carmaking.

Camrys produced at the Tsutsumi Plant, the mother of the Kentucky Plant, had already appeared on the American market to rave reviews. The car produced at Kentucky Plant would have to compete with an identical-looking car in the U.S. market. Indeed, the Camry was its own adversary.

The Big Three had almost an obsessive interest in the quality of the products coming out of the Fremont and Kentucky plants. The biggest reason that GM launched a joint venture with Toyota was to introduce TPS. At the start of the joint venture, GM sent an additional 5,000 engineers to the Fremont Plant to work hard to obtain expertise in passenger car manufacturing techniques. Soon, GM's main factory was overflowing with a deluge of Romanized signs and slogans for *kanban*, *kaizen* and *poka-yoke* (mistake-proofing)—the same ones used at Toyota's plants.

Based on this experience, GM set up a plant in Tennessee as a separate company to produce the Saturn line of passenger cars. Although production efficiency ultimately reached Toyota standards partly due to the active deployment of computer technology at the high-tech plant, quality still did not compare to that of Toyota vehicles.

GM only incorporated TPS in form. Information technology (IT) has been in the limelight in recent years, but cars cannot be made on IT alone. Using the human body as an analogy, the production floor is the muscle and bone, while IT is nerves. It is not possible to produce high-quality cars without strong muscles and bones, no matter how sensitive the nerves are.

U.S.-Japan auto friction flares up again

Partly because their U.S.-based production was going well in the latter half of the 1980s, there were times that Japanese automakers' exports did not even reach their quota under voluntary export restraints. This did not mean that U.S.-Japan friction over automobiles had abated.

While the number of finished car exports had definitely declined, the trade imbalance had conversely grown over the years. The U.S. trade deficit topped $160 billion in 1994. The deficit with Japan accounted for $65.6 billion—or 40 percent—of this, while automotive-related industries accounted for $36.1 billion.

In 1982 when export restrictions went into effect, the U.S.-Japan trade deficit was still just a bit over $10 billion, 90 percent of which was accounted for by automobiles. However, the deficit with Japan ballooned by nearly 600 percent, while the automotive-related deficit more than tripled, during the twelve-year period in which the restrictions were in place.

Even though the U.S. economy went on the upswing during the 1990s, the basic American perception was that the U.S. trade deficit with Japan would not go away until automobiles were brought under wraps. Consequently, just after the Tokyo Summit in July 1993,

President Bill Clinton and Prime Minister Kiichi Miyazawa agreed to launch the U.S.-Japan Framework for a New Economic Partnership with the objective of ameliorating the U.S.-Japan trade imbalance.

Toyota may have built an independent plant in Kentucky following the joint venture with GM, but all fingers would once again point at leading automaker Toyota unless it shook a leg and quickly made its next move. Increasing local parts supply from within the United States would be key to resolving the trade imbalance, but this would take time.

Toyota thus decided to import the J Car, a compact sedan developed by GM as a world car, on a scale of 20,000 per annum, which Toyota would distribute and sell through its own sales channel as a way to alleviate at least some of the criticism it was receiving from the U.S.

Bilateral trade had begun traversing a difficult path despite Toyota's desperate attempts. The tensions resulted from the collapse of LDP single-party rule and the formation of the Hosokawa administration—a non-LDP coalition—just after the U.S.-Japan Framework for a New Economic Partnership had gotten underway. U.S.-Japan relations took a cantankerous turn for the worse at the U.S.-Japan Summit meeting held in Washington in February 1994 when Hosokawa suggested that the two countries have a "mature, adult relationship," dismissing outright the numerical targets set out by the United States.

The Hosokawa administration collapsed in the spring of that year, but the Clinton-led Democratic Party suffered a historic beating in the November midterm elections. Big Three factories and auto parts suppliers, said to number upwards of 10,000 companies, are concentrated in the Midwestern states of Michigan, Ohio and Illinois. Primarily a Democratic stronghold, the whole region was carried entirely by the Republican Party. Clinton would not stand a chance of being reelected unless his party got these votes back. The Democrats then came up with a plan to win over its Midwestern constituency: stirring up friction from the White House.

Beleaguered by the aftereffects of the bubble economy, Japanese automakers at the time were compelled to restructure their operations. With yen appreciation, automakers' price competitiveness in the U.S. market, their cash cow, was on the decline, eating into profits. Over half of the eleven manufacturers of finished cars were incurring losses after the bubble burst, including Nissan, Mazda, Daihatsu, Isuzu, Fuji Heavy Industries and Nissan Diesel. The Big Three, on the other hand, recorded the biggest profits in the companies' histories in 1994.

In terms of microeconomics, the source of friction was nowhere to be found. It was a man-made phenomenon. Japan's Ministry of International Trade and Industry, quickly catching on to what the American side was up to, took a firm stance: "Japan has made unilateral concessions to resolve Japan-U.S. friction in the past. Washington's approach is to impose managed trade. We want to change how Japan always caves in to intimidation, which is the way political settlements are customarily reached. Negotiations can begin when the U.S. backs down from its numerical targets."

Toyota's awareness as an international corporation

This hawkish stance was the result of a political decision by then-Minister of International Trade and Industry Ryutaro Hashimoto (later prime minister). With the two countries failing to reach a common understanding, negotiations transformed into a stage for a "theological debate" over free trade.

On May 16, 1995, the White House invoked Section 301 of the U.S. Trade Act, announcing a list of sanctions that applied a 100 percent tariff to Japanese-made luxury cars. Since Japanese automakers had yet to undertake local production of luxury cars, it was estimated that Japan would incur a loss of $5.9 billion when sanctions went into effect.

While the three companies Toyota, Nissan and Honda were all exporting luxury cars to the U.S., Honda and Nissan were sitting on a massive inventory of unsold cars due to a downturn in sales. If it came down to it and sanctions were imposed, they had the option of temporarily withdrawing from the market under that pretext.

In contrast, Toyota's Lexus line of vehicles was flying off the lot. Toyota had already begun garnering praise as the company that would "surpass Mercedes-Benz in performance." Pulling out of the market with such a highly profitable car would be inconceivable. Although sanctions would go into effect on June 28, tariffs would be levied retroactive to May 20 with the invocation of Section 301.

Given the plight of the Japanese automotive industry, the

Japanese government sent a jolt to the United States by appealing to the newly-inaugurated World Trade Organization (WTO). Not to be outdone, the U.S. announced plans to countersue. Japan marched with elan into WTO headquarters in Geneva to whip up global sentiment but returned home with a sense of hopelessness after being brushed off by the U.S. in bilateral talks that began on June 12.

The White House was boiling with anger. Even the pro-Japan faction of the U.S. State Department began to criticize Japan's bearing towards negotiations, saying, "MITI's attitude is ridiculous. What are they thinking, kicking over the negotiation table without even trying to create a forum for agreement?"

Distrust between Tokyo and Washington was mounting. A summit of industrialized nations would be held on June 15 in Halifax, Canada. A U.S.-Japan Summit was planned to take place before this. Japan and the U.S. both declared that they would not take up automobiles as one of the themes of the summit, but it would inevitably become a topic of discussion whether it made the formal agenda or not. There was always a chance that the U.S.-Japan auto dispute could become the main item on the summit agenda.

The clock was ticking away until the sanctions were to go in effect. U.S. ambassador to Japan Walter Mondale swooped in to save the day. The ambassador proposed that the U.S. and Japan hold sub-Cabinet-level talks in Geneva on June 22-23 immediately after the summit and both parties accepted.

The Japanese side, however, would have to do something to break the deadlock before then. Ira Shapiro, chief negotiator for the American side, was considering adopting local parts content in place of numerical targets. Japanese automakers announcing a local parts procurement ratio in line with NAFTA standards would make it easier for the U.S. to drop its demands for Japan to increase the ratio of purchased parts it used in its vehicles. These NAFTA standards were that there would be no duties levied on goods exported from the United States to Canada and Mexico if the local parts procurement ratio were met—50 percent from 1994 to 1997, 56 percent from 1998 to 2001, and 62.5 percent thereafter.

On executive vice-president Hiroshi Okuda's order, Takeshi Nagae, director of Toyota's New York office, visited Shapiro at USTR headquarters on the morning of the 20th, two days before the sub-Cabinet-level talks were to begin, to tell him of Toyota's "New Global

Business Plan." The main provisions of the plan were to build a third plant within the U.S. and to increase from 700,000 to 1.1 million the number of cars produced in North America including Canada. Although the plan itself had already appeared in newspapers, Okuda's intention was for Toyota to get USTR to soften its stance by declaring that Toyota would comply with NAFTA standards upon constructing the new plant.

While Nagae described the plan, he left the phone connected between the USTR and Okuda's home line so Okuda could chime in with additional remarks. Shapiro saw this as a genuine attempt to reach an agreement, giving Okuda the feeling that Toyota would be able to avoid sanctions. Yet, with sub-Cabinet and vice-ministerial officials failing to reach an agreement for the sake of public appearance in talks held on the 21st and 22nd, the issue was handed over to ministerial-level talks between Hashimoto and USTR Representative Mickey Kantor.

Hoping for a resolution through the ministerial meeting, Toyota Chairman Shoichiro Toyoda, who served concurrently as Keidanren chairman, met privately with Mondale at the U.S. Embassy on the afternoon of the 27th in Japan to speak openly about Toyota's New Global Business Plan. Shoichiro's discussion with the U.S. ambassador set off heated debate within Toyota.

"We should stay loyal to MITI all the way and put off announcing the plan until we get a sign from MITI," went one argument.

"If we act in accordance with MITI's directive and then negotiations fall apart," ran another, "Toyota's going to get stuck with the blame. Toyota should therefore announce the plan in advance regardless of how the negotiations go."

Toyota definitely would have gone with the former argument back in the days when the company was assailed as the backwoods *daimyo* of Mikawa. By then, however, this was merely the mindset of a minority. "Rather than hide behind the authorities, we have to come out front and center and nip tensions in the bud early on to prevent trade frictions from recurring," asserted Okuda, who secretly supported Shoichiro. "This will only make Toyota stronger." Toyota already saw itself as an international corporation.

U.S.-Japan auto negotiations were distinctly anomalous within the context of the long history of bilateral trade negotiations. Government-level talks treaded a non-intersecting path for nearly two years with both parties as far apart as ever. It was resolved not because they thrashed out the issues to the very end to reach an agreement acceptable to both parties. What finally cleared the way for an eleventh hour resolution was the voluntary plan that Toyota put together itself.

Chapter 23
Crisis at Toyota

AFTER HAVING TAKEN THE FIRST step towards becoming an inter-national corporation, Toyota was able to respond astutely to trade tensions over automobiles. The reason for that was not completely unrelated to Toyota's baptism by fire at the hands of Japanese corporate raiders and American greenmailers during the bubble economy.

Spurred on by the Plaza Accord signed in September 1985, soon after Toyota made the decision to locate operations in Kentucky, the yen appreciated rapidly. Hovering around 240 yen to the dollar, the exchange rate a year later changed dramatically to 120 yen to the dollar. Incurring unrealized losses on dollar-denominated assets such as U.S. Treasuries, Japanese-affiliated firms sent their money straight to Japan where there was no risk associated with exchange rate fluctuations. This was the trigger that propelled Japan into a bubble economy.

The Bank of Japan moved to ease the money supply to rescue exporters, but this created the by-product of a massive amount of excess liquidity. Japan's low-interest rate policy was seen as an international commitment, soon bringing about a speculative mania based on expectations that low interest rates were there to stay.

Stocks and real estate became the main targets of speculation. Japan played host to a deep-seated "land myth" based on the belief that "the price of land will never go down." Supported by this myth, buying and selling for the purpose of resale was on the rise, sending land prices soaring. Banks increased lending using land as collateral. Before long, land prices were so astronomically high that it was said one could buy all the land in the United States with only the twenty-three wards of Tokyo (approximately 621 km^2).

Mitsubishi Estate Company's purchase of Rockefeller Center for ¥200 billion in 1989 became the symbol for Japanese companies' real estate spree both in Japan and abroad.

The stock market also took on aspects of the bubble economy. While stocks tumbled all over the world on the infamous Black Monday in October 1987, Japan was the first to slough off falling share prices. This inspired confidence in Japanese stocks, attracting excess funds from around the world to Tokyo. Trading at ¥18,996 (year high) in 1986, the Nikkei Index ticked ever upwards until it hit a historical high of ¥38,950 in December 1990.

A slew of wag-the-dog businesses put their main lines of business on the back-burner to concentrate on investing their financial assets to reap windfall profits. Everyone, even the general trading company Mitsubishi Corporation, known to be a rock-solid business, turned to *zaitech*, or financial engineering. The practice became so widespread that the head of Mitsubishi's finance department once went on recording as saying: "Our job is the same as that of sales and marketing. We'll contribute to the company by boosting profits through fund management (*zaitech*)."

Toyota's founding company falls victim to stock cornering

Toyota was zealously dedicated to manufacturing when the Japanese archipelago got carried away by the bubble economy. With reserve cash in excess of ¥1 trillion, Toyota was indifferent towards long-term high-yield financial instruments, not to mention *zaitech*, instead depositing all its money in the bank so as to maintain liquidity on short notice.

Gentaro Tsuji and then Masami Iwasaki, descendants of the "Hanai school," took over for Masaya Hanai, the first president (director of finances) of the "Toyota Bank," after his retirement. It was consistent with company policy that Toyota Motor Sales's Hiroshi Okuda would come to serve as Iwasaki's successor.

"Toyota is a manufacturer," Okuda would always say in media interviews. "Our responsibility is providing our customers with inexpensive quality cars. We therefore don't get involved with *zaitech*. Think about it rationally. Workers on the floor would lose morale if people from the finance department were sitting in an air-conditioned room watching the market to see if they're 'winning' or 'losing' at a time when the plant is working to cut costs by every single penny it can. A company that suffers from low morale in its core business is finished. One of the reasons that Toyota shies away from *zaitech* is to uphold Toyota's philosophy both at home and abroad of putting our heart and soul into making cars."

The scary thing about the bubble economy was that a company could get mixed up and fall victim to the madness no matter how careful it was. Toyota was pulled into the foray on two separate occasions.

The first was the stock cornering of Toyota's founding company, Toyoda Automatic Loom Works, at the hand of stock speculators. The one who cornered them was Nippon Tochi. President Kazuma Kimoto, along with Kazuo Kengaku, president of the members-only investment management firm Cosmo Research, and Yasuji Ikeda, president of investment firm Cosmopolitan, were extolled as the "Big Three" of the Kitahama district, the financial hub of Osaka. The three men were preeminent figures in Kitahama for their financial clout. After all, they could move over ¥100 billion anywhere they wanted to with the push of a button.

Nippon Tochi's main business was land speculation based on soaring land prices. Including its affiliates, Nippon Tochi was said to hold approximately 430 properties in real estate. It owned properties not only in Japan but in Hawaii, California and Texas. Most of the money the company put in stocks was borrowed against these extensive property holdings as collateral. The truth of the claim is not known, but Kimoto boasted that he was leasing his 10,000m² Beverly Hills mansion to actress Elizabeth Taylor.

Nippon Tochi surreptitiously began buying shares in Toyoda Automatic Loom Works in the mid-1980s when signs of the bubble economy were first starting to appear. Loom Works remained carelessly unaware of the shady dealings involving its own company's stock until the last minute because the stock purchases appeared under the name of a dummy securities firm. Nippon Tochi applied for a stock transfer at the end of March 1987. With 1.8 million shares, or 6.8 percent of all outstanding stock, Nippon Tochi boldly burrowed its way into becoming Toyoda Automatic Loom Works's sixth largest shareholder.

Sakichi Toyoda, the progenitor of the Toyota Group, founded Toyoda Automatic Loom Works to produce Toyoda-style automatic looms that he had invented. Moreover, the Automatic Loom Works automobile division was the predecessor of modern-day Toyota. The stock of *the* company that started it all for Toyota was cornered by a land shark of all people.

When Toyota leadership was informed of the facts behind the cornering, the first thing that came to everyone's mind was Taizo Ishida and his mantra that Loom Works was "my company." If he were still alive, this is what he would have said: "If I've told you once, I've told you a thousand times: protect your own castle. Of all things that could happen, my company gets cornered—what the hell? I can't face the generalissimo (Sakichi Toyoda) like this—even in the other world."

Although Toyota was not worried about being taken over, since strong shareholders held a majority of its stock, it was a bone stuck in its throat just the same. Kimoto's intentions were clear. With no intent whatsoever to participate in running the company, his sole objective was to force Toyota to buy back the stock at an inflated price. Just as they feared, he approached them privately about buying the shares.

Before the account settlement board of directors meeting in May, a flustered Toyota management brought in four companies—Toyota, Denso, Aisin Seiki and Toyota Tsusho—to quietly buy back the shares at the price Kimoto demanded. It is said that Kimoto made an enormous sum of over ¥10 billion on the deal. The incident may have received limited coverage even in the Japanese media, but gentlemen from the criminal underworld would not let this slide by so easily.

No one's pulling the wool over Toyota's eyes

"Corner the stock of Toyota's affiliates, and Toyota's sure to buy it back at a higher price."

The next target for cornering was Koito Manufacturing, a Toyota-affiliated manufacturer of lighting equipment. Toyota, as the company's largest shareholder at 19.02 percent, had sent in three directors, including a president. The first from the underworld to make a move was Mitsuhiro Kotani, the front of Kohrin Sangyo (later the Koshin Group), a *sokaiya* syndicate[38] hired to disrupt general shareholders meetings.

Speculators often target companies whose share price consistently trades low and who are experiencing internal discord among their top personnel. Koito was no exception. Kotani, planning to make a serious attempt at taking over Kokusai Kogyo, an enterprise involved with aerial surveys and civil design, did not have the means to get involved with Koito's stock. But he immediately sniffed out a pecuniary opportunity when a man associated with the founder approached him with a proposal to corner Koito's stock.

Koito's stock, whose average share price in the third quarter of 1987 was just over ¥600, began to go up in August, reaching ¥1,150 on October 7. Like they say in Japan, a snake's path attracts snakes. Knowing Kotani was cornering Koito's stock, Kitaro Watanabe, head of the Azabu Group, came in for a piece of the action.

With soaring land prices in the greater Tokyo area already peaking, real estate speculators strutted around as if they owned the place, buying stocks against land collateral and then buying even more shares using that stock as collateral. Koito's share price continued to rise, reaching ¥2,150 per share in March 1988, as Kotani and Watanabe teamed up to accumulate Koito's shares. Meanwhile, Watanabe approached Koito on the side, demanding that they buy back 20 million shares at ¥2,500 per share. He was flatly refused.

Dealing with the Koito issue on the Toyota side was none other than Hiroshi Okuda, the director of finances who had been promoted to "president of the Toyota Bank." Back when Toyoda Automatic Loom Works was reeling from being cornered, Okuda was engaged entirely in internationalizing operations as the head of overseas business and had nothing to do with domestic concerns. He was astonished to find out the course of events that had taken place.

Speculation that "Toyota was sure to buy back Koito's shares" began to mount not only among speculators themselves but also among politicians and even preeminent business scholars. Okuda, worried that Toyota would fall prey to politicians and society's criminal underbelly, strengthened his resolve early on, determining that "buying back Automatic Loom Works' shares and then Koito's

38. Sokaiya are organized corporate racketeers who use a variety of means, often revolving around the disruption or facilitation of general shareholders meetings, to either protect or exort money from corporations.

shares at inflated prices would not only make Toyota the laughing stock of the world but set it up to get ripped off again."

Watanabe, who knew nothing of Okuda's gritty determination to resist, continued making a push to accumulate shares believing that Toyota would ultimately take on Koito's stock. There was no one in the automotive industry who did not know Watanabe, the owner of Azabu Motor, which marketed Chrysler vehicles. But as a man connected to the underworld, he would be brushed off if he walked right in the front door and demanded Toyota buy back the shares.

Watanabe, who did not project the intimidating image typical of speculators and had instead an unguarded and humble demeanor, had a lot of close acquaintances in political and financial circles. Taking advantage of the contacts he had built over time, Watanabe tried to get in touch with Toyota through LDP faction leaders such as Secretary-General Shintaro Abe and Michio Watanabe, chairman of the former Policy Research Council, but Okuda refused to meet with politicians.

When the Recruit bribery scandal came to light in June 1988, setting the political world alight in a firestorm of controversy, the politicians that Watanabe relied on, now jittery about stocks, quickly distanced themselves from the Koito issue. Watanabe's speculations that he could use his political connections to get Toyota to take on Koito's shares at a steep price missed its mark.

Corporate raiders on the run

Watanabe had two options at this point. He could either resign himself to sustaining heavy losses and liquidate his position or accumulate more shares to pressure Toyota to buy them back at a high price as he had originally intended. Intrepidly choosing the latter, he aggressively moved to increase his holdings. Watanabe took over six million of Kotani's shares in early fall. Kotani let go of them because he needed additional funds to cover his intensified maneuvering to take over Kokusai Kogyo. Watanabe held more than 40 million shares going into October. Assuming it cost him an average of ¥2,500 per share to acquire, it meant Watanabe had already invested more than ¥100 billion.

Meanwhile, Toyota had been busy. Okuda was none too happy

that Mitsui Trust and Banking was providing Watanabe financial backing. When the Azabu Group bought out a hotel in Hawaii, Mitsui Trust formed a syndicate to loan Watanabe around ¥70 billion and sent a number of its bankers over to Azabu to advise on ways to improve its financial position.

Toyota and Mitsui Trust were both members of Nimokukai (Second Thursday Club), a group whose membership consisted of the presidents of principal companies within the Mitsui Group. When they ran into each other at Nimokukai, president Shoichiro Toyoda asked Ken Nakajima, president of Mitsui Trust, to exercise restraint in extending financing to Azabu, but Nakajima would not hear of it.

The issue became a topic of discussion at a Nimokukai meeting. One of the senior members of the group turned to Nakajima, offering a sharp rebuke for his complicity in the scheme. "What are you doing conspiring to corner the stock of one of Toyota's affiliates? Toyota's one of our own. This is a disgrace to the Mitsui Group. Cut the crap."

Although Toyota itself, long since a debt-free company, did not associate with Mitsui Trust, Mitsui financed a number of Toyota's affiliates, including parts suppliers and so forth. Mitsui Trust's past presidents invited the presidents of Toyota's affiliated parts suppliers to dinner every year at a long-standing traditional Japanese restaurant in Nagoya.

Okuda insinuated to Mitsui Trust's president that Toyota would assume its affiliates' loans and draw their business away from Mitsui if they did not stop financing Azabu. Pressured thus, Mitsui Trust did not quite pull back what it had already lent to the Azabu Group but could not provide new loans either.

The stocks that Azabu had cornered on margin were listed under the names of securities companies, and there were over thirty of them. Toyota put out a request in the trading community through Nomura Securities, Toyota's main broker. Nomura, acting on Toyota's concerns, leaned on every securities house to put a stop on Azabu's margin buying.

The trickiest part of cornering stocks is not so much when to buy but when to sell. There is only one formula for success. To hold on to the stock and keep it from tanking until finding a buyer. Although Watanabe had 100,000m² of land in the Minato-ku district, an area in which the price of land was remarkably high even by Tokyo standards, he had already taken out a mortgage on all the land to up to the allowable limit. Weighed down by interest payments on burgeoning loans, Watanabe was stretched thin.

He was nearly out of rope by the end of 1988. Selling off his shares on the market would lead to gargantuan losses. If there were any avenue at all to avoid taking a hit, it would be to have a foreign firm assume the shares. Using the connections he had at the time, Watanabe first sounded out Lee Iacocca, Chrysler chairman and Japan-car basher.

Iacocca's response was curt. "Koito? Never heard of 'em. Toyota would be one thing, but I couldn't care less about its affiliated parts suppliers."

Enter Boone Pickens

After a winding path of twists, turns and everything in between, Watanabe finally groped his way to prominent American investor Boone Pickens. On March 31, 1989, Boone Company jumped out of nowhere to become Koito's largest single shareholder with 32.4 million, or 20.2 percent, of its common stock. Pickens is a big-shot takeover tycoon who appeared at number eight on Fortune Magazine's list of top corporate raiders in 1987, ranking third in tactical resources and net assets.

Pickens started his career at Phillips Petroleum after graduating from university. He then struck out on his own to form Mesa Petroleum, which he expanded through a series of mergers, earning himself a reputation as a "piranha" for his David-versus-Goliath-type tactics in acquiring companies many times larger than his own. He was even celebrated as a national hero, appearing on the cover of Time Magazine in May 1985.

He was labeled as the "tainted hero of Wall Street" for his battle to acquire stocks in Gulf Oil, the fifth largest company in the United States in 1983. He apparently finagled hundreds of millions of dollars from Gulf Oil in a war that lasted over a year. News that the takeover tycoon had landed in Japan drew attention both in Kabutocho and Wall Street, which knew that Pickens was up to something.

The rumor mill was spinning at the Tokyo Stock Exchange in Kabutocho, quickly taking Pickens to task as a greenmailer. "Pickens is less an M&A man than a greenmailer who forces companies to take on cornered stock at inflated prices," some said. "Rather than get involved in management, Pickens's strategy is to exercise his right to speak as Koito's largest shareholder and hold out until Toyota says uncle and buys back the shares at a premium."

After Pickens himself arrived in Japan in April, he declared that he had "no intention of greenmailing Koito." He then put in an official request at a top-level meeting with Koito president Takao Matsuura to win three seats on the board, like Toyota. At the time, he did not exercise his right as a major shareholder to gain access to Koito's list of shareholders and accounting records, a common ploy used by the cornering party, and gave off absolutely no sign that he was planning to blindside Koito. Instead, he narrowed in on Toyota.

"Toyota's got Koito in the palm of its hand," he said at a press conference. "If Toyota has no involvement with Koito, then Koito would be more profitable." He also claimed, "What's causing the U.S.-Japan trade imbalance is a special brand of Japanese barrier called keiretsu."

Okuda was extremely apprehensive as to why Pickens would assume Azabu's holdings. "I wonder if Pickens really paid for Azabu's stocks," he mused. "Koito pays out 8 percent annually which would give Pickens no more than ¥300 million in dividends. The interest on loans for stock purchases is enormous. So who's going to defray the difference? Koito has more than a 60 percent share of strong shareholders, so Pickens can't get a majority no matter how many shares he accumulates. Would a guy like Pickens really do something that's economically implausible? Why would Koito's profits and share price go up if Pickens joined management? He couldn't possibly take the share price up to ¥4,000 without doubling the current return on sales. How could he make this happen without any experience in manufacturing? He still hasn't shown any kind of specific measures that he plans to take."

Okuda concluded, "Pickens must be in cahoots with Watanabe to greenmail Koito and split up the proceeds with the real owner of the shares. The two must have an agreement to transfer the title back to the original owner if the scheme doesn't work out. No matter how it plays out, they must have it set up so that Pickens doesn't lose a thing."

Okuda gave Koito and the man in charge of the case at Toyota strict orders not to comply with Pickens. "One Japanese company after another will become a target for hijacking if we give in to Pickens now. Don't cede a single inch no matter what he tells you to do! This isn't only a problem for Toyota. The future of every company in Japan is on the line!"

The reason Okuda issued such a forceful warning not to give in was that a number of Toyota directors held the bearish opinion that while buying back shares was out of the question, seats on the board perhaps needed to be given to a lead shareholder.

Meanwhile, some government officials feared that the Koito issue might cause trade tensions to flare up. In their view, Pickens's strategy was to leverage patriotic sentiment back home to pry open Japanese financial markets, thereby playing a modern version of Commodore Perry, who in 1853 used his flotilla to pressure Japan to open its doors to the world. They requested Nomura Securities Chairman Setsuya Tabuchi, dubbed "the Don of the securities world," for Nomura to find a company to assume Pickens's stocks before the matter got out of hand.

When Tabuchi reported this to Eiji Toyoda, he was cautioned in turn by the Toyota chairman: "No matter how you spin it, Pickens is a greenmailer. There should be no compromise."

Tabuchi later recollected, "For the first time in my life I'd encountered a genuine man of business with the ambience of a grown-up."

Why Pickens met with defeat

General shareholders meetings in Japan tend to center around specific dates. Around 1,500 companies held their shareholders meeting en masse on June 29, 1989. The most watched of them all was Koito's. Pickens, now the man of the hour, rolled in to the hotel where the venue was to take place accompanied by his wife Beatrice. A swarm of media over two hundred strong waited, joined by another fifty correspondents from American television networks and news agencies.

Just as predicted, Pickens laid out seven demands, including a provision for outside directors. Koito responded courteously to all of his demands, but unequivocally voted down with "majority opposition" his motion to appoint outside directors. But Pickens soldiered on, stating: "I'm determined to pursue Koito's long-term profitability. In the United States, people have started to realize that shareholders are the owners of the company, and that management is hired by the owners. The shareholder primacy to which I refer is likely to take root in Japan, too, at some point or another."

Koito somehow managed to defend itself in Round 1 of the Koito (Okuda) vs. Pickens (Watanabe) shareholder showdown. Pickens went on a tirade against Toyota—not Koito—at a press conference held after the general meeting and in a speech he gave at the Foreign Correspondents Club of Japan the next day: "The United States will take some sort of action against Japan if Japanese companies do not change their insular ways" and "I'll continue my assault until I am given full rights as a shareholder. The U.S. and Japan won't be able to maintain equitable trade relations as long as the Japanese market remains closed."

Although he was only in Japan for two nights and three days, it soon came to light that he had another reason for being there. He was firing up to run in the Texas gubernatorial race, the state where he was born and bred. Some observers commented that he also had ambitions for the White House if he could gain such a base. In any event, Pickens had calculated that it would be advantageous to his election bid if American media portrayed him as a shock troop commander forcing open the insular Japanese market.

But the road to the White House would prove a precipitous one. On August 30, two months after the shareholders meeting, Pickens announced that he was giving up his bid to enter the Texas gubernatorial election. Although he claimed that he was doing so "to throw all his energy into the Koito issue," the real story was that nabbing the Republican Party's endorsement would have been an uphill battle. President Bush's son had announced his candidacy.

Pickens announced in September that he had taken over ten million shares from Azabu. He then applied to transfer ownership of four million shares in the end of September, followed by another three million in October. His holdings in Koito had now reached 42.39 million shares, or 26.4 percent of all outstanding stock. His shareholding ratio would exceed 30 percent if he were to transfer over another three million shares.

Accumulating more shares would not grant him any kind of authority, but presented a new problem. Adding Pickens's shares in with those held by Koito's strong shareholders, fixed shares would top 90 percent and common shareholders would disappear. In that event, Koito would be in violation of the listing requirements for the Tokyo Stock Exchange.

The stocks would not be worth the paper they were printed on if the company were delisted. This would prompt an erosion of public confidence in Koito, setting up hurdles to raising funds from capital markets. Furthermore, Pickens would take a tremendous hit if the company's share price fell through the floor. After transferring the stocks, Pickens started to show his true greenmailing colors by taking legal action for raising dividends and examining accounts.

The decisive battle occurred at the general shareholders meeting on June 28, 1990. Pickens showed up with nearly fifty American shareholders in tow but stepped out partway through the meeting out of frustration about how it was being run. Adding insult to injury was the system requiring disclosure of the status of major equity ownership—the so-called 5 percent rule—which had gone into effect in December of the previous year. It was revealed that Boone Company had established a right of pledge to receive the purchased shares on loan from Watanabe. A mechanism was in place for Pickens, who had not paid a single cent, not to incur any losses. Okuda had been right from the start: Pickens was no more than a "hired foreigner" who had simply lent his name to the scheme.

"Okay, Koito, Toyota—I give up." After the Japanese economic bubble had burst, Pickens announced in an article in the *Washington Post* on April 28, 1991 his intention to return Koito's shares to Watanabe, a virtual declaration of defeat. With Mesa Petroleum's share price having fallen to a fifth of what it was during its heyday, he could no longer be bothered by Koito.

Perhaps his quest was just for a mercenary fee, but Pickens's defeat had to with his wrong choice of partner. Koito's share price at the time Watanabe divested the stock to Pickens was ¥3,375 per share, for a total purchase price of ¥1.4 billion. While Pickens did suffer an ostensible defeat, he was left fairly unscathed. Watanabe, on the other hand, was in dire straits. Although the Azabu Group was placed under the control of Mitsui Trust and Banking when the bubble burst, the firm ultimately collapsed.

The speculators glorified during the bubble years as "soldiers of fortune" met with a miserable end. Nippon Tochi's Kimoto, who had compelled Toyota to buy Toyoda Automatic Loom Works stock at a premium, was forced to commit double suicide with his wife on December 26 during the same year 1991 that Pickens declared defeat. Kengaku, who with Kimoto was one of the Kitahama Big Three, disappeared in January 1988. His body was found buried in concrete nine months later. Ikeda went missing in August that same year, 1988. His whereabouts remain unknown.

Finally, Koshin's Kotani, who conceived of the plan to corner Koito's stock, was sentenced to seven years' hard labor and went to prison in September 2003 for extorting and blackmailing Janome Sewing Machine Company. Watanabe, ranked as the sixth wealthiest man in the world by Forbes Magazine during the height of the bubble economy, lost virtually everything. Pickens held tough, however. Working his way out of a temporary pickle, he is said to have made an enormous amount of money on oil futures, which have risen sharply since last year.

Chapter 24
Okuda's Reform

THE BIGGER A COMPANY GETS, the more formal and rigid it becomes, fencing it into a bureaucratic structure more susceptible to authoritarianism. A firm with an entrenched bureaucracy loses its dynamism and begins to slide into decline. The only one who can break a company free from the undesired effects of bureaucratism is the chief executive.

Someone at Toyota was always secretly aiming for world-best, and that is former president and current senior advisor Hiroshi Okuda. While his term as president lasted just four years, from August 1995 until June 1999, Toyota never would have been poised to become the world's leading automaker had Okuda not been at the helm, nor would they even have shot for it. Fujio Cho and Katsuaki Watanabe, who succeeded Okuda, brought Toyota to the top tier of the automotive industry by running tirelessly along the course extrapolated from the one Okuda laid as the foundation of Toyota's global business.

So what kinds of strategies did Okuda devise to try to propel Toyota to the top? While there is no doubt that he had a natural gift for management, if he had not personally carried the banner at the head of his troops, his objectives would not have been realized.

An unconventional man with unusual ability

Toyota Motor and Toyota Motor Sales merged in July 1982. Okuda, originally from Toyota Sales, was appointed a member of the board at the newly-formed Toyota at the age of 49. Although he was not exactly the youngest of the young, it was still a special promotion occasioned by a merger.

The best thing to come out of the merger might have been the discovery of Okuda, a man of unusual and unprecedented ability. The one who found Okuda—who was said to have had little chance of making even the Toyota Sales board of directors had the Motor-Sales merger not taken place—was current Honorary Chairman Shoichiro Toyoda.

Okuda lived in Manila for six and a half years from 1972 to 1979. He first began associating with Shoichiro outside of work through Susumu Fujimoto, Shoichiro's son-in-law who had been transferred from the Ministry of Finance to the Asian Development Bank, headquartered in Manila.

"Why would they put someone that capable in Manila? I suppose that means Sales's human resources are that good," Shoichiro thought simply at the time. He had taken over the presidency of Toyota Motor Sales in the summer of 1981 to explore the possibility of a merger with Toyota Motor.

Top leadership from the Toyoda family are feudal lords in a sense. Although they treat their more capable employees well, as *sobayonin* or grand chamberlains, sycophants sometimes work their way into the fold. It is thus the lord's job to weed out the mere sycophants from their more valuable personnel. Eiji and Shoichiro Toyota were both good at doing this. Since joining Toyota Motor Sales, Shoichiro had his eye on Okuda after he repatriated from Manila as general manager of the Asia and Oceania division.

Toyota always gives its personnel a physical (background check) on the side when appointing them to the board. Toyota Motor Chairman Masaya Hanai, Eiji's right-hand man, ran the show when it came to the new Toyota's executive staff. Hanai objected to appointing Okuda to the board. "He was sent to Manila after fighting with his boss back when he was in the accounting department," Hanai said. "That was a one-way ticket with an open-ended return. He was ultimately banished for six and a half long years. I also hear he's just been sitting around doing nothing since getting back."

Even though he was turned down once, Okuda somehow slipped through the cracks and onto the board of directors with Shoichiro's strong support. When Hanai and Okuda later had the opportunity to sit down for a one-on-one, the older man realized he'd dozed, and flipped his assessment of Okuda 180 degrees: "No one like him exists at Toyota Motor. He just might be the person to carry Toyota into the future."

It did not take long before Okuda's outspoken speech and conduct, uncharacteristic of a Toyota Man, caught Eiji's attention. Eiji, Hanai and Shoichiro agreed shortly thereafter to send Okuda through all of Toyota's core departments. It was thus that Okuda's presidential training began.

During his tenure as board member and managing director, he kept an eye on the growing momentum for internationalization, serving as director of all the departments that the executive elite from the Toyota Motor of old would head by right, including the Overseas Operations Division, the Overseas Planning Department, the North American Operations Division, which manages Fremont operations as part of the joint venture with GM as well as the Kentucky Plant, Toyota's Canada office, and the Public Relations Department, all the while making decisions integral to internationalizing operations.

During his four years as senior managing director, Okuda supervised finance and accounting, domestic sales and marketing, and the various parts departments. After becoming executive vice-president, he rounded off his presidential grooming by adding external affairs, corporate planning, and information technology business to his résumé.

Anyone who manages Toyota's North American operations will become thoroughly acquainted with local operations. Serving as the head of purchasing affords an unadulterated understanding of the actual conditions of plants and car development. The company was able to get a numerical handle on the Toyota Production System largely due to Hanai's suggestion to place a plethora of accountants in plants, a major component of Toyota's distinct "squeezing a dry towel" approach to streamlining. Okuda's seventeen years spent in the accounting department before his transfer to Manila worked to his great advantage in helping him master the most crucial elements of management in a short period of time.

One of the fundaments underlying Toyota human resources is selecting employees for important positions and giving them a chance to succeed. Senior management is culled according to a system by which employees are given a chance to prove themselves, rather than nurtured along. Those who succeed rise through the ranks.

Shoichiro became chairman in September 1992 after serving

as president for ten years. Eiji then retired as honorary chairman. Shoichiro chose as his successor not Okuda but his younger brother Tatsuro. Blood is thicker than water, as the old adage goes. Although some had expected Okuda to be appointed, most employees knew down to their very core that someone from within the Toyoda family would assume the position since Eiji and Shoichiro's Toyoda clan had reigned Toyota for the preceding twenty-five years. Okuda's sun probably would have set had Tatsuro been in office long.

The top spot among the world's automakers that Okuda had been aiming for was largely premised on his assuming the presidency after Shoichiro. Tatsuro's accession essentially threw Toyota off track. Rather than mope or get impatient, however, Okuda continued unaffected full-steam ahead with the work given to him.

Shoichiro took over as Keidanren chairman, the "prime minister of business," in May 1994. There was a tacit understanding in business circles that Sony chairman Akio Morita would succeed Tokyo Electric Power Company chairman Gaishi Hiraiwa, while Shoichiro would succeed Morita. But Shoichiro quickly moved up in the order when, in a stroke of misfortune, Morita was taken by illness just after his informal appointment.

It was assumed that the ill-prepared Shoichiro would need to avail himself to Okuda—who had a wide network of connections outside the automotive world and scores of interesting things to talk about—as his right-hand man when taking up the Keidanren chairmanship. President Tatsuro's turn as chairman of the Japan Automobile Manufacturers Association had also come around. Tatsuro asked Okuda to serve as the chairman of standing committees, a position which exercises complete control over JAMA. But Okuda, being the person that he is, handed the job over to a fellow vice-president instead. Okuda did this because there would have been no one left to manage Toyota if he had devoted himself exclusively to the financial and industrial organizations as Shoichiro's and Tatsuro's lieutenant.

Eiji actively called for Toyota's board of directors to back up Shoichiro but, concerned about creating a duarchy, gradually reined in his advocacy. Yet, Eiji naturally could not just sit back and say nothing about Toyota's frustrating management in the wake of the bubble economy.

Shoichiro was swamped with work as Keidanren chairman, so

Eiji, after retiring as honorary chairman, had Okuda sit next to him at board of directors meetings to be the mouthpiece for Eiji's own views. Eiji had privately begun to consider appointing Okuda as the "post-Tatsuro" president. To that end, Eiji had Okuda sit by his side to initiate him in the final run-up to the presidency.

Okuda's aspirations

Tensions were initially high at the new Toyota after the merger between Toyota Motor and Toyota Motor Sales, while the big-company disease began to reach precarious proportions. Okuda had to make frequent visits to Toyota headquarters after his appointment to the board. Based on something that he became acutely aware of during his visits, he asked himself the basic question: "Why is everyone from the old Toyota Motor so pompous?" His job at the former Toyota Motor Sales—which was, just as the name suggests, a sales company—was to humbly bow his head before dealers and customers in order to sell cars.

At its headquarters in Koromo (Toyota City), however, there was no one to whom Toyota Motor had to bow its head. Top management from materials and parts suppliers, as well as subcontractors, would come to the purchasing department to pay their respects. The accounting and finance departments would get a constant stream of visitors from financial institutions trying to get their fingers wrapped around Toyota's massive store of excess funds. Toyota executives were mini-lords in the one-company town.

Habit can be a scary thing, especially when mini-lord executives genuflect before top Toyoda clansmen. Although this type of corporate climate began to fade for a time after the merger, it made an insidious comeback as the company expanded in scale. Perhaps because his work at the newly-formed Toyota was oriented towards the outside world, Okuda never became infected by the substandard atmosphere in Mikawa.

Toyota's situation grew more difficult with the collapse of the bubble economy. One could even say there were headwinds now. Regardless of fluctuations in the economy or exchange rates, Toyota had to follow through with its global plan to expand local production and parts procurement in the U.S. Going back on a commitment made to the U.S. government itself would threaten to reignite tensions between the two countries.

In even graver danger was domestic sales. Murmurs in the street—that Toyota had no appealing cars, that it was lagging behind in SUV business, and that it was only a matter of time before its share of the market dropped below 40 percent—were reaching critical mass. The hollowing-out of Toyota's domestic business would become a reality if sales fell below the 40-percent line. With a majority of Toyota's employees content in their comfort zone, however, they were cocksure that Toyota was an unsinkable battleship.

"Our company's sitting on ¥2 trillion of reserves. We'll be fine no matter what," ran the superpower mindset, identical to the GM of old.

Such a lethargic predisposition would be a prescription for decline—a far cry from aiming for number one. What then should the company do to elicit a sense of urgency among its staff, while at the same time inspiring them with solidarity? Okuda, who had to keep a watchful eye on all facets of the business in his capacity as executive vice-president, began to seriously consider this issue in February 1995. Soon after, president Tatsuro suddenly sank to the floor from hypertension while attending a party one night. The president's seat could not be left vacant for long during such challenging times. In August, Eiji and Shoichiro decided to appoint Okuda as Tatsuro's successor, judging that it would be an uphill battle for the ailing man to return as president. Okuda was already 62 years old.

At a press conference held on the occasion of his entrance into office, Okuda created a stir with a rather audacious comment: "I would have been happy to assume the position had I been ten years younger." Although some took this as an affront to the Toyoda family, what he really meant was: "The presidency requires a great deal of stamina, without which one would not be able to call forth the vigor and mental acuity the job requires. Youth is the source of this vitality." Having trained in judo as a university student and attained the rank of sixth-degree black belt, that was precisely Okuda's mindset.

"So that's what he really thinks, eh…ten years younger," Eiji thought at the general shareholders meeting in June at which he relinquished his board member status. "The president's job is demanding. Shoichiro and I are responsible for this because we are the ones who agreed to instate him. The best thing I can do to back him up is to stay entirely out of his business." He then sent out a cheer for Okuda. After carrying Toyota for the long haul ever since its inception, Eiji handed Toyota's future over to Okuda.

"I have to give everything I've got to my job at Keidanren," Shoichiro, too, confided to a close associate, knowing that Okuda would get the word. "Honestly, I don't have any time at all to think about Toyota. In the interest of avoiding a duarchy, I've given Okuda the power to shuffle personnel. Honorary chairman Eiji is a far more qualified person than me to consult about the company's business, seeing as he knows Toyota better than anyone else."

While Okuda had been given full powers by the two top elite of the Toyoda family, the company was still not where it needed to be for him to be talking about the global automotive throne. Shooting for number one would first require better positioning. In fact, taking Toyota to the very top during Okuda's tenure as president, which began after his sixtieth birthday, would be beyond hope. Underlying his "had I been ten years younger" comment was the sentiment, "I wish I could take Toyota to the top during my term as president." But when he realized that this would not be possible, he quickly changed course. "I'll lay foundations conducive to aiming for world leader even if it won't happen during my tenure."

This was the mission that Okuda, Toyota's eighth president, charged himself with. His managerial techniques were simple and readily comprehensible. He would devise the strategic plans for Toyota to become the world's leading automaker, but leave all the implementation to his staff. When a matter that affected the company's future needed to be decided, he would carefully canvas opinion far and wide, but run like a gale-force wind once the decision was made. Okuda always signed his name to account settlement transactions on the same day, before they had a chance to pile up. Despite an outward impression that he was "larger than life," Okuda also possessed cool and calm.

He took every chance he could get since becoming president on August 25 to appeal to personnel about the necessity for reform:

"Toyota faces an extremely intense environment. We are now at a monumental crossroads, and the way we respond in the next year or two will determine whether we'll continue to grow and expand in the twenty-first century or become a company of the past that prospered in the twentieth.

"As we move forward, I want you to think of the status quo as a bad thing. Trial and error is fine. I hope to judge the results of your bold challenges fairly. I want to overhaul managerial authority and resources so you can all take a chance and try your best."

The significance of a 40 percent share of domestic sales

One of the first things that Okuda had to act on as president was putting an end to Toyota's declining share of domestic sales (new car registration for passenger cars and above). Toyota's domestic sales faltered after posting a record 43.2 percent market share in 1987 before the bubble developed, and appeared set to fall below 40 percent in 1996 for the first time in fourteen years.

The terrifying thing about market share is that a company has its hands full just trying to put a halt to the downward momentum once it starts to slide. Turning it back around to an upward course is right next to impossible. Fully cognizant of this, Okuda preached to his staff about the importance of market share:

"Market share is essential. Whether we break 40 percent or not makes a world of difference. 40 percent may be only an arbitrary number. But businesses need a visible signpost. 40 percent is the one for Toyota. After laying out our objectives, we need to accomplish them. The company will become more and more vulnerable if we allow ourselves to be content with drawing up a blueprint but not acting on it."

One of the laws of an economy is that recessions work to the advantage of fundamentally strong companies, further consolidating the oligopoly of leading firms. Even so, Toyota's market share had dropped. For Okuda, who had prided himself on *"hanbai no Toyota"* or "Toyota the sales specialist," this was nothing short of humiliating. Number one in the world would be entirely out of the question on such shaky ground. First would be re-establishing solid footing, then launching out into the global market. This was the basic strategy that Okuda devised.

Ford Motor Company, which had been the first to sit atop the modern global automotive industry with its assembly-line production of the Model T Ford, plunged into the global market based on its success in the United States. Ford had enjoyed a 96 percent share of the Japanese market in the 1930s.

But consumers in Ford's U.S. market stronghold began to grow weary of the Model T's design. GM, on the other hand, released one fresh new model after another and usurped the lead from Ford.

Seventy-seven years later, GM was matched by Toyota. While it goes without saying that this was in part because Toyota itself made tremendous strides, GM's miscalculation was allowing its solid share of American sales to fall. Although it had a good 50 percent share of the market in its heyday, this deteriorated rapidly with the first oil crisis, to 30 percent, then 25 percent.

It would be tough for GM to take the lead back in all ways from Toyota without first putting a stop to its waning share of the U.S. market and setting it back on an uphill trend. Automakers' share of sales in their own countries is just that important.

The basis of Toyota's domestic sales strategy was to have consumers drive the Corolla family car as Toyota's entry car into the market, then have them switch over to the Mark II luxury vehicle (named the Cressida in overseas markets) after that. They would finally have consumers purchase the Crown, Toyota's flagship vehicle. The Crown's advertising slogan over the years was "*Itsuka wa kuraun*," or "One Day, a Crown." The bursting of the bubble, however, proved disastrous to the consumer buying cycle, something that Toyota previously had complete faith in.

Toyota was unable to keep up with changes in the market with its existing line of cars because more and more families wanted SUVs with roomier interior on account of family demographics or for leisure activities, rather than the status that goes along with owning a luxury sedan. Toyota found that what had previously been its strength had turned with the changing times into a weakness.

Upon assuming the presidency, Okuda gauged that "the times demand an expansion of the SUV market," directing the development team to scale up Toyota's SUV models. He also called for a return to the basics to clearly define the characteristics of Toyota's five sales channels. While Toyota had overtaxed itself up until then by making minor changes to the front grille design as part of a "twins and triplets strategy" to support the five channels, Okuda prescribed a change of course by shaping the same Corolla series into cars with a completely different exterior and image.

Meanwhile, he undertook new marketing techniques untrapped by successful experiences of the past. One of these was to set up auto malls, where cars from all five channels could be sold in one location, as well as used car outlets that sold rival brands.

Naturally, it would take time for the results of reorientations in manufacturing and sales structure to maifest themselves. Knowing this to be the case, Okuda continued to vociferously call for sustaining a market share of 40 percent. Toyota poured ¥100 billion into incentives in 1997 with the full understanding that rival automakers would criticize the measure as underselling at discounted prices.

In an about-face, Toyota moved to cut back on incentives in 1998. With its SUV lineup complete and a roster of models that sold well, Toyota made a 180-degree shift in policy towards improving the income structure of the Toyota Group and Toyota dealers.

Finally wresting back a 40 percent share of the domestic market in 1998, Toyota extended its share to 42 percent in 1999 despite having cut its incentive structure to half of what it was in 1997. Recapturing 40 percent had a significant impact on the company. One of the consequences was that personnel and dealers regained their confidence.

Okuda may not be an expert in automaking, but it is yet another field in which he demonstrated resounding leadership. Under his direction, Toyota released the Vitz (named the Yaris in overseas markets), a strategic small passenger car, in January 1999 as the first stage of the NBC (New Basic Car) Project launched just after Okuda's appointment. Toyota consciously developed the Vitz with an emphasis on standardizing parts and the modularization and systemization of production, cutting costs by approximately 30 percent compared to existing lines. This transformed the automaker's methods of development and cost-cutting practices. Toyota has since applied the same methodology that it successfully adopted for the NBC Project to develop other new lines, leading to further cost-cutting as the methods continue to evolve.

But this was hardly enough to elicit major change. One of Okuda's philosophies is that the risk of not changing is far greater than the risk of changing. The impetus for change comes only from a sense of crisis. If this sense of urgency starts to fade among company staff, then the president has no choice but to stage a crisis situation himself.

In August 1998, two years after Okuda took office, Toyota

launched the Virtual Venture Company (VVC), a project under the direct control of the president to develop cars specifically targeting young drivers. The catalyst for the project was falling below the 40 percent mark in 1997 despite having invested a massive amount of money in incentives.

One of the reasons cited for the slump in sales described above is a thinning out of Toyota fans among the younger generation. In years past, even if younger drivers started out with Hondas, they eventually switched over to Toyotas as they married, had children and got older. In time, however, Honda drivers exhibited the tendency to stick with Hondas even as they grew older. Toyota needed to increase its fan base among the younger demographic to recapture the market share seized by rival automakers.

Seeing the situation as a serious threat, in 1997 Okuda ordered his team to explore the younger demographic to deal with Toyota's eroding popularity among Japanese youth. Gathering eight assistant managers from not only development but from all departments, the team set out to conduct a number of studies towards finding a solution.

In July 1997 Toyota set up a VVC office in Sangenjaya, Tokyo—well away from headquarters in Toyota City—as a place to reach out to the younger generation. The office brought together forty people with an average age of 35. The task given to them was to look into products, marketing and image-building for the 21st century. Ten months later in the spring of 1998, a total of ten full-sized models—including everything from the starkly unconventional to the brightly-colored to more orthodox models—were carted in to Toyota headquarters.

Okuda made a snap decision then and there, telling the VVC director to productize three of the ten models, basing them on the Vitz. Okuda then proposed another challenge: "I know you usually need about 150 people to develop a single model. Let's see if you can't do it with just a couple dozen."

Ultimately, the project was undertaken with half the usual staff. The cars that they came up with were released as the WiLL line, a multi-industrial collaborative project involving five companies from different industries, including Toyota, Panasonic and others. Toyota brought three different cars to the market, starting with the WiLL Vi in 2000, followed by the WiLL VS and WiLL Cypha. VVC's new development technique naturally came as a major shock to some within the Toyota organization. "If VVC can do it with half the people, why can't our department?"

There was also another purpose for establishing VVC: speeding up development. VVC put all kinds of pressure on the departments directly involved. The latter then devised some sort of solution within their limitations, thereby prodding other departments to pick up the pace with their own projects so as not to be outdone.

The bB (short for Black Box), released in 2000 to target males in their twenties, is a prime example of this. Toyota was able to speed up the entire process by developing the car on the same platform as the Vitz and producing it with a fully digital design without having to build a prototype.

The same thing has happened in the U.S. in terms of the younger generation's departure from Toyota cars. American youth have started to view Toyotas as "boring, unstylish cars." Unlike for most developed countries, the younger segment of the American population is peculiar in that it will continue to expand in the future. The youth demographic, referred to as Generation Y today, will supposedly grow to 70 million people in the next ten years, surpassing the baby boomer generation. Brands tend to stagnate after a while as drivers mature over the years, which is the same phenomenon that occurred with GM and Ford.

Accordingly, Toyota launched the Scion brand in 2003 to target younger drivers. Starting with the release of the bB (named the xB in the U.S. market), Toyota continues to market the original Scion model (tC) today. Unlike the Lexus, which is sold through a network of exclusive dealers and which will be discussed in the next chapter, the Scion is sold as a "brand within a brand" at open booths set up within Toyota dealerships or in neighboring edifices. The idea is for young people who drive the Scion to eventually drive a Toyota and then a Lexus.

This series of initiatives is proof that Okuda's "Toyota is its own worst enemy" maneuvering has produced steady results.

Chapter 25
The Man Behind Lexus

IN ORDER TO MOVE A heavy object, you need a lever. The U.S. did not become the world's largest economic power because of the discovery of crude oil in Texas and the Gulf of Mexico, but because of the popularization of the automobile. Gasoline was the lever.

The Ford Model T, an historical masterpiece, was completed in 1908, five years after Henry Ford founded Ford Motors. Ford conceived the mass production system of assembly lines using a conveyor belt, winning him the title: "King of the greatest industry in history." Karl Benz may have been the inventor of the automobile, but Henry Ford was its foster parent.

The same year the Ford Model T was completed, William Durant founded General Motors (GM). Alfred Sloan revamped GM by introducing innovative business models such as multiple sales channels and the concept of annual styling changes. Sloan was the lever for GM to gain on Ford. GM eventually usurped control of the U.S. market from Ford and dominated the global automotive industry thereafter.

Two levers helped Toyota move to the top of the automotive industry: Lexus, Toyota's brand of luxury vehicles, and the Toyota Prius, a hybrid vehicle (HV) which combines a gasoline engine with an electric motor.

The Flying Salesman

It was out of necessity that Toyota decided to build the Lexus brand in the U.S. rather than in Japan.

Since 1981, Toyota had been forced into a voluntary export restraint of passenger vehicles to the U.S. After many twists and turns, it established a partnership with GM and started joint production, taking its first steps towards becoming an international business. Later, Toyota opened an independent plant in Kentucky for the local production of the Toyota Camry. But it would take time to reach satisfactory production levels and achieve Japanese-standard vehicle quality.

With restraints on passenger vehicle imports and the hoped-for local production taking time, Toyota Motor Sales USA's only option was to increase sales of small pickup trucks, which were not within the scope of import restraints. It was a strategy driven by necessity.

The Toyota Camry and Corolla were the two compact car models that had been planned for local production. Toyota's vehicle composition would not change by importing the compact luxury Cressida (Japanese name: Corona Mark II) and small pickup trucks, nor would its corporate image be affected. Yukiyasu Togo, who became president of Toyota Motor Sales USA after working in the Canadian sales office, felt an impending sense of danger about this business strategy. Togo thought, "Considering their quality, Toyotas are affordable and give customers the impression that they are getting good value for their money. Until now, Toyota has taken a low-profit, quick-return approach to the U.S. market. But with the high yen and voluntary export restraints, the approach will eventually come to a standstill. Before that happens, we should invest in luxury vehicle sales, which generate large profits. The mission of a car company is not merely to provide good quality cars inexpensively. It's also about allowing people to dream. I want to give Americans a dream with Toyota's luxury vehicles."

The story of Lexus's birth cannot be told apart from Togo. Like Kenya Nakamura, head of the Toyota Crown project, Togo was a man of talent. And like Nakamura, the story behind how Togo joined Toyota was an unusual one.

In 1957, at the dawn of motorization, Toyota participated in the Fifth Australian Rally Championship, a 19-day race over 17,000 km, with its newly released Crown Deluxe. One of the harshest races in the world, it was a great feat just to finish the race. This was the first time a Japanese car participated in an overseas rally. The Toyota Crown was able to reach the goal, a triumph highly praised by media.

The following year, in 1958, the Japanese newspapers *Yomiuri Shimbun* and *Osaka Yomiuri* co-sponsored the Round Japan Rally. This race was not about competing for speed but about stable driving skills. Points were given to teams that were able to drive fixed segments within specified time limits with the most accuracy while adhering to traffic rules.

The overall champion would win the privilege of participating in the Sixth Australian Rally Championship, held in August that same year. Three hundred teams, including semi-professional automobile clubs from universities such as Waseda, Keio, Nihon and Meiji, bid to enter the rally, which could only accommodate 50 teams.

Yukiyasu Togo had left Daiichi Trading (predecessor of Mitsui & Co.) to become president of his own business, called Toyo Bussan, which supplied synthetic building material. He entered the rally with his wife Misako, and after passing the selective examination, the Togo team was selected as representatives for the Kanagawa Prefecture.

To everyone's surprise, the Togo team won the overall championship, prevailing over the university automobile teams that were the rally's top contenders. Their victory was a result of Togo's driving skills, which put professionals to shame, combined with impeccable teamwork with his beloved wife in a time when female drivers were rare.

In August, the Togo team participated in the Australian Rally with a Crown sponsored by Toyota. An accident with a kangaroo resulted in their reluctant withdrawal from the race. Walking around downtown to kill time until all the teams had returned to Sydney, they came across a construction site where a movie theater had been torn down to make space for a parking lot. At the time, the Japanese film industry was in its heyday. But judging from the motorization trend, Togo was convinced that the demand for parking in Japan would also increase in the future. And because of high property prices in Japan, he imagined that multi-storey parkades that looked like Ferris wheels would be in demand.

As soon as he arrived back in Japan, Togo looked into multi-storey parkades and found a Swiss company that had a patent. He obtained a patent from them and arranged for a model to be made by a shipbuilding company that dealt with steel frames and iron. He then created a business model where Toyota would handle sales, and proposed it to Seishi Kato, managing irector of Toyota Automobile

Sales, whom he had met at the rally.

Kato was highly intrigued by Togo's proposal and urged him to join the research team at Toyota. He was recruiting Togo, who had left his previous job because he was tired of being a salaried worker. Although he declined at first, Togo was unable to reject Kato's offer and joined Toyota Automobile Sales as facilities manager when he was 36.

Although his multi-storey parkade project never materialized, Togo was recognized for his language and business skills. In 1971, he was transferred as vice-president to Toyota Motor Thailand, where anti-Japanese sentiments were rampant. The Toyota office had been set on fire during the increasingly violent anti-Japanese movement. Togo had been sent to salvage the situation.

Togo had anticipated difficulty. But when he met the Queen Mother at a tea party, he mentioned his interest in Buddhism. This lip service led him to practice asceticism at a temple which had ties to the royal family. Here, he shaved his head and eyebrows. He would wake up at 4:30 a.m., put on a yellow robe and go barefoot from house to house begging for alms. He would spend his mornings reciting sutras and listening to lectures by the chief priest. In the evenings, he would attend a wake if one was being held. At 9:00 p.m., it was complete lights-out. Togo was, and will always be, the only businessman-turned-monk in Thailand. It goes without saying that the trust gained through Togo's actions directly impacted sales results.

Without a triumphant return to Japan, Togo was then transferred to the sales company in Canada, a local subsidiary purchased by Mitsui & Co. in which Toyota had also invested. Mitsui's lack of automobile specialists had been causing strains in dealer relations and inevitable struggle. Togo was sent to put the sales company back on its feet.

Togo's sales philosophy was "First meet people. Meeting and speaking with people will help gain understanding, which will invariably lead to a sale." Togo made two key moves to make this happen. The first was to push Toyota Headquarters and Mitsui to make him president of the sales company. Purchasing a four-person Cessna was the other move.

Canada is a vast country with poor transportation, making it inconvenient to communicate with dealers. A private plane would allow Togo to travel in liberty without being tied to any schedule. He had already obtained his light aircraft license during his post-salaried employee days, so he himself took hold of the Cessna's control stick. Togo flew around the vast country, literally a flying salesman, increasing annual sales from 10,000 to 40,000 units within a short period.

Togo acquired his addiction to flying long distances during this period; after leaving Toyota, he set off on a round-the-world trip when he was 71, covering 32,000 km over 88 days.

A round-the-world trip in a light aircraft is a life-risking adventure. Cessnas are flown at low altitudes, putting them at the mercy of the weather. Encountering a thunderstorm, a Cessna's formidable enemy, requires finding an alternate airport and repeatedly making emergency landings.

In any case, the successful completion of a round-the-world trip in a Cessna requires thorough preparation, detailed planning, composed judgment and the will to accomplish the task. For Togo, a rally around Japan, a round-the-world trip in a light aircraft, and establishing a sales network for luxury vehicles had one common element: tackling something new.

Higher quality than a Mercedes and cheaper

Spring 1983. Two years had passed since the voluntary export restraints to the U.S. had been in effect. During a temporary visit back home, Togo shared his luxury vehicle idea with Chairman Eiji Toyoda and President Shoichiro Toyoda. However, the two maintained silence, not yet making the connection between Toyota's corporate image and luxury vehicles.

Togo was prepared to abandon Toyota and resign if the top two outrightly rejected his luxury vehicle idea. But he interpreted their silence as an indication to get a feel for reactions within the company. From then on, Togo pitched his idea to R&D and Sales executives every time he went back to Japan. But the majority of these executives doubted that Toyota could produce luxury vehicles of a higher quality than Mercedes-Benz or BMW and offer them less expensively. Even if they could produce such a vehicle, Toyota's corporate image as a mass-market automaker had stuck. Would Americans actually purchase a luxury vehicle made by such a company?

Executives from the technical side who were responsible for

development recoiled, and very few took Togo's idea positively. So
Togo switched gears and tried flattery. "I'm a salesman by nature
and don't know much about the technical side. But I'm convinced that
Toyota's technology, inherited from Kiichiro Toyoda, can hold its own
against Mercedes or BMW, and making affordable, quality cars is our
specialty. If we can gain control of the U.S. market, we'll gain control
of the global market. Let's join forces between the manufacturing side
and sales side to achieve this dream."

Eiji took pride in having realized Kiichiro's dream of making
a compact car for the global market with the Toyota Corolla. But
after realizing the founder's dream, Eiji had been forced to deal with
exhaust emissions regulations, international competition for the
compact car market during the 1980s, trade friction with the U.S.,
and internationalization. Even after becoming chairman, he did not
have the time to contemplate what kind of car Toyota could offer to
the world.

So when Togo proposed his luxury vehicle idea, Eiji was brought
to his senses. As the days went by, Eiji's car enthusiast spirit, which
permeated his 70-year-old body, was vividly revived.

From Eiji's point of view, tackling the luxury vehicle market
did not simply entail manufacturing luxury vehicles. Toyota had to
best the most prominent of cars, like the Mercedes S Class or BMW 7
Series, in terms of both quality and pricing. If he had been younger,
he would have jumped on this project and directed it himself. At the
board meeting in August, he bluntly stated what was on his mind, as
he usually did. "The time has come for Toyota to create a world-class
car comparable to a Mercedes or BMW."

This was Eiji's way of giving the green light. Okuda, the new
executive responsible for operations in North America, immediately
seconded Eiji's proposal. Okuda had been in Manila during Togo's
time in Thailand, so the two were close. When Togo first consulted
him in the spring, Okuda had agreed on the spot. "In order for Toyota
to become the world leader in the automotive industry, its corporate
image needs to change at some point. Successfully tapping into the
luxury vehicle market will elevate the quality and image of the
Toyota brand."

Luckily for Togo, Toyota's 50th anniversary was coming up in
four years, in 1987, and every department had been fumbling to find
a new project to mark the semicentennial.

At the time, four models were the mainstay of Toyota exports to the U.S.: the Corolla, Camry, Cressida and small trucks. The Toyota Cressida, a size smaller than a Mercedes or BMW, was popular among the post-war baby boom generation. As the baby boom generation aged and their income increased, their demand for an appropriate type of vehicle would need to be met. If Toyota were to tackle the production of a luxury vehicle, it would be the successor to the Cressida.

Manufacturing the ultimate luxury vehicle

Luxury vehicles in the U.S. had long been positioned as "cars driven by achievers of the American Dream," and carried dignity and composure. Traditional and distinguished brand names such as the GM Cadillac and the Ford Lincoln stood unrivaled in the market, and drivers tolerated small failures.

However, fuel efficiency regulations shook the foundation of these traditional brands. In order to meet regulation standards, luxury vehicles were also forced to downsize. As success symbols, luxury vehicles made by the Big Three were able to maintain their tradition but not their dignity. The emerging wealth class was also changing, shying away from overbearing designs and instead tending heavily towards German luxury vehicles that emphasized functionality, such as Mercedes-Benz and BMW.

So the R&D team at Toyota began designing luxury vehicles based on a new notion: functionality equivalent to German luxury vehicles with the quality and reliability only a Japanese car could offer, and at an affordable price to boot.

Because of these tough prerequisites, the preparatory phase took time. The executive committee gave their final go-ahead in January 1986, three years after Togo had proposed the idea. Although it was not made in time for Toyota's 50th anniversary, Eiji occasionally came to check the R&D team's progress and offered encouragement: "I want you to fully leverage Toyota's 50 years of experience in car-making to create the ultimate luxury vehicle."

The long development period allowed marketing to spend plenty of time on research, which indicated the need for a new sales network appropriate for luxury vehicles. A second sales network independent from the Toyota store was therefore established.

Naturally, the new sales network required an appropriate name. An U.S. consulting company was commissioned to offer a selection, from which Toyota chose "Lexus." Coined from the German word "luxus," it signified "luxury" or "first-class."

"Cambridge" was the choice initially favored over "Lexus." But it was soon eliminated due to its strong British image, and "Lexus" was quickly adopted. The name conveyed a sense of luxury, and with only five letters including L and X, it was easy to articulate and remember.

Toyota's luxury division, the Lexus store, was headed by Eiji's second son, Tetsuro Toyoda (current President of Toyota Industries). Leveraging Togo's know-how obtained in Canada to acquire dealers with the best reputation in the area, Toyota handpicked 100 dealers.

The new model was scheduled to debut in January 1989 at the Detroit Auto Show, and preparations were complete. But one week prior to the announcement, an online service company in New York called Lekis filed suit against Toyota for trademark infringement, claiming the name Lexus diminished their trademark name.

They were clearly after financial compensation. The Lexus mark was going to be sealed onto the engine several days later, and Toyota would be faced with a serious situation if they could not use the Lexus name. It would be easy to settle the case financially, but Togo's sense of justice did not allow this. So he decided to let the matter be settled in court, which ruled 2 to 1 in Toyota's favor.

The LS was the flagship Lexus vehicle, a sedan type with simple design and a Japanese aesthetic that offered novelty and surprise to the U.S. market. The LS sold 11,600 units in its first year and became the success story of a mass-market automaker entering the U.S. luxury vehicle market. Some critics esteemed that Lexus had overtaken Mercedes, and Lexus suddenly matured into a top brand within the luxury vehicle market.

Okuda, who had provided advice on establishing a new sales network, had been driving a Lexus since its experimental stages. Seeing sales growth increase year after year, he swore to himself, "I won't let anyone say, 'Toyotas may not break down, but they're only cheap mass-market vehicles' anymore."

But in order to become the world leader, Toyota needed a modern-day weapon in addition to the Lexus success.

Chapter 26
The Toyota Prius: Another Trump Card

DURING HIS PRESIDENCY, EIJI TOYODA aimed to establish "Strength" as Toyota's corporate image and declared "Global Ten," the goal to attain a 10-percent share of the global market. However, this ambition was criticized both internally and externally for being overly hegemonistic, and subsequent friction with the U.S. soon turned this into a taboo word within the company.

Toyota's third president, Taizo Ishida, advocated the idea that Toyota should "protect its own castle." This message was soon distorted into Toyota being "a self-centered company that only cared about itself," leading to criticism from society of being too profitable and from the industry for being too tough.

A respected car company

Toyota needed to find a new paradigm to replace "Strength." After trial and error, it decided on "A Respected Car Company." In the words of Hiroshi Okuda, Toyota's eighth president, it was about "business virtue." When a company begins expanding its horizon towards becoming world leader, its management vision is questioned more than anything else.

In order to improve Toyota's business virtue, Okuda advocated the importance of maintaining a harmonious relationship with society. With the 21st century about to begin, measures against global warming were becoming an urgent issue. Although global warming has various causes, neglecting the issue would only accelerate the environment's destruction. What Toyota could do as an automaker was to reduce the level of carbon dioxide emitted by cars.

In the U.S., 70 percent of crude oil is used as car fuel. Reducing fuel consumption would lead directly to reductions in carbon levels. Okuda's solution was for Toyota to tackle this problem head-on by offering the public a clean car with low carbon emissions. Unlike exhaust emissions regulations, carbon reduction levels had not yet been defined. If Toyota were to release the first clean car in the industry, it would become the epitome of a company in harmony with society.

At the end of the 20th century, the automobile industry considered the fuel-cell vehicle using hydrogen fuel to be the best candidate for clean cars. But based on the progress of infrastructure and development to date, the full-scale popularization of fuel-cell vehicles would take at least 20 years. On the other hand, hybrid vehicles (HV), which combined a gasoline engine with an electric motor, were considered a stopgap measure in advance of fuel-cell vehicles. Fortunately, Toyota's HV technology was more advanced than other automakers. Okuda was convinced that reducing carbon dioxide emissions would meet the needs of the times. Global warming would become increasingly severe, and automakers unable to cope with environmental issues would not survive. With this in mind, Okuda jumped on the HV idea.

Okuda also realized the importance of releasing the hybrid vehicle as early as possible, even if it meant sacrificing cost. By refining and perfecting HV technology, it could even be applied to bioethanol, diesel and hydrogen vehicles. And if Toyota's HV technology became the de facto standard, not only could Toyota rebrand itself, but the popularization of clean cars would accelerate. With the success of both the Lexus brand and hybrid vehicles, Toyota would become the world leader in the automobile industry.

The battery: a long-time Toyota dream

The collapse of Japan's bubble economy in 1993 was the impetus for Toyota to revamp its car designing process. Toyota was not smeared by the bubble because it had not been involved in money management or real estate spin-offs. But the strong yen combined with sluggish post-bubble domestic sales caused a rapid deterioration in business performance. Third-quarter performance results in 1993 dropped below 300 billion yen to the worst standard since the merger of the Toyota Motor Company and Toyota Motor Sales in 1982. Many automobile analysts made negative speculations: "With its enormous capital, Toyota may be able to mend the final profit figure. But if the yen continues to be strong and sluggish domestic sales remain long term, operating profits, which represent period earnings, could fall into the red."

In 1992, Tatsuro Toyoda became Toyota's sixth president. His decision to handle import sales for GM's strategic car, the second generation J-body (Chevrolet Cavalier), implied more than a strategy to reduce friction with the U.S. Tatsuro wanted to stimulate the company as much as possible, where stagnation was spreading like a disease. In order for Toyota to undergo a true transformation, its cars first needed to change.

Toshiro Kanehara, vice president of technology, was responsible for R&D. After the bubble had burst, he seriously contemplated the kind of vehicles Toyota ought to develop. In September 1993, Kanehara called a meeting of R&D executives and put out a manifesto: "There are less than ten years until the 21st century. Development methods which are merely an extension of the past will not be accepted in the new century. I want all of you to put your minds together and seriously think about what the next generation car should look like."

Coined from Kanehara's speech, the G21 committee was formed from across the technology department. G stood for Generation, while 21 represented the 21st century, an appropriate name for a research committee forming the shape of the future car.

When Eiji heard from Kanehara about the formation of a research committee, his intuition was that fuel efficiency and the environment would become two keywords in the 21st century. It reminded him of the million yen his uncle Sakichi had donated to the Imperial Institute of Invention and Innovation as prize money for inventions in 1924. Sakichi astounded the public with this donation, the equivalent of several billion yen today, which came from personal funds and not on behalf of the company.

Sakichi donated the prize money with the condition that the recipient be a Japanese citizen who could invent a storage battery capable of storing large quantities of electric energy. In energy resource-poor Japan, research on storage batteries had been conducted since the beginning of the Taisho period (1912-1926), but there was no outlook for its practical application. Sakichi's offer for funding was met with indifference and seen as a waste of effort. But he turned a deaf ear to such skepticism and instead held high hopes: "Japan is poor in fossil fuel resources but abundant in hydraulic power and other electrical power resources. If Japan were to invent a device capable of storing large quantities of electrical energy, it would become the world leader in industry."

Sakichi resolved to make this donation to the Institute of Invention in May that year, when he was in Kasumigawara, Japan, where he witnessed the stop-over of an American plane making a round-the-world trip. He was deeply amazed and expected this event to trigger rapid development of the world's aviation industry. "It is only a question of time for planes to play an important role in society, not only in terms of national defense, but also as a means of transportation. It is becoming increasingly important for Japan to invent an electrical motor battery before any other country. If the U.S. is able to fly to Japan in a plane using fossil fuel, Japan must push to the forefront and develop an electrical energy storage device."

The road to Prius

At the end of 1993, a full-time team was assigned to the G21 committee with Takeshi Uchiyamada (current executive vice- president) as team leader. Uchiyamada handpicked ten engineers from each section (Body, Chassis, Engine, Driving Force and Industrial Science), all young elites in their thirties, and entrusted them with the task of conceiving the ideal compact car for the 21st century.

Toyota has an unique chief engineer system for product development. The first chief engineer was Kenya Nakamura, who headed development on the Toyota Crown. Although the title *shusa* was later changed to the English words "chief engineer" (CE), the job still entailed bearing responsibility for the entire R&D process and remained unchanged since Nakamura's days. Although the G21 team was not developing a car, Uchiyamada set to work defining standards as if he were the *shusa*.

As Eiji had predicted, the two keywords were fuel efficiency and the environment. In fact, previous projects to reduce exhaust emissions had actually been about finding the balance between fuel efficiency and the environment, with wording being the only difference. Back then, the environmental issue had been cutting exhaust emissions, whereas in the latter half of the 20th century, carbon dioxide reductions became the major issue. In any case, the balance between fuel efficiency and the environment should always remain the automaker's mission in any given era.

In late fall of 1994, the project proposal for the ideal 21st century compact car was defined as "a direct-injection four-cylinder engine with twice the fuel efficiency of same-class cars."

This project plan was to be discussed at the vice presidents' meeting, then passed down to R&D, Production, Sales & Marketing, and Exports to form a company-wide opinion. However, as Toyota's answer to the 21st century, the majority of vice presidents agreed that simply doubling fuel efficiency did not carry much of a dream. It was easier said than done. Be that as it may, it was still a Herculean task to double fuel efficiency using an internal combustion engine.

Independently from the project planning by the G21 committee, the research center's electric vehicle (EV) R&D team was coincidentally conducting research on a hybrid system that combined a gasoline engine with an electric motor.

Although the electric vehicle predates the internal combustion engine, its short cruising range hindered its popularization. With the introduction of the Ford T Model, it disappeared from the market, which became dominated by the internal combustion engine. It again appeared in the limelight in the 1970s with the outbreak of the oil crisis and exhaust emissions regulations. Development of the electric vehicle was prominent in oil-poor Japan, where every automaker was conducting research towards the practical application of the electric vehicle. But with a lead battery, it was impossible to maintain fundamental vehicle performance levels. With the stabilization of oil prices and improved fuel efficiency using a catalyst device, EV research tapered before practical applications could be implemented.

However, the electric vehicle again found itself in the limelight in the 1980s, when the California Air Resources Board (CARB) introduced its plan for zero-emissions regulations. Automakers selling vehicles in the state of California would be required to sell a fixed number of units that did not emit toxic substances. Only electric vehicles would be able to clear these regulation standards. Toyota, Honda, GM and other automakers began developing and leasing electric vehicles that replaced lead batteries with nickel-metal hydride (NiMH) batteries, and expectations were high for the popularization of electric vehicles.

Compared to the lead battery, the NiMH battery had better energy and power density. But fundamental vehicle performances levels, such as cruising range, charge time, durability and pricing, were still substandard, and none of the electric vehicles could be sold as finished products. Eventually, the CARB regulations themselves vanished into thin air.

Still, Toyota continued its EV research, mainly as insurance for the future. In 1993, Toyota supplied electric vehicles based on the Toyota Town Ace to government offices and subsequently constructed an experimental EV version of the Toyota Majesta, but cruising range and other deficiencies inherent in electric vehicles had still not been resolved.

Third Sector Chief of the EV R&D Department, Masanao Shiomi, came up with a solution: an hybrid vehicle equipped with an engine and an electrical motor which would recharge the engine while driving.

With two sources of power, technical experts were fascinated by the HV system. But doubling the power source increased the vehicle's volume and weight, and would result in higher costs. This became the bottleneck for hybrid vehicles, preventing automakers from advancing beyond the experimental car stage and delving into mass production.

In that respect, the HV system developed by Shimi's team was fuel-efficient and had low exhaust emissions. It was designed to run on the electric motor when the engine requires power, such as during acceleration from a stop or when sitting in traffic, and once the engine could run efficiently, the engine would kick in. Kanehara's successor, Hiroaki Wada, vice president of technology, received a status report on HV development from Shiomi in late fall of 1994, around the same time he received the standards draft prepared by the G21 committee from Uchiyamada.

One day, Wada called a meeting with Uchiyamada and Shiomi to share his thoughts. "If we design a highly fuel-efficient hybrid vehicle and improve fuel efficiency by 50 percent as proposed by the

G21 committee, it would be great publicity for Toyota's research on environmentally friendly vehicles of the next generation. I want to design a hybrid vehicle based on the G21 committee's project plan and exhibit it at next year's (1995) Tokyo Motor Show."

Just in time for the 21st century

Uchiyamada did not have any objections to create a concept car, but he was somewhat opposed to combine the G21 committee's project plan with a hybrid vehicle. The project plan proposed what had been intended as the ideal car for the 21st century. The HV system, on the other hand, was still at the research stage, and there was no outlook for the practical application of the necessary technology. How could they fill this gap?

There was less than a year before the Tokyo Motor Show. If Toyota actually intended to sell this car in the future, it would be meaningless to have a show car with a hollow shell. Simply exhibiting a concept car required numerous problems to be resolved.

R&D expected to have the hybrid vehicle ready for the market in five years. At the beginning of Summer 1995, the concept car was still incomplete, but management was already considering its sale in three years. Then-president Tatsuro had fallen ill, and concerns for his unlikelihood to return to office were beginning to appear. Okuda, whose appointment as the next president was certain, was behind this aggressive schedule.

Okuda was promoted to president in August 1995, just after negotiations had concluded for the U.S.-Japan Automobile Trade Agreement. And immediately after, the HV concept car was exhibited at the Tokyo Motor Show.

Two things surprised show participants. The first was the Latin nickname "Prius," meaning "to go before." Most concept cars had uninteresting development codes, but this hybrid vehicle had already been given a nuance-rich name. Toyota's competitors quickly realized that this car was intended for the market. The second surprise was fuel efficiency, indicated to be 30 km per liter, which was based on simulation and not an actual figure.

Contrary to the splendor at the show, there were consecutive mishaps backstage. The battery, which ran the motor, was being developed in cooperation with Matsushita Battery. But the resulting prototype had only half the capacity of what Toyota had expected and could not be used for the show. As an emergency measure, it was substituted by a condenser.

After the motor show, full-scale test drives began at the Higashi-Fuji Technical Center test course. But for some reason, the car did not move at all. The Toyota Prius had three drive modes, engine, motor, and engine with motor, which were automatically controlled by a computer. Naturally, if there was a bug in the computer software, the car would not move.

Okuda began his serious push towards the sales of clean cars just after summer vacation in 1996, a year after he had been appointed president. Since his appointment, he had been advocating the necessity for internal reformation and had come up with one innovation after another to stimulate the stagnating mood within the company. The finishing stroke was the commercialization of the Toyota Prius. One day, Okuda called vice president Wada and unaffectedly conveyed his thoughts.

"The Toyota Prius will be launched in December 1997. It must precede the adoption of the Kyoto Protocol whose aim is carbon dioxide reduction. Otherwise, the significance of introducing a clean car will diminish. And it looks like the R&D team is aiming to improve fuel efficiency by 50 percent, but that won't be marketable. We'll have to double that."

Wada was troubled by Okuda's strong push. Although a year had passed since they had built the concept car and development was on a roll, technology such as the battery's output performance had yet to be fully established. And several parts that had been technically established had supply costs that were too high.

Wada transmitted Okuda's intentions to the CE, Uchiyamada, who responded: "I'll do everything I can, but if we face a technical limitation, I want the release to be postponed." Although Wada agreed, the Prius's early release was an order from the top down to the entire company and had to be achieved at all costs.

Okuda understood the difficulty of this task more than anyone else. At the time, more than 20 R&D projects including the hybrid vehicle were underway. But Okuda allocated 60 percent of company resources for the Prius project. Moreover, the R&D budget had no limit, and human resources were fully invested. In other words, the

Prius project had company-wide support.

The catchphrase for Prius's release was "Just in Time for the 21st Century."

Chapter 27

Preparing to Become World-Best

T HE AUTOMOBILE HAS ALL THE necessary elements for image-making. It is not performance, quality or price that creates the corporate image, but the branding. Although the automobile industry has OEM partners (who manufacture or sell products under its own brand), it does not have private brands (PBs), which are popular in the food and clothing industries.

GM's long reign in the automobile industry was due to the splendid branding in each of its affiliated companies, from the popularly priced Chevrolet to the luxury Cadillac. Branding is the added value that comes from consumer trust.

After the two oil crises, Japanese cars were beginning to enjoy tremendous sales throughout the world because of their low pricing, performance and quality. The reputation of Japanese cars improved each year, although there was a period when the Big Three ran a smear campaign against Japanese cars: "They might not break down, but they're only cheap mass-market cars."

In order for Toyota to grow its sales in the U.S. market, it needed to establish a new image to appeal its high performance and quality. This image was the very thing that would create Toyota's branding.

The rebranding strategy

Honda, coming to the U.S. market 15 years after Toyota, had successfully branded itself within a short period by introducing the compact Honda Civic, which was equipped with a compound vortex controlled combustion (CVCC) engine, during the first oil crisis.

In its December 1975 issue, *Reader's Digest* ran a feature entitled "From Japan—The 'Clean Car' That Saves Gas." Subsequent media praise of the CVCC as the "magic engine" with low fuel consumption and low pollution carried Honda's name to fame.

Due to its successive F1 victories, Honda has a strong image as a sports car maker in Japan. But in the U.S. market, Honda's branding was formed with the family car. New cars were purchased with high premiums, and their trade-in prices were also high. The high-grade Honda Accord followed the Civic and captured the hearts of yuppies in their thirties.

If Toyota wanted to become the world leader, it had to create branding in the U.S. market that surpassed Honda, and Okuda had finally found Toyota's trump card and secret weapon: the luxury Lexus and the hybrid Prius. The unit sales ratio in the U.S. was small, but the ripple effect could be immense.

Lexus's major sales point is its exceptional quality. With the exception of the SUV (sports utility vehicle) RX (Japanese name: Harrier), all of the units are still being exported from Japan, which involves currency risks, unlike locally produced vehicles. But because its customers are affluent, price imputations are fairly easy. In other words, its high quality ensures an appropriately high profit ratio. The profit made from one LS 460, Toyota's flagship luxury sedan, is the equivalent of several mass-produced Camrys.

Nearly 20 years have passed since Lexus was launched in 1989 as Toyota's second sales network specializing in luxury vehicles. Since then, Lexus surmounted several crises, such as the near-imposition of a 100 percent customs rate during the 1995 U.S.-Japan Automotive Conference. Unit sales continue to grow, and the Lexus brand enjoyed record sales in the U.S. in 2006 with 322,434 units, ahead of Mercedes (248,000 units), Cadillac (227,000 units) and BMW (216,000 units). Lexus had secured its positioning as the top brand for luxury vehicles in the U.S. market.

Meanwhile, the Prius epitomized Toyota's cutting-edge technology and played a major role in rebranding Toyota's corporate image. When the Prius was introduced to the U.S. market in 2000, environmentally-conscious intellectuals living on the West Coast flocked to make their purchase. News spread to Hollywood celebrities, who vied with one another to make Prius their private car and appeal their proactiveness on environmental issues.

When actor Leonardo diCaprio was nominated for an Oscar, he drove to the Academy Awards ceremony in a Prius. Each time its image appeared on TV, it reinforced consumers' image of Toyotas as environmentally friendly cars. Driving a Prius soon became a status symbol in the U.S.

Prius's image as an environmentally friendly car comes from its product excellence. The first generation Prius's gas mileage (10.15 mode) was 28.0 km, an astonishing figure for a gasoline car. After a full model change in 2003, the second generation had raised its fuel efficiency to 35.5 km, due to improvements in the system. The synergy between its product image and fuel efficiency helped the Prius mature into a mass-production model with 870,000 units sold worldwide (as of October 2007), mainly in Japan and the U.S.

Today, Toyota has broadened its range of hybrid vehicles to 12 models including the Prius, minivan Estema and Lexus LS 600h. As of May 2007, total sales has reached a million units. This is the equivalent of reducing carbon emissions by 1,500 times the volume of a domed stadium seating 50,000 people.

At present, Toyota stands unrivaled in the HV market. Toyota plans to pull worldwide sales up to 1 million units per year by the beginning of 2010, and to release hybrid vehicles for all model types by 2020.

The Achilles' heel of hybrid vehicles is the cost of the HV system, which is still relatively expensive. The selling price of the Prius is 400,000 to 500,000 yen higher than gasoline cars in the same class. But prices have been held down, with the first generation breaking even and profit margins kept to a minimum with the second generation. This has created a dilemma: the more units are sold, the more profit ratios are forced lower. But profits had not been taken into account in bringing the Prius to the market, which has resulted in Toyota's priceless rebranding as the maker of environmentally friendly cars.

The Toyota brand reaped the greatest benefits from the improved corporate image. With unit sales overtaking Chevrolet and Ford in 2007, Toyota became the top-selling brand in the U.S. Incidentally, Ford had been the top-selling brand in 2006, followed by Chevrolet. With their main models being large pickup trucks, SUVs and minivans, GM and Ford were hit hard by the stifling cost of gasoline. The Toyota brand surged to the top, finally ridding itself of the image as "merely cheap cars that didn't break down."

Toyota's response to industry realignment

At the dawn of the 21ˢᵗ century, Toyota's corporate image had dramatically transformed in the U.S., just as Okuda had hoped. All it had to do now was to sprint towards becoming the world's top automaker. But Okuda saw the need to first solidify Toyota's response to the industry's global realignment.

On May 6, 1998, a major incident took place which shook the global automobile industry. Chrysler, one of the legendary Big Three, and Daimler-Benz, manufacturer of luxury vehicles and full-size trucks, announced an unexpected merger. What the two companies announced was not a partnership but a full merger, which opened the final chapter to the automobile industry's global realignment.

The moment Okuda learned of this merger, he predicted that it would trigger the involvement of the world's prominent automakers in the industry's realignment. Japanese automakers would also be involved, and Okuda immediately understood the need to solidify Toyota's positioning before such events unfolded.

Okuda did not believe that Toyota needed to take initiative in the industry's imminent realignment. It was actually the contrary. He thought of the message advocated by Ishida, "Protect your own castle," and put it into action by spreading it throughout the Toyota Group.

Okuda started by making Toyota the primary shareholder in two affiliates, turning them into subsidiary companies: Daihatsu Motor, a light motor vehicle manufacturer, and Hino Motors, which was suffering from stagnating full-size truck sales. He then turned his attention to Denso, Toyota Industries and Aishin Seiki, subsidiaries wholly owned by Toyota. These subsidiaries could be described as *jikisan hatamoto*, or samurais in direct service of their shogun. Okuda's strategy was to send chairmen and vice chairmen into these important automotive parts manufacturers to strengthen group ties through people.

If these takeovers, mergers and acquisitions through stock purchases became established in Japan, Toyota's stock market capital would be higher than the Big Three combined. But this did not rule out the possibility of a takeover. Although the actual chances of Toyota being bought out were slim, the affiliated automotive parts manufacturers were still vulnerable.

Okuda had had a bitter experience in the Koito Manufacturing case. At the time, Okuda stood at the head and successfully drove them out, but there was no guarantee that a similar nightmare would not occur again.

As Okuda predicted, the announcement of the cross-Atlantic merger kickstarted the realignment of the automobile industry. Ford formed the Premium Automotive Group, adding British Jaguar and Land Rover as affiliates. And in March 1999, Ford purchased the passenger vehicle division of renowned Swedish automaker Volvo to solidify its luxury car class.

GM could not afford to fall behind and purchased 50 percent of Saab's passenger vehicle division in 1990, when the Swedish aircraft and automaker separated. In 2000, Saab became a wholly owned subsidiary of Ford. Scania, Saab's commercial vehicle division, had first become affiliated with Volvo, but eventually became part of the Volkswagen group. Incidentally, in 2005, GM paid 1.55 billion euros to dissolve its five-year affiliation with Fiat, claiming that the partnership had produced few results.

Nissan: the focal point of the realignment

Nissan, one of Japan's leading automakers, became the focal point of the global realignment. Nissan's misfortunes began when Yutaka Kume, who became president in 1985, mistook the company's temporary recovery during the bubble period as the real thing. Not only did Kume pursue reckless overseas projects inherited from the former president, he diversified and increased the number of domestic facilities.

Yoshifumi Tsuji, who inherited an excess of facilities and enormous debt from Kume, was unable to return the budget to the black even once during his four years as president. The matter was now in the hands of Yoshikazu Hanawa, Nissan's "Last Prince."

Bearing the hopes of the entire company, Hanawa assumed office as president in 1996. He immediately vowed to increase Nissan's domestic market share to 25 percent in 2000, but none of the employees could believe the president's promise.

Far from establishing plans towards rebuilding, Hanawa was pressed to find funding. Nissan's interest-bearing debt had mushroomed to 2 trillion yen (non-consolidated) and 4 trillion yen (consolidated). Convertible bonds, issued at the peak of stock prices, were stagnating in the sluggish stock market. Instead of increasing in value, they became debts with imminent redemption terms. In Fall 1997, the domestic financial crisis came to a head, and banks became even more reluctant to lend. Even the Industrial Bank of Japan (now Mizuho Bank), its main bank, was unwilling to give out new loans.

Hanawa secretly asked the accounting department to calculate the amount Nissan required to survive. The answer was 800 billion yen. When Nissan was turned down by its main bank, its last hope, Hanawa abandoned hope for an independent recovery. In order to survive, Nissan would have to resort to foreign investment. Hanawa braced himself for the worst. Renault, DaimlerChrysler and Ford were three companies that came to mind as potential partners. Nissan was already negotiating a business partnership with Renault which did not involve any capital funding.

Hanawa set his eyes on DaimlerChrysler. Nissan had originally been in negotiations with Daimler-Benz regarding the sales of its subsidiary truck manufacturer, Nissan Diesel Motor. Negotiations had been concluded before the holiday season in early May and only required signing. Then, Daimler-Benz's sudden merger with Chrysler was announced, and signatures for Nissan Diesel Motor had been delayed.

Hanawa became impatient and went to see Chairman Schrempp at Daimler's German headquarters. Going under the pretense to congratulate him for the inauguration of the new company, Hanawa's real aim was to obtain Schrempp's signature for the Nissan Diesel deal. But to Hanawa's surprise, Schrempp was not only prepared to invest in Nissan Diesel but in the Nissan group itself. Unlike Renault, Daimler had plenty of capital. The vanity of Nissan's employees, who took pride in their products, would be satisfied. Excited, Hanawa returned to Japan, where Ford Chairman Wayne Booker was waiting for him.

Since 1998, Nissan and Ford had been jointly developing RVs and had formed a close relationship. Ford's aim was to win back the world leader position from GM. In terms of profit, Ford had managed to momentarily overtake GM. But in revenues, it was all Ford could do to slightly narrow the gap.

If luck was on its side, the automobile industry's global realignment would offer Ford the chance to regain its status as world leader. President Jack Nasser saw a partnership with Nissan as the perfect opportunity to pursue GM and sent Booker, Nasser's superior during his days at Ford Australia, to Japan to investigate possibilities.

Booker dropped hints of Ford's interest in a partnership with Nissan and returned to the U.S. Ten days later, Hanawa went to see Booker at the Ford headquarters in Detroit to start partnership negotiations. Nasser, who had heard the latest developments from Booker, formed a special team to take a closer look at Nissan's state of financial affairs.

The road to Renault

With three candidates on its list of potential partners, Nissan was prepared to enter negotiations at any time with Daimler, Ford and Renault, in order of preference. However, negotiations did not proceed as Hanawa had hoped.

At the beginning of 1999, Renault sent word that 40 billion yen was the maximum amount of capital funding it could presently offer. Immediately after, Schrempp arrived in Japan with co-CEO Robert Eaton (former Chrysler head) under the pretense of announcing the newly formed DaimlerChrysler.

At the press conference the next day, the two confirmed their intention to continue partnership negotiations with Nissan, including capital funding for the Nissan group. But this was only lip service. Their real intention was to postpone partnership negotiations until both sides of the new company could be reconciled.

But Nissan was running out of time. Financing was becoming difficult with each passing day. When Hanawa understood that the partnership with Daimler was going to take time, he flew on his own to Detroit and negotiated directly with Nasser. At the end of the discussions, Nasser requested Hanawa to write a letter of intent which Nasser would use to persuade Chairman Clay Ford, who was taking a cautious stance towards the partnership with Nissan. In describing the letter, Nasser employed the word "proposal." Hanawa mistook this for an actual detailed proposal and wasted more than ten days.

Misunderstandings with DaimlerChrysler were dispelled and negotiations were imminent, which were scheduled to begin on March

10. Schrempp suddenly came to Japan and broke off negotiations on the capital tie-up with the Nissan group and Nissan Diesel Motor, then immediately left Japan. This had been within the scope of Hanawa's expectations. What surprised Hanawa was U.S. ratings provider Moody's reaction. Moody's downgraded unsecured long-term loans issued by Nissan from Aa3, the lowest grade of eligible investments, to Ba1, below investment grade. With such low ratings, Nissan would no longer be able to issue corporate bonds in the U.S. market.

The Ministry of International Trade and Industry (now Ministry of Economy, Trade and Industry) had been closely observing the hectic developments surrounding Nissan. Nissan's insolvency looked inevitable to then-minister Kaoru Yosano, who analyzed information published daily. Yosano instructed the Ministry to investigate the effects of the worst-case scenario.

But when one door is shut, another is opened. In the evening of the day Hanawa learned of the downgrading by Moody's, he was contacted by Renault's Schweitzer about the prospect of an increase in capital funding for Nissan. Specific figures would be decided at the board meeting on the 16th, but Nissan was requested to sign a freeze agreement beforehand. Could Hanawa meet him in Paris on the 13th?

A freeze agreement was to ensure that Nissan would not enter negotiations with other companies during the contract period. Until the moment he boarded the plane to Paris, Hanawa hesitated a great deal between prioritizing the partnership negotiation with Ford and taking Renault up on its new proposal. In the end, Hanawa chose Renault to maintain credibility.

The realignment also affected automakers at the core of the automobile industry. In light of Nissan's affiliation with Renault, Fuji Heavy Industries dissolved its partnership with Nissan. Competition unfolded between GM and Ford to secure partnership with Fuji Heavy Industries, who chose GM in the end. After similar twists and turns, Nissan Diesel became affiliated with Volvo.

Schrempp had a burning desire to expand DaimlerChrysler. Once the merger was on track, he singled out Mitsubishi Motors and succeeded in making it an affiliate in 2000. However, confrontation arose in 2004 regarding additional investments to salvage Mitsubishi, and Daimler subsequently withdrew its funding. Fortunately for Mercedes Benz, Mitsubishi had separated its full-size truck division,

Mitsubishi Fuso, allowing Mercedes Benz to finally purchase its truck division.

As if predicting Nissan's future, Okuda gave a profound speech at the end of 1998. "The 21st century will not be an extension of the 20th century. Instead, it will be about the survival of the fittest. The remaining two years will be the final preparatory phase for Toyota to rank among the main players." At a time when the world's automakers were panicking over the making and breaking of alliances, Toyota was steadily preparing itself to become the industry's world leader.

Chapter 28
Reaching for the Throne: Multidimensional Strategy

IT TOOK 60 YEARS FOR Toyota's annual world production to reach 5 million units. But Toyota was able to produce nearly the same number of units within the next ten years thanks to eighth president Hiroshi Okuda, the driving force behind global management.

In the 1980s, Toyota's overseas strategy was to prioritize the U.S., the world's largest market, a strategy that bore fruit and gained momentum. Okuda's style of global management was not only to invest in people and money, but to pour in as many management resources as possible.

Because of the wide reach of the automobile industry, less developed countries tend to consider it strategic and impose higher customs rates. Implementing local production that helps build the country's automobile industry is the only way to tap into these markets. These countries readily welcomed Toyota's expansion because of the local implementation of the Toyota Production System (TPS).

When Okuda was confident that Toyota was capable of simultaneously carrying out several overseas megaprojects, he decided to apply the production and sales know-how he had acquired in the U.S. to conduct multidimensional diplomacy for local production in emerging markets. In 1999, when domestic sales shares were on the rise and Toyota's response to the global realignment was more or less defined, Okuda strongly urged each department with overseas operations to pick up speed on their overseas expansion.

Prime minister of business: the Toyota CEO

The presidents of many Japanese companies serve as both CEO (Chief Executive Officer) and COO (Chief Operations Officer). The chairman monitors management executives and is usually removed from the business frontline.

Toyota was able to position itself as the next world leader because of Okuda's absolute authority as president. However, as soon as Okuda was named chairman of the Japan Federation of Employers' Associations (JFEA, now the Japan Business Federation, JBF) in May 1999, he turned over the presidency to Fujio Cho at the board meeting held after the June stockholders meeting and became chairman.

Because the leader of the Japanese business world must ensure neutrality, there was an unwritten rule for the JFEA President to not concurrently be president of their parent organization. So when Okuda became leader of the business world, he followed suit and withdrew from Toyota's presidency, a position that carried both CEO and COO responsibilities. In reality, it was physically impossible to wear both hats.

When the Japanese economic bubble burst in 1991, the majority of economists predicted that it would take ten years for complete recovery. But there was no sign of improvement after seven or eight years, and the financial crisis of 1997 only made matters worse. Companies were exhausted and too preoccupied to consider wage increases. JFEA's role was to be the labor advocate of "the Japanese Company" by presenting wage increase guidelines to labor and management and directing spring offensives. Okuda had become the chief executive of this organization.

The work of the prime minister of business is arranged by the minute. And in 2000, it would be Toyota's turn to serve as chairman of the Japan Automobile Manufacturers Association (JAFA). The possibility of amalgamating the JFEA and the Japan Federation of Economic Organizations (JFEO) had started to surface, and the financial world unanimously saw Okuda as the most qualified candidate to be the first chairman.

Even if Okuda had the right to represent Toyota as its chairman, he would have very little time available to engage in its business management. Fearing that Toyota's dream of becoming world leader was going to end as a dream, Shoichiro Toyota made a nonchalant comment at the press conference to announce the new president. "Although Toyota is not looking to adopt the American management system, we could say that Mr. Okuda is now the CEO, with Mr. Cho as the COO."

Unimaginably hectic days began for Okuda. When he assumed office as JFEA Chairman, he appealed his management philosophy to both sides. To the employer side, he called for management with a long-term outlook that respected basic rights. And to the labor union side, he called for the pursuit of open-mindedness in interactions with management instead of doggedly pursuing financial gains through wage increases, which had been a common occurrence in the past.

In May 2002, after completing concurrent postings as chairman for both JFEA and JAFA, Okuda became the first chairman of JBF, which was founded by the amalgamation of JFEA and JFEO. When the (Junichiro) Koizumi administration formed in 2001, it was Okuda's turn to serve as member of the Council on Economic and Fiscal Policy, whose chairmanship was served by the prime minister. As a business expert, Okuda's role was to be the driving force behind Koizumi's structural reforms. In order to implement these reforms, Okuda had to fight with bureaucrats and politicians and hold his own.

During this time, Okuda did not take his eyes off Toyota. From Monday to Thursday morning, he was in Tokyo and fulfilled his role as the prime minister of business. On Thursday evenings, he would make an appearance at Toyota headquarters and listen to the week's reports. On Fridays, he would attend meetings at headquarters or summon leaders from relevant departments and give them instructions. On Saturdays, he would enjoy a game of golf or a meal with leaders of associated companies to establish mutual understanding and friendship. He squeezed in overseas trips to examine the progress of his global management strategy. Okuda's hecticness was superhuman.

The secret behind the rapid growth

Global Ten, Eiji's goal for Toyota vehicles to obtain 10 percent of global market share, was achieved at the end of the 20th century, in 2000. Once a goal is achieved, leaders of a corporation must establish the next goal. Shortly after the start of the 21st century, in April 2001, Toyota defined "2010 Global Vision," the goal to increase global market share to 15 percent within ten years.

At the time, GM's global market share was just under 15 percent. So this was an indirect declaration of Toyota's desire to become the world's auto leader. Toyota intentionally avoided provocation by using the words "world leader."

In theory, even if Toyota obtained 15 percent of the global market, GM could still have a higher share and maintain its world leader status. Be that as it may, it was like playing musical chairs. If Toyota increased its market share, another automaker would lose those shares.

Toyota had produced 5.89 million units in 2001, which was over 2 million units less than GM. Everyone in the industry was convinced that Toyota was simply no match and could not possibly overtake GM in ten years' time. However, this was when Toyota's growth began. The secret behind Toyota's rapid growth was that it had been pouring its energy into producing 500,000 to 600,000 more cars each year. Every year, in effect, Toyota founded a new automaker larger than Fuji Heavy Industries. According to Toyota's calculations, these new companies would be comparable to Nissan in five years' time.

The U.S. was Toyota's second home ground. Toyota's U.S. unit sales overtook Chrysler in 2006, and Ford in 2007. Market share in 2007 jumped to 16.2 percent, while GM's market share was at 23.5 percent. Toyota had narrowed the gap to 7 points.

The media was too preoccupied with the competition between GM and Toyota for world leader status to notice that Toyota had overtaken GM in unit sales for passenger vehicles in the U.S. This was a ground-breaking event in the automobile industry.

When founder Kiichiro Toyoda stepped down from presidency to take responsibility for the 1950 labor disputes, his only regret was Toyota's inability to produce passenger vehicles that were accepted by the world. He had once told Eiji Toyoda, his favorite disciple: "Trucks are secondary to cars. An automaker is a company that makes cars."

Eiji overcame setbacks suffered by the Toyota Crown when it could not be properly driven on American highways, and paved the way by developing the Toyota Corolla. Using the synergy between Lexus and the Prius as his trump card, Okuda succeeded in making Toyota the top leader of the U.S. passenger vehicle market.

BRICs, emerging markets, and Formula One

From the moment he assumed the presidency, Okuda's challenge was to tackle the Chinese market, which was certain to overtake the U.S. market.

Although Okuda recognized the importance of the Chinese market, he had prioritized the U.S. He had not been mistaken in his strategy. If he had prioritized the Chinese market over the U.S., Toyota may have become the top automaker in China but would not have been in a position to target world leader status.

This theory is proven by Volkswagen, who was the first overseas automaker to launch local production in the U.S. in the 1970s. But it did not meet expectations, so Volkswagen sold its plant to Chrysler and focused its management resources in China. Although Volkswagen became the undeniable top automaker in China with over 50 percent market share, it was largely overtaken in the U.S. by automakers who had entered the market later.

"Toyota feels strong nostalgia for China. We cannot give up the Chinese market. The 'last bus' for the locally produced mass-production car in China has already left, but I hope we can catch up with it somewhere. I'd like to visit China as soon as possible."

Reading Okuda's presidential aspirations in a magazine article published shortly after he assumed office, Eiji secretly flew to Beijing in his private jet and met with General Secretary Jiang Zemin. He promoted Toyota as an automaker that not only made finished cars but that had exceptional know-how in the parts industry. By suggesting honest strategies for Toyota's entry into the Chinese market, he was laying the groundwork for Okuda's visit.

Authorization from the government and joint ventures with a local company were prerequisites for a foreign company to undertake local production in socialist China. At the time, Shinji Tanimura's song "Subaru" was gaining popularity in China. General Secretary Hu Jintao was a big Tanimura fan and had sponsored several of his concerts in the Great Hall of the People. Knowing this, Okuda asked Tanimura, who had also been in Toyota commercials, to accompany him to China in order to create a strong bond with the Chinese head of state.

At Hu's suggestion, Toyota joined forces with Tianjin Automobile and later with state-run First Automobile. In exchange, Toyota was able to launch its first overseas production of the Prius. In 2010, preparations will be complete for a local production capacity of 900,000 units per year. Despite Toyota's late start in the Chinese market, it succeeded in catching up with the advance party in no time.

Toyota's Europe strategy also gained momentum at the start of the 21st century. Although its local production in the U.K. fell behind Nissan and Honda, once on track, Toyota became the first Japanese automaker to open a plant in France. And in 2005, Toyota opened a compact car plant in the Czech Republic under joint management with PSA Peugeot Citroën. The Toyota Yaris (Japanese name: Vitz) was selected for production at this plant. A compact car which had been developed per Okuda's instructions as Toyota's global strategy model and designed by Greek Sotiris Kovos, the Yaris was a novel car.

In order to raise awareness for its vehicles, Toyota has been participating in Formula One (F1), the most prominent of automobile races, since 2002. Instead of merely supplying engines, Toyota has been using its technology to assemble its own race machines from engine to body and forming an all-Toyota team to participate in F1 races.

Although the Toyota team has yet to stand on the center dais of the podium, Toyota purchased the Fuji Speedway at the base of Mt. Fuji to denote the seriousness of its F1 participation. Toyota eventually managed to wrest hosting rights for the Japan Grand Prix, held at Fuji Speedway since 2007, from Suzuka Circuit in Honda's home town.

Toyota's rivals are storied veteran teams like Ferrari, which produces cars to win F1 races and uses their prize funds to invest in F1. It is no ordinary feat to stand at the podium's summit with 14-time constructors' champion and "F1 geek" Ferrari as a rival. But these F1 races will not promote Toyota's sales until Toyota stands on the podium.

In Russia, Toyota became the first Japanese automaker to go into local production. Okuda was aware that its failure would not be fatal for Toyota. Rather, he was strongly determined that the faster Toyota expanded into Russia, the bigger the results would be. In 2005, President (current Prime Minister) Putin's attendance at the groundbreaking ceremony in Saint Petersburg received much attention.

For many years, Toyota had suffered deficits in the European market. But the tide has changed in the last few years and Toyota has yielded profits due to the low yen and high euro, as well as satisfactory sales in Russia. Toyota first released the luxury Lexus, but the locally manufactured Camry also became very popular and is selling at a rapid pace. The local plant held a line-off ceremony in Dec 2007, and the construction of a second plant nearby, with an annual production of 200,000 to 250,000 has already been decided.

The second plant is estimated to go into operation in spring 2010. With emphasis on the Toyota RAV4, a popular SUV model in Russia, compact car models such as the Corolla and the Yaris are also scheduled to be manufactured there. Combined with the first plant, annual local production is estimated to be 300,000 units, with overhead investments exceeding 100 billion yen.

Compared to GM, Ford and Renault, who entered the market before Toyota but with annual productions remaining between 60,000 and 80,000 units, the scale of Toyota's local production in Russia is overwhelming. This is unimaginably swift for Toyota, which had previously been more cautious than its own motto of "knocking on a stone bridge before crossing it."

The Corolla, Camry and Yaris are Toyota's Top 3 global strategy cars. In 2006, the Corolla sold well throughout the world with 1.45 million units produced and sold. The Camry did well in the U.S. with 750,000 unit sales worldwide. And the Yaris, with its main battlefield in Europe, had worldwide unit sales of 560,000. The combined unit sales of these three models is just under a third of Toyota's overall figure.

Toyota actually has a hidden best seller: the IMV (Innovative, International, Multi-Purpose Vehicle), which was developed for emerging markets. The IMV has a secure space frame designed to withstand bad roads and can be mounted with three body styles: pickup trucks, 3-seat minivans and SUVs.

The production of pickup trucks had been dispersed all over the world, but Toyota unified them into one category and concentrated their production in Thailand and other ASEAN countries, from where they are exported to countries all over the world.

By geographically concentrating the complete process, from parts supply to sales, Toyota has been able to reduce costs and therefore vehicle prices. Pickup trucks recorded 700,000 units of sales in 2006 and surpassed the Camry in 2007. At this rate, pickup trucks will exceed 1 million unit sales in a few years.

The remaining BRICs, Brazil and India, have not been left out of the picture. Brazil was the first country where Toyota implemented local production. The 4x4 Land Cruiser has been the model manufactured there, causing sales to be sluggish for many years. But the production of the Corolla is now in full swing at the plant, and a second plant with an annual production of 100,000 units is scheduled to be built in 2011.

Suzuki stands unrivaled in India, whose population is second only to China. Toyota's market share there is less than 3 percent, but plans are in place to build a plant in the Bengal region exclusively for the production of low-cost cars. With an estimated annual production of 100,000 units, Toyota is aiming to obtain 10 percent of market share.

Toyota's strength is its ability to steadily increase profits as it expands on a corporate scale. Toyota's third-quarter performance results (consolidated) in 2007 showed over 2.2 trillion yen operating profits, which indicate the core business's earnings, for 24 trillion yen in sales. More simply put, Toyota increased sales by 10 trillion yen and net profits by 1 trillion yen in the past six years, the equivalent of creating a business comparable to IBM America in six years.

2007 became a memorable year for Toyota. Just before its 70th anniversary on November 3, Shoichiro Toyoda succeeded Eiji in joining the ranks of the automobile industry's most prominent leaders. But the greatest commemoration that year was the rise of Toyota as the world's top automaker. Although Toyota's global unit sales that year was 9,366,418, just 3,000 shy of GM's unit sales, Toyota produced 9.49 million units, outrivaling GM by 210,000 units and placing it at the top for the first time.

Epilogue
The Wounded Forerunner

Toyota's third quarter performance results in 2008 showed 26.3 trillion yen in sales, a 10 percent growth from the previous year. But operating and net profits, respectively at 2.27 trillion yen and 1.7 trillion yen, only showed marginal increases.

Toyota's sneeze was caused by the sudden chill that came over the U.S. market due to subprime loans and high oil prices. The automobile demand in the U.S. had been a reflection of the prosperity of the latter half of the 1990s, and estimates had been high at around 17 million units per year. The tide has turned and demand estimates for 2008 will certainly fall below 15 million units for the first time in 13 years.

The largest decline is in the full-size truck division, where the demand for SUVs suddenly dropped due to high oil prices. In the second quarter of 2008, GM and Ford, whose strengths are in this market, suffered deficits of 15.5 billion dollars and 8.7 billion dollars respectively.

The Big Three's slump is indicated by U.S. sales figures in July 2008. The combined market share of eight Japanese automakers reached an unprecedented 43.0 percent, overtaking the Big Three's market share for the first time.

2008 marks an important anniversary for the U.S. automobile industry: the centennial of both GM's foundation in 1908 and the Ford T Model's debut, considered the "immortal car" in automobile history. Normally, festivities would be in order, but there was not an ounce of a celebratory atmosphere at either company.

The year 2008 will probably be carved into the history of the automobile industry as the year of humiliation for the Big Three. Not only did they suffer enormous deficits, Toyota overtook GM in the first half of the year by 270,000 units and rose to the top of global unit sales at 3.83 million, while Volkswagen overtook Ford, jumping to third place. Chrysler, who dissolved its merger with Mercedes-Benz and placed itself under an investment fund umbrella, has disappeared from the Top 10.

However, Shoichiro Toyoda from the founding family, Okuda, Chairman Fujio Cho and President Katsuaki Watanabe are all aware that Toyota did not rise to the top due to its own strength but because of its rivals' self-destruction. Consequently, they are unmoved by their status and instead have an acute sense of an impending crisis.

The pitfall of international business

In the 1980s, Japan won an overwhelming victory in the international competition for the compact car market. The Big Three had successfully created the shift towards compact cars but were unable to produce high-performing, quality compact cars that could compete with Japanese cars. Cadillacs and Lincolns were the U.S. automakers' milk cows and only hope, but they were soon overwhelmed by Toyota's Lexus and Europe's Mercedes-Benz and BMW.

The Big Three's final refuge was in the highly profitable full-size pickup truck and SUV market, which has an annual demand of over 3 million units, primarily in Texas and other southern states. Because these models are produced in facilities which GM and Ford have paid off, profit is estimated to be around 10,000 dollars per unit. The Big Three preserved their dignity with easy profits in this market.

Until the 1990s, there was a narrow but distinguishable gap between Japanese automakers and the Big Three. But Toyota did not overlook this profitable market, which had been considered the Big Three's stronghold. At first, Toyota was extremely cautious about expanding into this field and, as usual, followed its cautious management philosophy of tapping on a stone bridge before crossing it. Taking soft, stealthy steps, Toyota first started local production of the mid-size truck Tundra (now full-size) at the Indiana plant which began operations in 1999.

Although the Tundra's sales growth was not satisfactory, Toyota purchased a vast 2,000-acre property in San Antonio, Texas, in 2003 to build a plant for the exclusive production of full-size trucks, which was completed in November 2006.

So what gave Toyota the confidence to expand into the full-size truck division?

In 2001, Toyota headquarters announced its plan to acquire 15 percent of global sales. American managers in command on the front line at Toyota USA like Jim Press (previously Managing Director, now Vice Chairman of Chrysler) jumped at this opportunity: "Toyota is no longer a Japanese company. It is deeply rooted in the U.S. and users see it as an American company. It's time for Toyota to stop focusing on cars that fill the gap left by the Big Three, and to supply cars that compete head on. We should no longer let the Big Three monopolize the highly profitable full-size truck market."

Dealers also wanted large vehicle models that would follow the Lexus. Japanese headquarters wanted to nurture the HV market with the Prius, but dealers were wary of its unpredictability. With less than 1,000 units supplied from Japan, it was impossible to move out of trial sales and there was not enough business. Dealers unified in their request for Toyota to build a full-size truck plant in the U.S. and promised to accept responsibility for sales.

Offering large profit margins that would contribute to increased market share, the production of full-size trucks seemed like an attractive idea to Toyota's management. This was the moment the Toyota locomotive lost its brakes and became a runaway train.

The Tundra, Toyota's full-size truck produced at the Texas plant, did not have a favorable start. Toyota's compact cars had several selling points: they had high standards in performance and quality, and they never broke down. The Lexus combined these selling points with Japanese taste and a silent engine. The Prius was featured as an environmentally friendly car with good gas mileage. Contrarily, full-size trucks and SUVs did not have Toyota's usual features. Without the Toyota emblem, their fuel efficiency was not much different from GM or Ford vehicles. The only way to grow unit sales as a latecomer to this division was to offer sales subsidies.

The brakeless locomotive began its runaway. In February 2007, only three months after the Texas plant had gone into operation, Toyota decided to build its eighth U.S. plant in Blue Springs in Union County, Mississippi, for the production of the mid-size SUV Highlander.

The mission of an automaker is to make vehicles that meet

consumer demand. But Toyota was expanding into the gas-guzzling large vehicle division while simultaneously promoting low-emission eco-cars. Getting both divisions off the ground was like running full speed on brittle glass.

High oil prices broke one side of the brittle glass, and the shards came flying towards Toyota. Toyota's first-quarter performance results in 2008 showed 2.18 million in global production, but sales decreased by 4.7 percent due to the then-high yen, and net profits slumped steeply, by 28.1 percent, due to the rising cost of raw materials such as iron and steel.

In order to stop sneezing, you need to take medicine. In Toyota's case, the medicine was a review of the production system in North America. First, production lines of full-size trucks at the Indiana and Texas plants were stopped for a three-month period from August. Operations were also stopped at the Alabama plant, which produced engines for large-size vehicles. At the Mississippi plant, which was still under construction, the production model was switched from SUVs to the Prius, whose demands could not be met with exports from Japan. Amidst high oil prices, the Prius has become so popular that it took six months to deliver after the contract was signed.

Production of the Highlander will be switched to the Indiana plant, and production of the Tundra, currently carried out at both the Indiana and Texas plants, will be unified at the Texas plant by Spring 2009.

These three plants will suspend operations for three to four months, affecting over 5,000 line employees. GM and Ford have responded to the recession by plant closures and layoffs. Nissan, who had been at the helm of the expansion into the large vehicle division, suffered a larger blow than Toyota and requested the voluntary retirement of 1,200 employees.

Under Toyota's management philosophy, employees are the company's treasure, so implementing layoffs or voluntary retirement would be difficult, even for its overseas plants. Within Japan, employees in domestic plants can be reshuffled to other plants, but this solution would not be suitable in the U.S., which is vast. Toyota decided to continue employment at plants while operations are suspended and have employees undergo training or explore improvements to the Toyota production method.

When Toyota faced a crisis prior to capital liberalization in the late 1960s, then-president Taizo Ishida boasted that Toyota could hold a sports day every day for six months and still survive. Motorization began soon after, and Ishida's claim was never tested. If Ishida saw Toyota, 40 years later, holding an extended sports day in the name of training and production method improvements, perhaps he would smile wryly and say, "I've been saving up for sports day. The cost of holding a sports day in the U.S. is nothing. If you look at it as tuition for Toyota's leap towards the future, it's pretty cheap."

High oil prices have changed the Toyota landscape. Within Japan, the shift away from cars is progressing quietly and certainly. Increases in raw material costs are not reflected in the product the way they ought to be. The European market was expected to grow slightly compared to the previous year, but the resulting downward trend was inevitable due to feature models approaching their last years. In Asia, the Chinese market is expected to continue its growth, but the influence of high oil prices will inevitably halt this growth to only a slight increase. The Near and Middle East, Africa and Oceania are the only markets showing favorable growth.

Under such changes, Toyota adjusted its 2008 estimates for global unit sales to 9.5 million units, 350,000 units lower than originally predicted, including 200,000 less units in the U.S. Although there is a subtle increase compared to the previous year's figures, the decline in speed is evident.

The post-"world leader" challenge

In choosing the world's top automaker, we tend to focus on production units and unit sales. But in both name and reality, it's about the automaker with the best quality and quantity, in both business performance and product. High oil prices may have caused Toyota to sneeze, but the Big Three caught very bad colds (performance decline). With no prescription medicine available, there is no sign of their recovery (strategy to stop the deficit).

Although Toyota is expecting a 30 percent decrease in profits in the third quarter of 2009 compared to the previous year, it is still capable of producing annual profits of over 1 billion yen. This difference is apparent in its stock price, 30 times the value of GM.

Subprime loans and high oil prices are man-made calamities

for the automobile industry. If the top automaker cannot respond appropriately to such calamities, it will end up as a badly wounded frontrunner.

Toyota's response to high oil prices is the expansion of its eco-car production, which created Toyota's corporate image as an environment-conscious company. Starting with hybrid vehicles already on the market, Toyota is engaged in the development of all technologies, including bioethanol, diesel, electric and fuel-cell cars.

The race to develop environmental technology is just at the start line, but Toyota is the only automaker in the world committed to a wide range of development. As the Japanese, U.S. and European governments hammer out strategies to reinforce fuel efficiency regulations to reduce carbon dioxide levels, it is no exaggeration to say that environmental technology is the key to the industry's realignment in the 21st century.

Automakers will fall behind if they cannot cope with fuel efficiency regulations when they are implemented in Japan, the U.S. and Europe. Although Toyota was not proactive during the industry realignment in the 1990s, it recently acquired Isuzu after the dissolution of its affiliation with GM. Toyota's aim was to acquire Isuzu's diesel technology.

With rising oil prices, hardly a day goes by without some news of eco-car development, giving the impression of a sudden emergence of talent and achievements. To those unfamiliar with the actual situation, Toyota may appear to have lost its predominance in this field. But taking a closer look, most of the stories are about technologies at the experimental stage. Latecoming developers have yet to realize that even if these technologies can be commercialized, the path to mass production is thorny.

In the last few years, the spotlight has been on electric vehicles, considered the ultimate eco-car because of their zero carbon dioxide emissions. Although the electric vehicle predates the gasoline engine, its implementation has been hindered by its short cruising capacity (mileage). The key to improving this cruising capacity is in the lithium-ion battery, which has high energy density and storage capacity. Although widely used in notebook computers and cell phones, these batteries have the risk of exploding. Extreme caution must therefore be exercised in their application in automobiles, which have the inherent risk of accidents resulting in injury or death.

Automakers who had a late start in developing environmental cars are aiming for a sudden reversal and putting their energy into developing electric vehicles. The battery, the heart of the electric vehicle, is being jointly developed with electronics and battery manufacturers. But information on the progress of battery development is not readily available.

All eyes are on Toyota, who has made the most progress in this field with the successful commercialization of a hybrid vehicle. The third generation Prius, scheduled to undergo a full model change in Spring 2009, will be equipped with a nickel-metal hydride (NiMH) battery like preceding generations, a result of placing the utmost importance on safety. But with the implementation of the lithium-ion battery coming into sight, Toyota's new hybrid passenger vehicle, scheduled to be released in Fall 2009, will carry the new battery.

Plug-in hybrids and electric vehicles use the characteristics of the lithium-ion battery to their advantage. The battery can be charged with home electricity and runs uniquely on electricity for short distances. When battery power becomes insufficient, the gasoline engine kicks in to generate power.

At the 2008 North American International Auto Show held in Detroit, Toyota announced plans to commercialize its plug-in hybrid vehicle by 2010. But internally, it had already been decided to sell the application of this plug-in hybrid technology as the new Prius model, whose sales will be moved up to Fall 2009. Its biggest advantage is the ability to run at least 150 km after charging overnight. With that much cruising capacity, it could be used as the electricity source for an in-town electric vehicle. The development of limited-purpose electric vehicles is also beginning to come into sight.

The lithium-ion battery has many convenient applications such as hybrids, plug-in hybrids and electric vehicles. The race to develop eco-cars will grow more heated, but Toyota's fundamental strategy against global warming will continue to be the hybrid system. Toyota's undeniable strength is the sale of nearly 2 million hybrid units, which provides abundant information and mature technology.

Toyota's future challenge will be the application of the HV system to full-size tucks and SUVs. Toyota had originally planned to apply the HV system to large vehicles but abandoned the idea because the present NiMH battery could not support their rough and diverse usage.

Toyota then switched to the idea of using diesel engines, whose fuel costs were less expensive than gasoline. But the price difference between diesel and gasoline grew to be negligible, and development was almost shelved. Recently, however, the outlook for the commercialization of the lithium-ion battery has revived efforts to improve fuel efficiency using the HV system. If this project succeeds, Toyota will succeed in distinguishing itself from the Big Three in the large vehicle market, using fuel efficiency as its selling point.

High oil prices prompt Okuda into action

If oil prices continue to rise and high prices become established, not only will the automobile industry shrink, but the world's economy will be unable to emerge from the slump. Toyota, with an environmental strategy centered on hybrid vehicles, cannot remain at the sidelines of surging oil prices.

In the beginning of Summer 2008, the possibility of oil prices reaching 150 dollars per barrel carried the world into utter confusion. Okuda decided to take action. He met with government authorities and royal family members in Saudi Arabia and two other oil-producing Gulf states to present his opinion.

"If we let speculative funds run rampant, oil prices will not stop at $150 but climb as high as $200 per barrel. In such a case, it will no longer be a question of global warming for automakers but rather of survival, and they will have to resort to non-gasoline cars. If this happens before oil reserves are exhausted, oil-producing countries will suffer more than consuming countries. In my opinion, a good compromise between oil-producing and consuming countries would be between 70 to 100 dollars per barrel. Proven oil reserves are said to last about 40 years. If oil prices stabilize, automakers will make headway on energy-conserving cars currently in development as measures against global warming, in which case oil reserves will last at least 70 years. But if automakers move away from oil before then, oil-producing countries will certainly experience hindrances in their nation building."

Oil-producing countries understand better than any other countries that reserves will be exhausted sooner or later. This is the very reason why Saudi royalty have purchased hybrid-drive Lexus cars as examples of energy conservation for their citizens. What Okuda proposed to the Saudi king was a production increase. He projected that if Arab Gulf states increased oil production and other oil-producing countries followed, speculative funds would move away from the futures market.

The Saudi king accepted Okuda's proposal and announced a production increase at talks between Middle Eastern oil-producing countries and consuming countries at the Energy Forum held in June. Unfortunately, Saudi Arabia's intentions were not understood by neighboring countries, so oil prices did not decline right away. Okuda then made another trip to the Middle East during the Toyako Summit in July to meet with the heads of the three Gulf countries he had neglected to visit on his previous trip. Over two months, he visited Saudi Arabia, United Arab Emirates, Kuwait, Qatar, Bahrain and Oman, and appealed for them to increase oil production. Okuda's repeated efforts proved effective. By the time the summit ended, speculative funds began to move away from the futures market and oil prices have started to decline.

Toyota's real enemy: arrogance

Toyota founder Kiichiro Toyoda established his company with the determination to make a compact car accepted by the global market, using Japanese brains and skills. Three-quarters of a century after the formation of the automobile department of Toyota Industries, Toyota stood at the summit of the automobile industry. However, it had not been smooth sailing all along but a succession of crises.

War, labor disputes, the founder's sudden death, capital liberalization, industry realignment, the world's strictest emissions regulations, oil crises, Japan-U.S. trade friction, internationalization, environmental issues... Toyota not only surmounted each crisis but used it as a springboard for growth. Fortunately, there have been no crises since the U.S.-Japan Automotive Conference in 1995. The majority of current employees were hired after Toyota became "Toyota of the world" and have only experienced its success in climbing to the top.

Toyota's real enemy is not GM or other rival companies, nor trade friction. It is the arrogance that comes from employee complacency.

Precisely because of its rapid growth in the past ten years, Toyota employees' awareness is not yet suitable for a top runner.

At the end of 2006, the gigantic high-rise in front of Nagoya Station was completed. Corporate functions including production, development, domestic sales and exports were centralized in the Nagoya area between the cities of Nagoya and Toyoda. Little by little, bureaucracy has become rampant. From now on, Toyota will be put under enormous pressure, something it had not experienced before taking the top spot. When high oil prices stalled production and sales, employees unfamiliar with past crises could only cower.

Toyota's management was highly praised by Jack Welch, CEO of GE for 20 years, who turned the company into the world's best business. The essence of Toyota's management is in its continuity. Toyota's history can be categorized into three periods: struggle, growth and the leap forward. The leading figures in each period were: founder Kiichiro and restorer Taizo Ishida during the period of struggle; Kiichiro's favorite disciple Eiji during the period of growth; the duo of Shoichiro, from the main branch of the Toyoda family, and Okuda, the non-Toyoda family member, during the leap forward.

But a change of generations will definitely take place. The time is drawing near for the leaders of Toyota's leap forward, Shoichiro and Okuda, to retire from the management stage. What kind of era awaits Toyota after the leap forward?

Toyota's immediate goal is to acquire 15 percent of world share. Despite its status as forerunner, sales are still just over 9.36 million units, the equivalent of approximately 13 percent of world sales. Okuda secretly put together another unofficial Toyota plan called the 3-3-3 Plan, whose threefold points are: 30 trillion yen in sales, 3 trillion yen in operating profits and a dividend payout ratio of 30 percent.

Whether it's acquiring 15 percent of world share or the 3-3-3 Plan, Toyota's circumstances have changed dramatically since these goals were conceived. Toyota's headlong rush, which has brought it thus far, will not suffice. Toyota needs to first reconsider whether it even needs to set target values, now that it sits at the top of the industry.

Perhaps Toyota must aim instead to become the world's best business, as opposed to automaker, through its craftsmanship. A new strategy will be required for this. The question is, who will draw up the proposal, and who will play the supporting roles? Toyota has set sail for a new journey. How will a new captain steer the boat?

About the Author

Masaaki Sato has no peer when it comes to reporting on the Japanese auto industry, his prominence dating back to the 1980s when he was on the auto beat for *Nikkei* (the Japanese *Wall Street Journal*). He is the author of several highly regarded histories, including one on the early days of home video technology (VHS vs. Betamax) that has been adapted to the big screen. His magnum opus is *The House of Toyota*, on which the current volume builds specifically for an overseas audience. *The Honda Myth: The Genius and His Wake*, winner of the annual nonfiction Soichi Ohya Award, is also available in English from Vertical.